MW00679841

São Paulo

UNIVERSITY PRESS OF FLORIDA

Florida A&M University, Tallahassee

Florida Atlantic University, Boca Raton

Florida Gulf Coast University, Ft. Myers

Florida International University, Miami

Florida State University, Tallahassee

New College of Florida, Sarasota

University of Central Florida, Orlando

University of Florida, Gainesville

University of North Florida, Jacksonville

University of South Florida, Tampa

University of West Florida, Pensacola

University Press of Florida

Gainesville · Tallahassee · Tampa · Boca Raton · Pensacola · Orlando · Miami · Jacksonville · Ft. Myers · Sarasota

São Paulo

Perspectives on the City and Cultural Production

David William Foster

The publication of this book is made possible in part by Arizona State University, Tempe.

Printed in the United States of America on acid-free paper

This book is printed on Glatfelter Natures Book, a paper certified under the standards of the Forestry Stewardship Council (FSC). It is a recycled stock that contains 30 percent post-consumer waste and is acid-free.

16   15   14   13   12   11   6   5   4   3   2   1

Library of Congress Cataloging-in-Publication Data
Foster, David William.
São Paulo : perspectives on the city and cultural production /
David William Foster.
    p. cm.
Includes bibliographical references and index.
ISBN 978-0-8130-3665-6 (alk. paper)
1. Brazilian literature—History and criticism. 2. Literature and
society—Brazil—São Paulo. 3. São Paulo (Brazil)—In literature.
4. São Paulo (Brazil)—In motion pictures. I. Title.
PQ 9522.S36F67 2011
869.09'3588161—dc22

                         2010054049

The University Press of Florida is the scholarly publishing agency for the State University System of Florida, comprising Florida A&M University, Florida Atlantic University, Florida Gulf Coast University, Florida International University, Florida State University, New College of Florida, University of Central Florida, University of Florida, University of North Florida, University of South Florida, and University of West Florida.

University Press of Florida
15 Northwest 15th Street
Gainesville, FL 32611-2079
http://www.upf.com

Contents

Illustrations

São Paulo

Introduction

São Paulo, Brazilian Megacity

Non ducor duco.

⚙ Motto of the city of São Paulo.

Afinal, São Paulo não era uma cidade nem de negros,
nem de brancos e nem de mestiços; nem de estrangeiros
e nem de brasileiros; nem americana, nem européia, nem
nativa; nem era industrial, apesar do volume crescente das
fábricas, nem entreposto agrícola, apesar da importância
crucial do café; não era tropical, nem subtropical; não era
ainda moderna, mas já tinha mais passado. Essa cidade que
brotou súbita e inexplicavelmente, como um colosal cogumelo depois da chuva, era um enigma para seus próprios
habitantes, perplejos, tentando entendê-lo como podiam,
enquanto lutavam para não serem devorados.

⚙ Sevcenko, *Orfeo extático na metrópoli* (31)

By most accounts São Paulo is not a user-friendly city, and it may even be
viewed as hostile. The paradigmatic megacity (along with Mexico City or
Tokyo), São Paulo has grown exponentially in the past one hundred years,
such that something like eighteen million inhabitants now occupy the

greater metropolitan area (a good characterization of the city is provided by Faria; Rebollo and Silva discuss the gendered city). Some of this growth is attributable to foreign immigrants, brought in mostly to work the expanding coffee plantations, but the emerging industrial base east of the city is also a factor (see Patrícia Galvão's novel, *Parque industrial*, discussed in this book; foreign immigrants figure prominently in the novel). Both Jews and Italians have been coming since the last quarter of the nineteenth century, with a particular spike in Jewish newcomers in the context of European fascism and the policies of Getúlio Vargas's Estado Novo in the 1930s (on the arrival of Jews during the period, see Lesser, *Welcoming the Undesirables*).[1] Japanese immigrants, on the other hand, began entering during World War I, and their arrival was largely the result of circumstances in Japan at that time and the Brazilian need for cheap agricultural and industrial workers (on the arrival of the Japanese, one hundred years ago as of this writing, see Lesser, *A Discontented Diaspora*). To whatever extent immigrants may have been encouraged to concentrate in rural areas, they or their immediate descendants have since flooded into major metropolitan areas, where they have joined that other great force powering the growth of São Paulo: internal migration, as millions of rural Brazilians have sought to escape from the material (and, in many cases, the spiritual) poverty of the outback and similar nonurban settings, and tried to find a new life, generally precariously and often disastrously, in the burgeoning urban cores of the country. Where most Latin American countries have only one magnet city (as the Argentines say, "God is everywhere, but he only holds office hours in Buenos Aires"), Brazil has half a dozen such centers. But none is more voracious in its absorption of new arrivals from both overseas and the countryside as São Paulo.[2]

The first decades of the twentieth century were the turning point for the explosive growth of São Paulo, which now serves as the financial center of the country—as well as of all Latin America—and, in its suburbs, as the country's industrial center (on the feverish 1920s in Brazil, see Sevcenko, *Orfeo extático*). Brazil industrialized early, well before other Latin American societies thought that it might be better to produce the goods of modernity at home rather than import them from abroad (as did, say, Argentina until well into mid-century). São Paulo, as a consequence, moved away from being the rather tranquil center of the coffee-plantation society of the region, a society that had its roots in the colonial period as much as did the sugar plantations in the Salvador de Bahia and the Northeast and the cattle ranches in the southernmost Rio Grande do Sul; dairy farming emerged after the colonial period in the state of Paraná, immediately to the south of the state of São Paulo, but it was of a whole with a rural economy that, as in most of Latin America, dominated daily life and economics until the twentieth century.

One cannot rehearse here the complex theories relating to the transition from a rural economy to an industrial, capitalist one in Latin America.[3] Suffice it to say, however, that Brazil, long marginalized in Spanish-speaking South America for its linguistic as well as other sociocultural and historic differences, leapt far ahead of other nations in the post–World War I period, and though São Paulo became the center of the development of urban capitalism, it also began to gain on Rio de Janeiro, the legendary cultural center of the country. A growing premium was placed on the arts, and their increasing complexity mirrored the increasing complexity of São Paulo life in general.[4] The establishment in 1935 of the Departamento de Cultura de São Paulo (São Paulo Department of Culture), with the participation of artists of the caliber of Mário de Andrade,[5] discussed in this volume, was an important milestone in affirming the growing importance of São Paulo as a cultural center to be reckoned with.[6] The establishment in 2006 of the Museo da Língua Portuguesa (Museum of the Portuguese Language), the only museum in the world devoted entirely to a language, was part of the continuing affirmation of that importance.

Culturally speaking, as is now widely acknowledged, the turning point for São Paulo came with the Semana de Arte Moderna (Week of Modern Art), the city's equivalent of the 1913 Armory Show in New York City (see Bastos's comparative comments on the two events). Both events showcased a culture driven by firm concepts of modernity that challenged traditional artistic values in themes as much as in forms. These shows asserted the city's occurrence as the upstart vis-à-vis what will be insistently seen by the latter as the waning influence of its ancestor, Rio de Janeiro in the case of Brazil, Boston in the case of the United States. Held between February 11th and 18th, 1922, São Paulo's—at first only São Paulo's, later all of Brazil's—Semana de Arte Moderna brought together a mélange of artistic efforts, although it is now mostly remembered for painting and poetry (major documents of the Semana are reproduced in the *Caixa modernista*; see also standard treatments like Nist; Wilson). Perhaps it might be correct to discern a certain exaggeration of that program's immediate effect on Brazilian cultural production. But there is no question that, at least for the São Paulo artists involved and their enthusiastic audiences, something new was being touted, and it was being touted as inescapably Brazilian and, therefore, as the real beginning of an unimpeachable national culture. Where one could speak before of a transition toward a distinctive national culture in the decades between the separation from the Portuguese Empire and the early twentieth century, the Semana de Arte Moderna served to impose an irreversible paradigm shift.

This paradigm shift was, in the end, what was going on with São Paulo as a whole in the period in question, and one could catalogue significant processes in all areas, with a summation of those processes being evinced in the very nature of the change in everyday life of the people of the city. To be sure, since capitalism distributes wealth unevenly, there is unevenness in the accession to modernity of the people of São Paulo when viewed in individual material terms and not just in terms of the creation of a new social imaginary, which deals more in ideals than realities. Yet the emergence of the contemporary city of São Paulo has resulted in an enormously complicated lived environment: one with numerous textual ruptures (not just the difficult terrain, some of which has been adjusted), unchecked urban sprawl and its attendant traffic congestion, barriers created by a freeway and throughway system that often does not respect earlier rationally conceived street layouts, layers of insecurity, and, above all, one of the worst manifestations of air pollution in the world. It would probably be an outrageous extension of the Anglo-American antiurban belief to say that the citizens of megalopolises are alienated from each other and from their environment, but few can effectively grasp the immensity of this city. Such magnitude may not produce psychological alienation, but it does mean that few occupants live the city as a whole.

One of the major developments in the period after the Semana de Arte Moderna that confirmed São Paulo's new, vital role in Brazilian life was the creation in 1934 of the Universidade de São Paulo, now one of the best higher-learning institutions in Latin America. Brazil did not have anything like a university system until the twentieth century, preferring before that to affirm its continued ties with the mother country by sending its sons (as only males were allowed to study) to the flagship Portuguese university, the Universidade de Coimbra. However, as the pool of university-ready Brazilians began to include significant numbers of the sons of immigrants with no reasonable tie with Coimbra, the German community in Curitiba founded its own state university in 1910, the Universidade do Paraná. Although it would be several decades before Brazil began to develop a federal university system, at which time Paraná was incorporated into a system that includes universities nationwide, when São Paulo decided to create its own university, it did so as a municipal undertaking made possible by new local wealth, and the school has remained outside the federal system to the present day, standing as a symbol of São Paulo's sense of a unique urban identity.

While São Paulo and other cities had professional schools and institutes prior to the establishment of Paraná and the USP (to use its current acronym), there was nothing like the sort of comprehensive university that Spanish-American societies such as Argentina, Mexico, Colombia, and Chile had established as part of the project of attaining independence from Spain—comprehensive universities in the sense that they are descendants of the medieval institutions of Paris, Oxford, Salamanca, Bologna, and, of course, Coimbra. The USP stands as a symbol of a certain level of academic—and, indirectly, cultural—sophistication that was very much a part of the Paulista (relative to the state of São Paulo)/Paulistana (relative to the city of São Paulo) imaginary that was firmly in place by the fourth decade of the twentieth century. While there are now many universities in São Paulo, the USP remains something like a symbol of what the city has become in the national mosaic.

The essays brought together in this volume all focus on the city of São Paulo, in the triple dynamic of cultural production: the critical representation of society, the analytical interpretation of the internal dynamic, and the principled imagination of alternative ways of living. They do not propose to be a history of the cultural production of São Paulo, which would require a multivolume encyclopedic approach, nor do they pretend to be a carefully balanced survey of all possible modalities or genres of cultural production, which would require the efforts of diverse specialists in the face of ever-expanding manifestations of cultural responses: as the city grows exponentially, its culture—especially when culture is seen in the broadest terms possible and not only as a socially elite and institutionally privileged Culture—likewise grows exponentially. One would be hard put to know where to begin—after obvious categories such as fiction or film or theater—compiling an adequate bibliography of cultural production. Perhaps it is an important postmodern perception to recognize that such a bibliography cannot now or ever be compiled.

Rather, I have prepared a series of essays that capture some of the most characteristic cultural products that index São Paulo. There is much that is personal in the choice of these manifestations, both in terms of my own professional capabilities and what I have found to be the most instructive texts. Some of them are well known, while others are presented here as deserving of greater attention than they have customarily attracted. This is particularly true in the case of individuals whose names are associated with São Paulo, but whose work has so far escaped detailed analysis, such as Claude Lévi-Strauss's photography of the city.[7]

The volume opens with an examination of the poetry of Mário de Andrade devoted to the city of São Paulo. Andrade was responsible for a wealth of artistic materials important to the emergence of a national Brazilian literature in the context of the Semana de Arte Moderna, perhaps none more notable that his antiheroic novel *Macunaíma* (1928), which deals with the experiences in São Paulo of a visitor from the indigenous interior.[8] While *Macunaíma* provides a memorable Bakhtinian interpretation of the city and has been widely studied, much denser in terms of a poetic engagement with the city is the volume of poetry studied here, *Paulicéia desvairada* (Hallucinated São Paulo; 1922), a work whose title points, with its head noun, toward an epic vision of the city, which is, in turn, parodied by the accompanying adjective: *desvairada*, meaning "hallucinated" or "delirious," counters such grandiose visions (indeed, *Hallucinated City* is Jack E. Tomlin's title for his translation of the text). A work directly tied by date to the Semana de Arte Moderna, *Pauliceia* is the first significant literary interpretation of São Paulo in Brazilian literature. But Andrade's collection of poetry is essentially a highly artistic rendition of the city by one of Brazil's great men of letters. Chapter 2, devoted to Patrícia Galvão's writing on São Paulo, turns to a more proletarian and materialistic experience of urban life.

One of the most controversial figures of the Semana de Arte Moderna is Patrícia Galvão, the only woman writer of note associated with the movement, which was in most regards resolutely masculinist (mention must, however, be made of the important participation of the women painters Anita Malfati and Tarsila do Amaral). The story of Galvão's involvement with the Brazilian Communist Party, which frequently condemned her for pursuing a personalist agenda in opposition to party discipline and despite the fact that she paid for her political commitments by being the first female political prisoner in Brazilian history, exemplifies the complexity of her personality. As part of the revolt against the bourgeois values of her family, Galvão left the family home in Santos to live in São Paulo, where she had extensive ties to the industrial proletariat that accompanied the capitalist development of the city. The result was her socialist realist novel—one of the few signed by women in Latin America—*Parque industrial* (1933; the Brazilian Communist Party obliged her to publish under the pseudonym Mara Lobo). Although the Brazilian academic establishment continues to pay little heed to this important early feminist figure, Galvão now enjoys a secure place in any history of women's writing in Brazil, and her novel, a veritable chorus of women's voices, is a significant representation of both immigrant districts of São Paulo, such as Brás and Moock, and the industrial parks that were developed there, presumably to take advantage of cheap immigrant—especially women's—labor. The discussion of *Parque industrial* is followed by an examination of a previously unknown document by Galvão, an autobiographical account that serves to reinforce her importance as a voice of women's urban experience. Galvão's feminist interpretation of São Paulo is strikingly complemented by the brilliant photographic work of Hildegard Rosenthal, who had a very keen eye for the daily public life of the city.

Another near-forgotten woman's representation of São Paulo is that offered by photographer Hildegard Rosenthal. In a certain sense, it is incorrect to call her a photographer, since this implies not only a professional engagement, but also an extended commitment to the art, both of which were untrue for Rosenthal. Arriving in Brazil in 1934 as a refugee from the Nazis (although she was not Jewish herself, she had married a Jew, Walter Rosenthal), she soon moved in important artistic circles and found herself persuaded to begin photographing her new home. During a span of only nine years, 1938–47, Rosenthal took thousands of images of São Paulo before abandoning her undertaking in order to raise a family. Records show that it was not until 1974 that her photography was first shown at the Universidade de São Paulo. The Instituto Moreia Salles inherited her archive upon her death in 1990 and published the first representative volume of her photography. In 1975, the Museu de Arte de São Paulo undertook a retrospective. Rosenthal's importance lies in the fact that her photographic gaze was both that of a foreigner and that of a woman, at a time when São Paulo was still very much a man's city.[9] Indeed, the degree to which São Paulo favored the masculinist gaze is evident in the photography studied in chapter 5, which will examine Claude Lévi-Strauss's focus on the architectural landscape of the city.

Equally important for his foreigner's gaze on the city was the French-Jewish intellectual Lévi-Strauss, whose brief tenure at the newly founded Universidade de São Paulo was the launching pad for his anthropological work there. Lévi-Strauss first arrived in São Paulo in 1935, but his anthropological work is best represented by *Tristes tropiques* (Sad Tropics; 1955), a work that went on to have a major place in the development of twentieth-century anthropology. As part of his field work in Brazil, Lévi-Strauss took many photographs with indigenous themes, which he considered important as notes for his subsequent interpretations, but unimportant as creative productions themselves. Many of these photographs are included in *Saudades do Brasil* (Nostalgia for Brasil; 1995), which has received considerable attention as part of Lévi-Strauss's fieldwork. However, while attention has been devoted exclusively to the anthropological material, *Saudades do Brasil* includes a number of the photographs Lévi-Strauss took of São Paulo during his brief residence there, photographs that are an important part of the record of changes that took place in the city in the latter half of the 1930s. These photographs were subsequently reproduced along with others in the book *Saudades de São Paulo* (Nostalgia for São Paulo; 1996), which is quite obscure, at least to judge by its absence in international libraries (World-Cat lists only 14 holdings worldwide, as compared to 528 for *Saudades do Brasil*). The contrast between the gaze of the two foreigners—Rosenthal and Lévi-Strauss—is instructive. Lévi-Strauss, coming from Paris, appears to be more fascinated by the emerging metropolitan built environment (his image of the 1924 Edifício Martinelli, the first skyscraper in Latin America, is perhaps the best known). While Rosenthal did photograph aspects of the built environment (such as Getúlio Vargas's 1940 manifestly fascist-inspired sports stadium, the Estádio do Pacaembu near downtown São Paulo), she was more interested in the individuals who moved in the public space, capturing notably the masculinist cast of the city at that time and even using her female assistant as a subject to add more heterogeny to the cityscape.

The four writers, two Brazilian and two foreign, two men and two women, are representative of the modernist interpretation of the emerging metropolis, soon to be megalopolis.

As a transition from the culture of modernism to that of postmodernism, chapter 6 focuses on film. Certainly, film is the modernist cultural medium par excellence and is the most truly original and pervasive of art forms in the twentieth century as a whole, vying in the latter half with the related genre of television (indeed, films are often a staple of television programming). Yet film also served as a major vehicle for the questioning of modernism, most decidedly for the incoherencies of the city as it created great swaths of social malcontents and dissidents unable to find a place for themselves in the sort of modernist city contemplated by *São Paulo, sinfonia da metrópole* (São Paulo, Symphony of the Metropolis; 1929), Adalberto Kemeny's and Rudolf Rex Lustig's paean to the city of Brazil's future; Kemeny and Lustig were both European immigrants.[10] *São Paulo*, while it does not turn its gaze away from some unpleasant urban realities, such as a brief prison scene, is unrelentingly jingoistic and upbeat, with the rapid transition of images a correlate of the presumed intense rhythms of Brazil's new center. This gaze will, however, give way to an intense filmic production anchored in São Paulo that will underscore the city's dysfunction, despair, and seemingly insuperable violence.

Madalena Schwartz was another important foreign photographer of São Paulo. She too was a Jewish refugee (from Hungary, via Buenos Aires), and although she did not begin working in photography until late in her middle age, she went on to become Brazil's most important portrait photographer, working extensively in publicity and producing images of some of Brazil's most prominent citizens. However, Schwartz also developed a personal artistic line to her photography. Working exclusively in black and white and venturing into the outback, she might be said to be Brazil's first eco-photographer. Of interest to this study, however, is her perspective on marginal urban groups; she is famous for her images of often marginalized Afro-Brazilians, such as the singer Clementina de Jesús and the spiritual leader Mãe Menininha do Gantois, as well as the transvestite performance group, Dzi Croquettes, whose creative resistance to the censorship of the 1964 military coup won them an international audience. Again, Schwartz's work, as that of a foreigner and a Jew, is important as a site of a highly innovative gaze on urban phenomena. Unlike Rosenthal, who tended to focus on street life, and Lévi-Strauss, who was fascinated with the built environment, Schwartz was very much the intimate portraitist. Yet she too captured the enormous complexity of urban life. Regina Rheda, to be discussed in chapter 8, also focuses on individual lives, but she does so by relating them to one of the great architectural icons of São Paulo, the Edifício Copan.

If the 1927 Martinelli is the signature building of early Brazilian modernism, the one representing its high point is the 1960 Edifício Copan, originally an Oscar Niemeyer project (although he later abandoned it) designed to commemorate in 1954 the four hundredth anniversary of São Paulo. The largest residential structure in Brazil (it even has its own postal code), the Copan has not always weathered well and experienced a notable decline with the abandonment of the old city core in the late 1970s and 1980s (the

Copan is located only a few blocks from the original central city square, the Praça da República). However, downtown São Paulo is experiencing something of a comeback, including a refurbishing of the downtown and enhanced security, and the Copan has now regained some of its former attractiveness, which for some is signaled by the disappearance of the evangelical sect that had made its home in the theatrical space that was part of the original building design. Depicting the Copan before its more recent rejuvenation, Regina Rheda's short stories index the decline of the Copan as part of the decline of downtown São Paulo; it is a descent that is very much antiphonic as regards the modernist city represented by the cultural production examined in the first segment of this volume. In chapter 9, the interpretation of São Paulo, following the emphasis of Galvão and Rosenthal, returns to the streets of the city, with Emílio Eduardo Fenianos's enormously original urban expedition.

Eduardo Emílio Fenianos has authored what may be considered a significant postmodern book about São Paulo. Since São Paulo is a city of cultural experimentation dating back to the Semana de Arte Moderna, it is not surprising that Fenianos saw the potential for expanding on a grand scale the more modest experiment he had attempted in his native Curitiba (Curitiba is Brazil's fifth major demographic concentration and the capital of the state of Paraná, the home of the Cataratas de Iguaçu [Iguaçu Falls]) a few years earlier. Fenianos's project, dubbed the Urbenauta, was to spend three months living in his jeep and touring his native city in order to produce a book interpreting its urban nature; this he did in 1998 under the title *O Urbenauta: manual de sobrevivência na selva urbana* (The Urbenaut; Manual for Survival in the Urban Jungle), and his account is accompanied by a series of photographic dossiers on each of Curitiba's neighborhoods, many of them still ethnic in nature.

In 2002, Fenianos published *Expedições Urbenauta: uma aventura radical* (Expeditions Urbenaut: A Radical Adventure), which dealt with a greatly expanded version of the aforementioned undertaking in São Paulo, wherein he spent a year traversing the streets of the city's dozens of official divisions and neighborhoods. If it is true that most people live large cities on a very local level—the site of their residence and the site of their workplace, connected only by some form of private or public transportation that does yield itself to familiarity with the points that intervene between home and work—the Urbenauta's "radical adventure," designed to attain a comprehensive understanding of the city, is unique.

Graphic humor and narrative are particularly modern cultural genres, and their content, format, and parameters of legibility are characteristically urban: the material details of the cityscape are rendered in all their complexity as part of both foreground and background of the stories told in the successive snapshots of the strips of graphic narration. Although Fábio Moon and Gabriel Bá have worked extensively in various graphic genres, from the gothic and fantastic to the illustration of literary classics, the *De:Tales: Stories from Urban Brazil* confirms their interest in the narratives of the megalopolis. Significantly written and published originally in English (I do not know if there are plans for a Brazilian edition in Portuguese), *De:Tales* (a title that plays on both "such and such" and "details") is a collection of twelve short stories in graphic form that focus on the tensions of urban life set against the backdrop of the often staggeringly daunting city that São Paulo has now become. Moon and Bá's São Paulo is no longer a dynamic model for the development of Brazilian modernity, but rather a labyrinth of human ciphers and their conflicting and frequently self-annihilating passions and emotions.

The reader will have noted by this point that there is a particular absence in this book of traditional narrative genres such as fiction and theater. With the exception of Patrícia Galvão's novel *Parque industrial* (*Industrial Park*), virtually ignored by academic criticism, and Regina Rheda's stories under the title of *Arca sem Noé* (And Ark without Noah), the immense bibliography of narrative fiction is not represented here (for São Paulo in literature, see Rosso; *Cultura paulista*). Nor can the lack of attention to theater—São Paulo is now the undisputed theater center of Brazil, with hundreds of new works performed every year—be overlooked. Rather than focus on these traditional genres, which have already been studied extensively by other scholars, my goal has been to place emphasis on forms of cultural production that are somehow unique to the city of São Paulo. This has meant the inclusion of Andrade's poetry on São Paulo, a singular contribution for its day in terms of thematic focus, and Galvão's novel, which remains an isolated feminist contribution to urban social realism. Likewise, the concern for urban photography is inflected by the way in which some of the most important contributions to the genre were made by foreigners, precisely at a time when São Paulo had come to define itself as one of Latin America's great immigrant centers.

Finally, this volume's attention to film, graphic narrative, and the chronicle of an urban *dérive* underscores some of the particularly singular ways in which the city of São Paulo is being represented and interpreted.[11] Film is, of course, now a firmly entrenched cultural genre, but it is its visual capacities that have been most intriguingly put to use in surveying lived human experience in the city. By contrast, graphic fiction and the chronicle do not yet possess as extensive a bibliography as film has by now accumulated. Nevertheless, they are represented here as part of a conviction that they, as well as other yet-to-be-identified emerging genres, will someday be characteristic of the cultural production of São Paulo. São Paulo has come a long way since Mário de Andrade and Patrícia Galvão participated, respectively, directly and indirectly in the project of the Semana de Arte Moderna and its enormous derivations for Brazilian art. São Paulo now competes quite vigorously with Rio for honors as the cultural capital of Brazil, and it will continue to be important to recognize that fact. The essays brought together in this volume are one example of that recognition.[12]

My first and most enthusiastic acknowledgement is always for my students, including my research assistants Kyle Black, Assen Kokalov, Eduardo Muslip, and Caridad Rodríguez. Charles St. George assisted me magnificently in the preparation of the final manuscript. I am, as always, grateful to the research programs at Arizona State University, which have supported my work for almost fifty years; this project received special support of the Jewish Studies Program. Material presented here was also developed as part of funding received from the National Endowment for the Humanities, Summer Seminars for College and University Teachers, for my 2006 seminar on Urban Brazilian Narrative. I am grateful for funding provided by Arizona State University's Barrett Honors College. My Portuguese Studies colleagues Isis McElroy and Clarice Deal have provided me with invaluable insights and information, and colleagues in Brazil—Jaime Ginzburg, Denize Araujo, Márcio Seligman-Silva, Silvana Garcia, Lizandro Calegari, João Luis Ourique—have provided intellectual and material support for this study. Work on the final version occurred when I was the Ednagene and Jordan Davidson Eminent Scholar in the Humanities at Florida International University. As always, Naomi Lindstrom is my best and most rigorous first reader. I hope someday my young grandsons, James Gustaf Svoboda and George William Foster, will want to read it!

1

Mário de Andrade

On Being São Paulo-Wise in
Paulicéia desvairada

When Mário de Andrade published his book of poetry *Paulicéia desvairada* in 1922,[1] São Paulo was only beginning to present the interesting urban landscape that a European flâneur like Claude Lévi-Strauss would find intriguing enough to photograph a decade later (see chapter 5). As part of a constellation of Latin American cities that profited immensely from the great expansion of capitalism on the continent from the latter part of the nineteenth century on, São Paulo also benefited from the particular burst of prosperity that accompanied the post–World War I years. Along with Mexico City and Buenos Aires (Buenos Aires in particular), São Paulo became one of the seats of a fully affirmed project of modernity that was only made possible by an unusual influx of wealth and the prosperity and its derivatives that such wealth provides, such as the material needs of cultural production: individuals with the wherewithal to produce culture and individuals with the leisure and sociopolitical horizons to consume it.

Culture unquestionably became a commodity in areas of Latin America that included São Paulo. And wherever a sociology of culture may be interested in examining the way in which culture begins to function as part of an overall structure of commodification, it becomes important to examine how the materiality of culture also exists as a thematics of that very cultural production. Certainly, material aspects of culture are present in the works of Machado de Assis a generation before, and, indeed, Machado's literature is significantly understood to be possible as a consequence of the very nature of the society he describes, with its own high level of prosperity and the preoccupations that come with and are made possible by such a socioeconomic level (see Trigo on Machado's Rio de Janeiro).

Certainly Brazilian prosperity was carried to a higher power by post–World War I developments, as the economic base shifted (it had actually begun to do so by the early part of the twentieth century) to São Paulo and a less feudal and more bourgeois society. It is the absolutely primum mobile axiom of Brazilian culture that modern Brazil has as its paradigmatic reflex the Semana de Arte Moderna in February 1922, an event of which Mário de Andrade was himself one of the prime movers, and unquestionably one dimension of Andrade's *Macunaíma* (1928) concerns the other major shift in Brazilian society, from the rural outback (the *sertão*) to the metropolis. Although Andrade's œuvre manifests ample interest in traditional aspects of Brazilian culture, such as his work on folklore and traditional music, one of the singular aspects of his production during the third decade of the twentieth century is his "discovery" of the city as a realm of human experience worthy of being interpreted via poetry (Perrone, "Presentation and Representation" surveys Andrade's interest in São Paulo and critical estimations to it; he also links Andrade to other vanguard poets versifying the city; see "Performing São Paulo").

Indeed, it is significant that *Paulicéia desvairada* is Andrade's first book of poetry,[2] as though the discovery of the city and the investment in the most privileged form of literary production, poetry, were to have coincided. Poetry is, of course, the undisputed genre of Brazilian modernism (as also with the Latin American equivalent, *vanguardismo*), and in this case what is of interest is the conjunction of the "unpoetic" texture of the modern metropolis with the privileged Orphic voice. What, then, becomes of interest is the way in which Andrade provides an interpretation of the texture of the dynamically evolving São Paulo of the 1920s: the very title of the collection connotes the nonplacid nature of its movement. What is not at issue is merely the way in which the city is thematized or "represented" (Perrone, "Presentation and Representation"), as though the individual poems (there are twenty-two in all) were pictures in an exhibition of landscapes, local-color settings, and typical occupations and pastimes. Rather, of concern are the material aspects of the city as they become the stuff of poetry:

its semiotic processes, rather than its meaning effects; the urbanization of poetic language, rather than the poetization of the cityscape (as Suárez and Tomlins assert, 55).

In order to elaborate what might be understood by the urbanization of poetic language, one can begin with the following postulates:

1. Such a semiotic process means the incorporation into poetry of the fullest parameters of the city. But whereas, were they to concern themselves with the city at all, Romantic poets engaged in pathetic fallacy and Parnassian poets idealized the cityscape in terms of Arcadian gardens and the landscapes of refined and privileged taste, modernism finds its preferred anchor in the city and its evolving modernity. The very fact that Andrade organizes this collection of poems around the city of São Paulo is significant. The history of Brazil has been a southward displacement of urban centers, from the colonial Salvador de Bahia to, first, the imperial and, subsequently, the late nineteenth-century early republican Rio de Janeiro, to the São Paulo that emerges early in the twentieth century as the financial center of the country; it is significant to note that Brasília may now have been the official capital of the country for fifty years. Yet it has never become anything other than a bureaucratic enclave, with none of the iconic, mythic, or symbolic associations attributed to the three historical centers of the country. Indeed, although one can speak of a filmic production specifically associated with Rio de Janeiro, one is hard put to recall a major work of poetry like *Paulicéia desvairada* devoted to Rio or to Bahia.[3] Andrade's poetry is characterized by an emphasis on the ethos of the city, and on the engagement of the poetic voice with its material realities: "Tenho os pés chagados nos espinhos das calçadas . . ."[4] (the opening verse to "Colloque sentimental" [Andrade, Poesias completas 99]).[5]

2. It is inevitable that the language referring to the material reality of the city appear cited, if not used in a body of poetry on the city. As Andrade says in one of the affirmations to be found in the "Prefácio interessantíssimo" ("Extremely Interesting Preface"), a sixty-six paragraph meditation that fronts *Paulicéia desvairada*,[6]

Escrever arte moderna não significa jamais para mim representar a vida atual no que tem de exterior: automóveis, cinema, asfalto. Si estas palavras freqüentam-me o livro não é porque pense com elas escrever moderno, mas porque sendo meu livro moderno, elas têm nele sua razão de ser. (Paragraph 52 [74])[7]

With such a statement, the difference between the mundane and the lyrical is undermined. Whereas the latter refers to an aesthetic realm removed from the "hallucinations" of everyday life, the focus on the texture of the everyday life of the city—the "Paulicéia desvairada"[8]—brings with it inevitably the specific *stylus humilis* of the language of urban existence (see Schelling 77–79 on Andrade's conceptions of primitivism and language). The purpose of Andrade's poems would seem not to be to write directly about the machinery and devices of modern life—he specifically rejects the futurism of Marinetti, so associated with "singing" the machinery and devices of modern life (paragraph 12 [60])—but if their appearance is inevitable in describing the cityscape, their physical presence and their visual and auditory features (their integral contribution to urban noise) is inescapable.

3. Andrade's commitment to Brazilian Portuguese is legendary (see Pinto). To be sure, the term "Brazilian Portuguese" means many different things and refers to numerous concurrent developments of the language: as a part of the natural evolution of any spoken language, especially a deterritorialized one in contact with many other languages (indigenous languages, the languages of immigrants, and the prestige languages of alternative cultural models, none of which may be immediately evident to the imperial establishment, past or present); as a part of the pedagogical association with an academic norm (adherence to the imperial norm, but nevertheless conscious of irreversible local developments); and as part of the conscious creative projects of literati. Such developments may refer as much to the lexicon (which is often what is most understood as the stuff of regional variants) as they do to pronunciation (immediately evident, but often underrated as literarily significant) and morphosyntax (usually referred to unsystematically).

For example, Andrade refers to "A língua brasileira é das mais ricas e sonoras. E possui o admirabilíssimo 'ão'" (paragraph 34 [67]).[9] Since the diphthong "ão" is not exclusive to the phonology of Brazilian Portuguese, one wonders whether Andrade is referring to a certain Brazilian phoneticization in which, rather than a nasalized [a], what is articulated is a nasalized [ï].[10] Of course, Andrade could simply be referring to this phonologic combination in all dialects of Portuguese, but the nationalism of the qualifier is noteworthy. There is throughout the "Prefácio" a string of allusions to language. A particularly alluring one implies a rejection of Portuguese academic standards, a commitment to the spontaneity of the spoken language, and, in the fashion of the Modernistas, the bootlegged nature of national varieties:

A gramática apareceu depois de organizadas as línguas. Acontece que meu inconsciente não sabe da existência de gramáticas, nem de línguas organizadas. E como Dom Lirismo é contrabandista. . . . (paragraph 49 (73)[11]

Certainly, there is a snide remark about Portuguese academicism contained in the following affirmation:

Pronomes? Escrevo brasileiro. Si uso ortografia portuguesa é porque, não alterando o resultado, dá-me uma ortografia. (paragraph 51 [74])[12]

While Andrade does not specifically refer in these prefatory notes to the quality of a geolect typical of modern São Paulo, existing criticism on *Paulicéia desvairada* has repeatedly observed how its linguistic cadences constitute an important index of the urban manifestations of Brazilian Portuguese,[13] a phenomenon that could be borne out by the examination of other important literary works of the period anchored in São Paulo.[14]

4. One of the overarching features of *Paulicéia desvairada* is its divided attitude toward the city. On the one hand, Andrade is unquestionably enthralled by the dynamic modernity of the metropolis, while at the same time he is appalled by the bourgeois vulgarity that modernity enables, as much in regard to conventional manners and morality as the ostentatious theater that is an integral part of the consumerist imperative of modernity. Thus he is able to enunciate, as the very first verse of the inaugural poem ("Inspiração" ["Inspiration"]) of his collection, "São Paulo! comoção de minha vida . . ." (83).[15] Yet, two verses later, in one of the recurring motifs of *Paulicéia desvairada*, he refers to "Arlequinal! . . . Trajes de losangos . . . Cinza e ouro . . ." (83).[16] Although other phrases are used with exclamation marks, "Arlequinal!" is placed as though it were an epiphoneme of "São Paulo!," which is repeated as the penultimate line of the poem: São Paulo = Arlequinal! = São Paulo! References to arlequinal, either as an adjective or nominalized adjective, abound in the collection, appearing more than a dozen times (see Kossovitch 94–111 on the importance of this motif in Andrade's writing). Portuguese, like English, allows for this word to refer to the harlequin both with the specific sense of type of comedic performer and in an extended sense as anything that is characterized by the clownish, the buffoonish, and the farcical, with the comedic shading off into the grotesque.

Andrade's third poem, "Os cortejos" ("The Processions"), states as its fourth verse "Horríveis as cidades!" (84),[17] while Andrade's acerbic "Ode ao burguês" ("Ode to the Bourgeois Gentleman") is one of the most famous poems of the collection. It begins with the verse "Eu insulto o burguês!"

(88),[18] and ends with the triple imperative "Fora! Fu! Fora o bom burguês! ..." (89).[19] To be sure, one associates ambivalent attitudes with the city, modern or otherwise, and the metaphor of the fall from divine grace instituted by St. Augustine's trope of the City of Man is an abiding figure of Western culture. Jorge Luis Borges, Andrade's contemporary (see the comparative study by Rodríguez Monegal), may have been unstintingly elegiac in his poems to the city of Buenos Aires in *Fervor de Buenos Aires* (1923), but the simple fact is that one associates with the evocation of the alternating pattern of seduction and repulsion by the city that *Paulicéia desvairada* evinces, much in the same fashion as other contemporary writers (Salvador Novo and Federico García Lorca, for instance) portray places like Mexico City and New York. Not until the Mexican Carlos Monsiváis's 1995 collection of essays *Los rituales del caos* is the Latin American city (now more postmodern or extra-modern than modern) given its due, with the full extent of its tumultuous nature endorsed. Much more customary was the sort of urban interpretation promoted by the Peruvian Sebastián Salazar Bondy's 1964 essay *Lima la horrible* or the Argentine Ezequiel Martínez Estrada's 1940 essay *La cabeza de Goliat*.

Richard Morse, in his marvelous "biography of São Paulo"—a subtitle that serves to grammatically animate the city in much the same way that Andrade does in *Paulicéia*—writes that:

> in São Paulo, as in the whole Western World, the early years of this century were marked by childlike exuberance, by naive conceptions of "happiness" and cultural refinement, and by the naive belief that these commodities were inevitable rewards for pecuniary success in a world of increasingly numerous and remunerative opportunities. The most vital foreign influences were not those in which the city passively acquiesced but those which answered its new rhythms of life. (202–03)

It would now be appropriate to examine how these primes regarding the urbanization of a Brazilian poetic voice are carried out in representative texts of the two dozen compositions that make up *Paulicéia desvairada*.

To a certain extent, Elizabeth Lowe is correct in identifying Andrade's "Romantic pose in relation to the city that he embraced and rejected with equal passion" (94)—that is, insofar as regards a measure of pathetic fallacy. Lowe does not explain what she means by a "Romantic pose," although one suspects that it has to do with the emotional engagement of the poet with the cityscape. Yet I would insist that this is not so much a

São Paulo: Perspectives on the City and Cultural Production

measure of reading into the city the turbulence of the poet's own soul, but rather, in a more Whitmanesque way, the manner in which the poetic voice engages with the awesome array of spectacle the city presents (I believe this is the case with DiAntonio's concept of Andradian "primitivism," a stance often associated with the romantic). If the recurring synthetic motif of this spectacle is the Arlequinal, the dazzle of the harlequin's outfit and comportment provide the best cipher of that spectacle. Thus, in the following text, "Paisagem No. 1" ("Landscape I"; there are four), the poetic voice recounts a personalized engagement with the city:

> Minha Londres das neblinas finas . . .
> Pleno verão. Os dez mil milhões de rosas paulistanas.
> Há neves de perfumes no ar.
> Faz frio, muito frio . . .
> E a ironia das pernas das costureirinhas
> Parecidas com bailarinas . . .
> O vento é como uma navalha
> Nas mãos dum espanhol. Arlequinal . . .
> Há duas horas queimou Sol.
> Daqui a duas horas queima Sol.
>
> Passa um São Bobo, cantando, sob os plátanos,
> Um tralalá . . . A guarda-cívica! Prisão!
> Necessidade a prisão
> Para que haja civilização?
> Meu coração sente-se muito triste . . .
> Enquanto o cinzento das ruas arrepiadas
> Dialoga um lamento como o vento . . .
>
> Meu coração sente-se muito alegre!
> Este friozinho arrebitado
> Dá uma vontade de sorrir!
>
> E sigo. E vou sentindo,
> À inquieta alacridade da invernia,
> Como um gosto de lágrimas na boca. . . . (87–88)[20]

There is an internal contradiction between the first and the second verses: while it is certainly understandable for the poet to see São Paulo as a version of foggy London, and a London that is anchored in the tight personal relationship implied by the possessive adjective, the second verse refers to the fact that what he is contemplating is characteristic of the middle of summer. I would suggest that what is going on here is that the middle of São Paulo's summer (January and February) marks England's deepest winter— the period, of course, of the deep fogs of London (at least before current air pollution controls). So what the poet perceives is that the São Paulo summer, with its combination of temperatures averaging in the mid-nineties and its equally high index of humidity, produces a shimmering atmosphere roughly equivalent to the fabled London fog. Thus, the air perfumed by the semitropical flowering vegetation that is one of the city's hallmarks (particularly evident in downtown green spaces such as the Praça da República and the Parque Trianon [officially, Parque Siqueira Campos], not to mention the many other impressive parks the city has to offer) is as though replete with flakes of snow, and, as a consequence, that air is cold, very cold.

This long introductory stanza pursues the image of, to indulge directly in an oxymoron, a tropical cold with the conceit of that cold cutting like a straight razor in the hands of a Spaniard. The moment of contemplation is a period between the sun of two hours ago and the sun of two hours hence, as though this were a customary interlude in the heat of the day during which the temperature somehow dropped, producing an inverse climatological bell curve (since a natural one would rise until afternoon and then fall off). The image of the legs of the dress-shop girls (marked by poverty, malnourished, and rachitic) seeming ironically to be those of dancers reinforces the transformative gaze here—a gaze in which the texture of the city during the summer imposes a transformation as though one were seeing winter—because the mundane transit of the shop workers was like the graceful movement of a highly trained dancer. In general, there is a transformative perception here in favor of a highly erratic poetization of the cityscape.

Yet I have insisted that the tenor of *Paulicéia desvairada* is not the poetization of the urban setting, but rather the incorporation into a poetic discourse of the texture of urban life. Thus, in the three stanzas quoted above, the material reality of the city intrudes on this poetic vision,[21] driven by the metamorphosis of the poet's São Paulo in the summertime into the topos of foggy London in the winter, to specify some of its less "poetic" circumstances. These include the "São Bobo," an example of the homeless demented, singing to himself under the ever-present canopy of banana trees—an integral part of the city's landscaping and a form of natural shade for street people who have no hope of any other sort of protection from the sun—and the presence of the city police, who serve as a reminder of the specter of imprisonment for the disorderly, an imprisonment necessary in order to preserve the civilization of which the city is a paradigm. São Paulo in the 1920s was undoubtedly more beset by problems of disorderliness, including specifically those that accompanied rapid growth driven by the influx from both abroad and the interior, than São Paulo of recent decades, in which violent crime is a permanent part of the city's fabric (on violence in São Paulo in the twentieth century see Caldeira).

Such images reaffirm the perception of wintry cold, but it is much more of an emotional chill than a meteorological one: the grimness of the cityscape (the perfumed flocks have been forgotten) and the wind of social reality engage in a dialogue of lament. Andrade's stanza is not itself a lament, since it evokes a mood rather than articulating a response to that mood, but it is metapoetic in the sense of juxtaposing the discourse of the poem to that articulated by the streets themselves: the literary poem cites, so to speak, the material poem of the now decidedly unpoetic streets. That is, the lyricism of the opening stanza now must engage implicitly in an antiphony with the details of social reality, which cannot be evoked jejunely by poetic tropes. Whereas the social reality of the proletarian shop girls poetized them as dancers, nothing remains here to poetize—not the urban demented, not the city police and the reminder they bring of the consequences civilization imposes on disorderliness, not the (presumedly) ragged banana trees (hardly the spreading chestnut/elm/oak trees that provide shade in a topical Arcadian landscape), and certainly not the shivering grayness of the windswept streets.

The second stanza implies a mood swing (verse fifteen, "Meu coração sente-se muito triste . . . ," becomes verse eighteen, "Meu coração sente-se muito alegre!"): the ellipses of verse fifteen are something like the orthographic antonym of the exclamation point of verse eighteen, which, in addition to the explicit movement from "triste" to "alegre," is sustained by the pairing of the partially phonetically similar "arrepiadas" (verse sixteen) and "arrebiado" (verse nineteen). Such a mood swing is indicative of Andrade's profoundly mixed feelings about the city of São Paulo, the interplay of embrace and rejection Lowe refers to (there is much that is schematic in Andrade's poems; see Foster, "Some Formal Types"). Of course, if I may be subjective, a certain amount of cold does lift the spirits in the face of the oppressive realities of the city. But no further elaboration is given, and the poem concludes with the stanza inaugurated by the pithy declarative "E sigo," because this is the poet's relation to the city: he continues to traverse it, continues to perceive it, and continues to feel the emotions of attraction and repulsion it produces. Whatever it is that he has synthesized about the city as a wintry gloom, it leaves a taste of sadness in his mouth, and that is the closing image of the poem—urban reality is always more likely to produce a sensation of sadness than happiness. Neither an idealized landscape nor one of disillusionment, neither utopian nor dystopian, Andrade's São Paulo is always the mixed image of the harlequin: panache signalling grotesque farce.

The opening line of "Colloque sentimental" might serve as a hypogram (see below) for the totality of *Paulicéia desvairada*:

Tenho os pés chagados nos espinhos das calçadas . . .
Higienópolis! . . . As Babilônias dos meus desejos baixos . . .
Casas nobres de estilo . . . Enriqueceres em tragédias . . .
Mas a noite é toda um véu-de-noiva ao luar! (99)[22]

A "hypogram," as developed by Riffaterre, is often understood to be the title of a poem, an abstract of what perception of meaning or sentiment it will develop. "Colloque sentimental" certainly functions appropriately in this regard, announcing that the poem is constructed around a conversation that brings out a range of feelings—in this case, contrary ones about the city that are in line with the general stance taken·by the poetic "I" in *Paulicéia desvairada*. However, the hypogram of a poem may be one of its key verses, typically its opening one, which serves as a sort of "thesis statement" (in the case of untitled poems, of course, it is common to give as their title, if solely for purposes of indexing, the first line). In this case, however, the opening line of "Colloque sentimental" is not so much a hypogram of this one poem as it is of all two dozen compositions. This is so for the following reasons: First of all, it echoes for the poem the global anchoring in *Paulicéia desvairada* of the role of the poetic "I" as a poetic "eye" (I mean to make nothing of the fact that in English these are homonyms). Throughout, the poet is an observer engaged in scrutinizing, often at considerable emotional cost (and, here, physical cost), the burgeoning city at a time when São Paulo is undergoing the transformation from center of the state's plantation economy to a modern industrial hub, which in turn will serve as the springboard for the city's emergence as the financial capital of the entire continent. The poetic I as inquisitive eye will scrutinize the contrast between the older seignorial city and a metropolis teaming with proletarian workers, including immigrant masses; between the rawness of the texture of this evolving urban scene and the paradigmatic image of Paris (which was as much a model to the old plantation aristocracy as it was to the new vanguard generation); between the modern exemplars of Paulistana life and the motif of Babylonian excess and decadence.

Second, the poet is an incarnation of the homo viator, the individual who roams the world and reports on what is to be perceived. Certainly, the topos of the homo viator is customarily linked with the motif of the journey of life, and it is often embedded in a bildungsroman as the major device for generating the experiences that lead to the protagonist's character formation (as such, Andrade's *Macunaíma* is very much a parody of the modern bildungsroman). However, the homo viator is a potent poetic trope that captures one process for contemplating the world and thereby producing a perception that validates the poetic effort. It is the experience, as the opening line of a traditional Appalachian carol has it, of the individual who can say, "I wonder as I wander out under the sky." In this case, there is not an explicit reference to seeing, but there is to wandering, as the Belle Époque flâneur has been replaced by the individual who breaks free of the former's limited prestige circuit (to continue with the conjunction with the image of Paris, the Walter Benjamin upper-bourgeois realm of the arcade, often transformed in a balmier Latin America into the pedestrian mall of which the aristocratic Buenos Aires Calle Florida of yore is the paradigm [Cócaro and Cócaro]) in order to literally stumble through the streets.

The way in which the poet stumbles through the material reality of the streets, literally wounding his feet on their rough edges (this is one of the finest images in all of Latin American poetry, as it refers to an interaction with the physical city), is carried out in the paired elements that make the poem a colloquy, in the basic sense of the word. For example, one such paired element can be seen in the contrast between the hustle and bustle of popular São Paulo neighborhoods (Brás, Bom Retiro) and Paris, by which one understands not all of Paris (which, on this level, would certainly present no fewer examples of the rough edges of urban life than would São Paulo, and indeed, because of its age, even more), but the Paris of the patrician image of privilege, elegance, and orderliness (as in Higonnet). By contrast, if the term "Paris" refers to the realm of the flâneur and congeners and descendants, "São Paulo" is synonymous with popular areas such as Brás, the paradigm of the industrial districts to the east of the central core (the Praça da Sé), and Bom Retiro, the Jewish quarter to the north anchored by the Parque da Luz and its train station, which is, to use an American metaphor of teaming throngs, the Grand Central Terminal of the city (see the essays by Diafèria et al.).

Another contrasting element functions along the same lines: the drains (presumably fetid) of the city and the handkerchief sweetened with French perfumes which the "count" holds to his nose to mask the urban miasma. Indeed, it is reasonable to believe that the "count" here, who is given a tour through some areas of the city ("Venha comigo então"), is not a French visitor, but rather an example of the (often pseudo-) upper-class individual, still clinging to what remains of the pre-Republic aristocracy (whose sway was not long past, as the Republic dates from 1889, and Andrade's book from 1922). The "count's" point of reference is elegant Higienópolis, but he has descended to the urban Babylon to enjoy the company of a prostitute ("Esqueça um pouco os braços da vizinha . . ."). The poetic "I" here presumably equates himself with the prostitute, since "vizinha" must belong to the deictic sphere of the speaker and not that of the client. (Note that Higienópolis is, in reality, a major avenue and not a district, although the name is often used as such, to evoke part of the prosperous neighborhood of Consolação, to the west of the central core—that is, on the other side of the industrial area evoked by the reference to Brás. The very name Higienópolis, of course, points to how this part of the city is reputedly healthier than the fetid realms to the east, and elsewhere Andrade will refer to the Jardins, a large and very prosperous area to the southeast of Consolação and south of the central core.)

Finally, the synecdoche of the material reality on which the poetic "I" wounds his feet are the paved streets of the city. One could certainly wound oneself and endanger one's health on the mud tracks of a forgotten village, but here specific mention is made of one of the singular characteristics of the built environment of the urban landscape, the paved street. Such an improvement for transportation is not without its problematical aspects, however, and, in the sprawling environment of the Latin American megalopolis, such installations are rarely kept in optimum conditions. There are often potholes and open trenches that have been there for so long that they veritably deserve a bronze plaque to commemorate them as national monuments to the problems of maintaining the infrastructure of the city. Another detail of the problematical infrastructure of the city is that of standing or trickling fetid water, an example of the imperfectly or incompletely channeled waste that is as much a result of the occupants of the city as it is of the installations of their built environment (that is, as much a problem of leaking "used" or "black" water as it is of leaking incoming "white" water that often becomes contaminated by the construction substances of buildings). Andrade here uses that water as a metaphor for the nameless tears of the occupants of the unfortunate neighborhoods into which the "count" has ventured: "Estas paragens trevas de silêncio."

The sentimentality to which "Colloque sentimental" refers is hardly of the sublime order of Romantic poetry (if I may once again restrict the characterization Lowe makes of *Paulicéia desvairada*), but rather the impressionistic reactions of the poetic "I" to the features of the city that wound him both emotionally and physically. Once again, the material reality of the cityscape, the "cogumelo das podridões," is imported into the discourse of poetry as part of the urbanization of its semiotic dynamics. *Paulicéia desvairada* is hardly a hymn or an ode to the city. If modern São Paulo/São Paulo of an emerging high modernity is the realm of the bourgeois triumphant ("A digestão bem feita de São Paulo!" ["Ode ao burguês" 88]), the poet can neither simply sing its accomplishments, as Walt Whitman did in the case of New York, or denounce its depredations, as—to continue the example of New York—Federico García Lorca was to do less than a decade later in *Poeta en Nueva York*. Andrade is manifestly interested in the city of São Paulo as a complex human space, not merely as a forum for projecting one or another social interpretation. That this is manifest may be understood by the many ways in which he focuses on fundamental aspects of the city—both the joy of their vitality and the despair of their ugliness: "Esse espectáculo encantado da Avenida"[23] ("O domador" 92 [the reference is to the Avenida Paulista, the main financial corridor of the city]) versus "Formigueiro onde todos se mordem e devoram" ("A caçada" 94).[24] The final verse of the closing poem of *Paulicéia desvairada* serves as a summary statement of Andrade's ambiguous poetic interaction with the city: "Oh! este orgulho máximo de ser paulistamente!!!" ("Paisagem No. 4" 102).[25]

Aside from the triple exclamation point, a rhetorical insistence not found elsewhere in the collection, what is notable about this verse is the grammatical solecism it involves, a solecism that bears the poet's final statement. The point is that this verse does not close with a nominal or adjectival predicate, the grammatical accompaniments of the verb "ser," but rather with an adverbial complement. Adverbial complements may grammatically be used with the other essive verb in Portuguese, "estar" (which may also take an adverbial complement, but not grammatically a nominal one), and such a construction expresses the status, in terms of manner or mode, of the subject at a particular moment. However, by using an adverb with "ser," the poetic "I" affirms, as grammar books usually explain it, the "permanent and ongoing quality" of the subject of the predicate. Jack Tomlins, in his translation of *Paulicéia desvairada*, seeking a way to render such a solecism in English, opts for, "Oh! this supreme pride in existing São Paulo-wise!!!" (75), although the adverbial marker of the complement is lost ("-wise" functioning in English to mark adjectives). I will not venture to try to improve on Tomlins's translation, since capturing solecisms in translation is a particular stylistic challenge. Suffice it to say that Andrade's closing trope is fully characteristic of the way in which he has written about São Paulo, both transmitting his ambiguous feelings and succeeding admirably in converting a complex modern cityscape into the linguistic event of poetry.

2

The Feminization of Social Space
in Patrícia Galvão's *Parque industrial*

> O bonde se abarrota. De empregadinhas dos magazines.
>
> Telefonistas. Caixeirinhos. Toda a população de mais
>
> explorados, de menos explorados. Para os seus cortiços
>
> na inmensa cidade proletária, o Brás.
>
> ❂ Patrícia Galvão, *Parque industrial* (26)

Patrícia Galvão's novel, *Parque industrial* (1933), is, as noted by the critics who have devoted attention to it in recent years, a textual anomaly. It is now possible to see, as K. David Jackson has done in his superb study of the novel (included as an afterword in the translation he did with Elizabeth Jackson), that *Parque industrial* is coextensive with many aspects of the vanguard movements of the 1920s and 1930s and echoes a spectrum of social concerns common to a period of savage capitalism in São Paulo (Dean, passim). Known almost universally as Pagu,[1] Galvão, although she came from a solid petit-bourgeois household, was from an early age very much a social rebel. Unconventional in her personal life and defiant in her stance toward patriarchal authority, her conduct earned her not only several periods of imprisonment under dreadful conditions at the hands of the state, but also a tumultuous relationship with the Communist Party, from which she ultimately broke (Cancelli, passim, "Pagu"). Although there is good scholarship now available on Galvão's life (1910–62), without there yet being a definitive biography, one of the best sources is the enormously successful film by Norma Bengell, very much characterized by the feminism of the post-dictatorship. *Eternamente Pagu* (Eternally Pagu; 1987) perhaps best captures the spirit of this key figure in a history of female cultural producers in Brazil (see my analysis of the film: Foster, *Gender and Society* 83–96).

The reader will find in the afterword to the Jackson and Jackson translation of *Parque industrial* an extensive characterization of the structure of the novel, its relationship to the social and artistic movements of the period, and references to critical reactions to it, including a discussion of how, "Considered taboo, Pagu's novel fell out of history" (127). Patrícia Galvão, regrettably, remains virtually nonexistent in Brazilian literary history. This is not because she was a woman, since there were several important female artists during the period who attained significant recognition and who have become part of the cultural record, none more prominently than Tarsila do Amaral, who is considered an absolutely crucial figure in the avant-garde movement of São Paulo that was marked by the all-important 1922 Semana de Arte Moderna ("Tarsila do Amaral"). Nor is it because of her voice of social denunciation, since Raquel de Queiroz's novels on the plight of the northeastern peasantry during this time are classic examples of Brazilian socialist realism, which included some of the most famous writers of the period, beginning with the internationally renowned Jorge Amado (who, like Galvão, also broke subsequently with the Communist Party). Even Sílvio Castro's three-volume *História da literatura brasileira* (1999) fails to mention Galvão, and she is only accorded two passing references, with no mention of her novel, in the extensive volume on Brazilian literature in González Echevarría and Pupo-Walker's *The Cambridge History of Latin American Literature*. Nor is Galvão included in classical studies on the modernist movement, neither that of the Brazilian Martins nor that of the American Nist. Quinlin, in her study of Brazilian women writers, devotes only a brief paragraph to her (and incorrectly cites the date of publication of *Parque industrial* as 1931) (52). Likewise, Ferreira-Pinto makes no more than a passing reference to Galvão's interest in the female body in her monograph on gender and desire in Brazilian women writers.[2]

Perhaps one way of approaching the historical fate of Galvão's novel is in terms of its feminist perspective. While Jackson makes a point of noting that Galvão did not consider herself a feminist—she even made fun of those women of the period who did ("Afterword" 143)—this is a matter of what scope of ideological commitments is to be understood by the word, especially as it would have been used in the period of the novel. As Jackson's examples of Galvão's scorn make obvious, Galvão, a member of the Communist Party at the time the novel was written, saw feminism as a claim exercised by bourgeois women on masculine privilege, not a revolutionary movement of social justice (this point is also made by Besse in her discussion of Galvão [180]; see also Bloch 191). To this day in much of Latin America, "feminist" is frequently understood in this sense (and, moreover, as an American posture), and it is only the evolution of a radical feminist commitment that has connected women's issues specifically with revolutionary movements. Certainly, during Galvão's day, feminist concerns, including those which today we would recognize as part of radical and liberatory concerns, were viewed as inconsequential and even antagonistic to the sense of a truly socialist revolution. Clearly this is why Galvão herself had so many conflicts with the Brazilian Communist Party, which she renounced in 1940 after her final—and longest—imprisonment.

Galvão published *Parque industrial* under the pseudonym Mara Lobo, as the novel could not be sanctioned as having been penned by a member of the Communist Party. Why this is so must be the object of an adequate critical analysis, and I would propose that the key lies in the way in which Galvão feminizes social space and essentially tells the story of women who inhabit it. Indeed, it would be impossible to think of any other Brazilian novel before or contemporary with *Parque industrial* in which such an extensive representation is given of the social life of women; the fact that Galvão's novel focuses on their urban workplace is even more remarkable. Doreen Massey outlines some of the relationships between women and geography in the following terms:

> From the symbolic meaning of spaces/places and the overtly gendered
> messages they transmit to straightforward exclusion by violence, space and
> places are not only themselves gendered but, in their being so, they both
> reflect and affect the ways in which gender is constructed and understood.
> The limitation of women's mobility, in terms both of identity and space, has
> been in some cultural contexts a crucial means of subordination. More-
> over the two things—the limitation on mobility in space, the attempted

consignment/confinement to particular places on the one hand, and the limitation of identity on the other—have been crucially related. (179)

In terms of this position, I would understand the feminization of space in three ways: 1) the demonstration that a particular space has been assigned/consigned to women (that is, the home, or within it, the kitchen and the nursery); 2) the ways in which some spaces are reassigned to women for reasons that benefit the patriarchal/masculinist order of the world (that is, the factory when it becomes appreciably advantageous to have women doing certain types of work for lower wages than men, such as the Mexican *maquiladoras* or the textile factories in Galvão's novel [Besse 146–47]); 3) the struggle by women to usurp space customarily assigned/consigned to men, to the rigorous exclusion of women (for example, the altar, military barracks, the boardroom). There is a fourth possible meaning, and this is the reinterpretation of feminist space (in the first sense above) by men equally insistent on crossing the gender barrier; it is not so much a question of the masculinist expropriation of those spaces, but a measure of the feminization of some men (male nannies, for instance). In sum, a "feminized social space" is a space *(re)assigned* to women, in which case one can examine the way in which women function/struggle within that space against masculinist domination; or it is a space *appropriated* by women, in which case one can examine what women do with the space they have made their own. It is important to note that Galvão's novel entertains both propositions, since, in the first place, *Parque industrial* focuses on one example of a microcosm of women created by capitalism—the workplace confined (principally) to women—and, in the second place, the novelist narrows the real-life social realm such that only women's stories are told, as though individuated men did not exist.

It is noteworthy that there is only one significant male character—Aldredo de Rocha, whom Jackson sees as patterned on Galvão's lover (and then-husband) Oswald de Andrade ("Afterword" 140–41)—but the novel mocks his attempt to transform himself from a bourgeois citizen into a sympathizer of the proletariat. Other references to men are secondary and circumstantial. This is a novel of women's lives—women who are depicted as downtrodden factory workers in the industrial park of Brás (which is located immediately east of the central core of São Paulo as defined by the Praça da República);[3] women who inhabit the margins of society because of their status as prostitutes, women of color, immigrants, or the destitute

Figure 2.1. *Os operários* (The Workers), by Tarsila do Amaral.

and dying; and even women who are agents of a savage capitalism because they are in a position to exploit other women. The women of *Parque industrial* move in the public space primarily because they must do so to earn a living, though often they are not even successful in their attempts to survive. That Galvão's novel gives voice to these women, often through the narrative practice of directly quoting their human discourse, made it unacceptable in its day for both the conservative establishment and the Communist Party, and has guaranteed its continued effacement from academic histories of Brazilian literature to the present day.

Galvão inaugurates her novel with a direct defiance of the masculinist point of view regarding the importance of industrial development in São Paulo. This she does in the form of two juxtaposed epigraphs.[4] The first is from the "ESTATISTICA INDUSTRIAL DO ESTADO DE SÃO PAULO," dated 1930 and signed by one Aristides do Amaral, who is identified as the "Director" (Galvão, *Parque industrial* [1981] 1). This is typical chamber of commerce boilerplate, extolling the growth of industry in the state in the decade following World War I, but noting the decline prompted by the recent economic depression (for a detailed analysis of the growth of industry in São Paulo during this period, see Dean). As such, it is a masculinist discourse not so much because it speaks of business in terms of capitalistic waxing and waning, but because this process is devoid of meaning on the level of direct human experience. Jackson is correct in observing that Galvão's novel is a counter-discourse to the business narrative (128). *Parque industrial* portrays human suffering as a consequence of that narrative—Galvão seeks to tell the stories of a spectrum of individuals whose lives are impacted by the business narrative and show how their misery is inversely proportional to the prosperity of industrial development. Indeed, one must underscore this ironic proposition, intrinsic to Galvão's socialist/ communist labor perspective, to the effect that human misery makes capitalism work, and when capitalism does not work (that is, when recession and depression occur), human misery simply increases, but in this case proportionally. Human misery is never absent from the universe of (the) *Parque industrial*.

Thus, Galvão's second epigraph, in her own voice, is the promise to offer a counter-discourse:

A ESTATISTICA E A HISTORIA DA CAMADA HUMANA QUE SUSTENTA O PARQUE INDUSTRIAL DE SÃO PAULO E FALA A LINGUA DESTE LIVRO, ENCONTRAM-SE, SOB O REGIME CAPITALISTA, NAS CADEIAS E NOS CORTIÇOS, NOS HOSPITAES E NOS NECROTERIOS. (*Parque industrial* [1981] 1)[5]

The counter-language Galvão offers is thus her novel as a textual whole, which may be viewed from many different angles as the story of the individuals absent from the statistical summary as well as an exposé of the correlation between that summary and human misery produced by the processes for which those statistics stand as signs. One can speak of alternative realities, the account of the underbelly of industrialization, of the eloquent silences of those too drained and, in many cases, deformed by work to speak—something like a catatonia of exploitation—while at the same time referring to the stridency of those voices that have found forums to speak out against their exploitation, from the loose social bonds of the workers to the more formal structures of the unions. Actually, Jackson sees both discourses embedded in the novel, since he recognizes the material evidence of São Paulo's modernity, the description of which intersects with the vast array of human suffering that makes modern materialism possible:

> The novel is both a document and a memoir of the lower depths of the industrial park of Braz, where the author grew up in the 1920s. Names of streets, squares, theaters, and factories become points of reference within a novelistic map of the city. Limousines, trolleys, and cinemas appear as the totems of society's fetish for modernity on the surface of a proletarian world of injustice and suffering. (127)

What remains to be studied, however, are the diverse aspects of the language—language as a social phenomenon[6]—the novel speaks, and this is what I propose to focus on in the remainder of this chapter. I will seek to characterize the substance of a female urban discourse (that is, speech in the spatial context) as it is embodied in Galvão's *Parque industrial*, and particularly how that language represents a feminization of the social space the novel describes (Unruh enumerates the many female spaces of the novel, see "Las aguilas musas" 275).

The "feminization of social space" does not only refer to the inclusion of women—or the inclusion of the representation of women—although such an operation is surely of considerable importance. Nor does it simply mean cultural production by women, which should bring with it inevitably a feminist point of view with respect to social space: women may not necessarily be feminist. Yet, to the extent that it is likely impossible for a social subject marked as a woman not to experience the historically fundamental difference of women's lives, it would be difficult to understand how any cultural production by women would not in important ways differ from that produced by social subjects marked as men.[7] And, I repeat, all this is possible without necessarily producing what might properly be understood as feminist: that is, adhering to one consciously theoretically grounded agenda or another (see the papers in *Mapping Desire* for approaches to gender and geographic space).

Minimally, the feminization of social space ought to overcome the way in which the richly textured representation of women's lives is so impressively absent from cultural production. For example, if one recalls the major Brazilian work of naturalism—one that, like Galvão's *Parque industrial*, provides a complex sense of urban life—Aluísio Azevedo's novel *O cortiço* ("The Tenement"; 1890), the masculinist perspective is particularly evident. For Azevedo's book is reputed to be the first work of Brazilian literature—indeed, of Latin American literature—to represent lesbianism (Reis). However, Azevedo's novel is hardly sympathetic toward the subject of lesbianism, as it is seen as one more social malaise that preys on the miserable of the earth. That said, *Parque industrial* also provides an unflattering portrayal of lesbianism.[8] But the point I would make here is that Galvão at least treats it in a broad context relating to an array of issues in women's lives, and not just as the de-gendered misfortune that it is in Azevedo's novel. In the latter, it is one of an inventory of misfortunes that are not essentially marked by gender, even if it is, in this case, the matter of the abuse of one woman by another. Women's lives are not the point of Azevedo's novel, but rather all the lives of the tenement house as a microcosm of social exploitation and the meanness of the existence of those who suffer under it.[9] A woman character is only another example of life in the social abyss, and Léonie, the lesbian seducer, although she can be generous toward the young woman she seduces, is never presented in any way other than, in conformance with emerging deviant theories of the period, as a sexually violent man who happens to inhabit a female body and thus as yet another agent of exploitation. In such an inverted formulation, a lesbian can never be anything other than a male social subject who happens, monstrously, to occupy a woman's body, and one looks in vain for any sense of lesbianism as part of a continuum of women's lives, something that does not come, at least in the case of Brazilian literature, until well into the latter half of the twentieth century (see Foster on a writer like Márcia Denser, for example; *Gay and Lesbian Themes* 94–97). Galvão does not exactly provide a defense of lesbianism in the case of Eleonora, but she is presented within the context of the social world of women and the manner in which relationships between them occur is counter to masculinist primacy. Indeed, Eleonora tells her husband to make himself scarce because she is going to be receiving Matilde (62).[10]

However, although I will return to the lesbian dimension of *Parque industrial* below, I wish to use it at this point to make what is probably the most salient point with regard to the feminization of social space, and this is its concomitant queering in conjunction with the necessary representation of women's lives. By queering I mean the questioning and, by extension,

the undermining of masculinist primacy in the representation and enact-
ment of social experience. The feminization of social space cannot mean (as
seems to have been the case for feminist human geographers like Doreen
B. Massey) only the "correcting of the balance" by incorporating women's
lives and whatever this means for male privilege in cultural production and
scientific inquiry. Rather, it must bring with it some measuring of the questioning of sociosexual roles and the imperative to see the world in terms
of the feminine/masculine binary, no matter what the calculus of the interaction of male and female might be. Since feminism is almost universally
understood to involve a questioning of the construction and interpretation
of gender roles, it is also inevitably a process of examining what masculinist ideology considers to be the fixity of such roles, bringing with it, first,
the destabilization of what "male" and "female," "masculine" and "feminine"
encompass, and, consequently, a blurring of their distribution in human experience and social space (for a more detailed survey of these issues, see
Jagose, especially 119–25)

I am not arguing that all of this is what takes place in *Parque industrial*,
although I would underscore that the queering of sociosexual roles in
Galvão's novel is present to the extent that the author is not content to limit
women's experience to the narrow confines dictated by male imperatives.
This is evident in the ways in which women in the novel seek to be agents, if
only imperfectly and sometimes disastrously, of their own lives. To be sure,
women are not part of the work force as a measure of any feminist independence, since they must work out of harsh economic necessity. Rather, I am
referring to instances when a woman like the Lithuanian immigrant Rosinha undertakes a vocal role in the struggle for worker's rights (see below).

Moreover, the way in which male figures are notably either lacking or
minimized in the novel is significant in undermining patriarchal masculin-
ity—if not, to be sure, in the real world, at least in the universe of this narrative. Indeed, the scandal for the still predominantly male critical establishment—and the predominantly male readership it represents—is what
most assuredly accounts for the way in which Galvão's novel, along with
her other cultural production, has either been diminished or ignored by
the Brazilian academic establishment. By the same token, when a vanguard
poet like Augusto de Campos authors the only comprehensive assessment
of Galvão's artistic accomplishments, it highlights in stark contrast her absence from the bulk of conventional literary scholarship. It is only during
the past decade that a feminist-oriented interest in Galvão has emerged (see

Furlani's testimonial, which has already gone through several printings; Bloch provides a general characterization of Galvão's bohemian character).

What I would like to turn to at this point is an examination of the many ways in which *Parque industrial* represents the feminization of social space, beginning with the direct way in which, as a feminist proletarian novel, it sets out to provide an account of women's participation in the workplace. The fact that this dimension of the novel was problematical at the time—a time when proletarian literature, like the vast majority of cultural production, was dominated by male voices, with their questionable account of women's history—is emblematized by the way in which Galvão was forced to publish her novel under a pseudonym in order (vainly, as it turned out) not to violate the authoritarian directives of the Communist Party in which she was attempting to hold an honorable place.

Galvão's interest in women's experiences in the factory workplace is evident in a number of ways in the novel: in terms of the details of the workers' routine, in their double discrimination (first as wage earners and then as women; see Helena Solberg-Ladd's famous 1976 documentary film, *The Double Day*), and in their oppression at the hands of the male supervisors who represent the way in which the factory is an integral part of patriarchal society.[11] The vignettes along these lines are of documentary use in constructing a social history of the time. This is so even though they are vignettes, a construction in conformance with the basic discursive principles of Galvão's novel, as opposed to the sort of full narrative embodiment that one might expect to find in a more properly realist novel of the time, such as the masculinist texts of Jorge Amado. Yet they are more significant when, rather than contributing to the mosaic of proletarian workplace life in general, they capture the interaction between women in that setting.

For example, in the opening sequence of the novel (it would not be completely accurate to call these major divisions of *Parque industrial* chapters), Bruna, exhausted from a late-night dance she has attended, is scolded by the male foreman for speaking idly with a fellow worker, when in reality the latter has merely warned Bruna that the distraction produced by her bleariness is going to cause her to have an accident. The setting is introduced as a jail: "Na grande penitenciária social os teares se elevam e marcham esgoelando" (18). When Bruna is being reprimanded by the foreman, she is powerless to defend herself:

—Malandros! É por isso que o trabalho não rende! Sua vagabunda!
Bruna desperta. O moço abaixa a cabeça revoltada. É preciso calar a boca!
Assim, em todos os setores proletários, todos os dias, todas as semanas,
todos os anos. (19)[12]

This is a pretty standard denunciation as proletarian novels go. However,
Galvão's novel becomes truly innovative in the next fragment:

—Va lá na latrina que a gente conversa.
A moça pede:
—Dá licença de ir lá fora?
—Outra vez?
—Estou de purgante.
As paredes acima do mosaico gravam os desabafos dos operários. Cada
canto é um jornal de impropérios contra os patrões, chefes, contramestes e
companheiros vendidos. Há nomes feios, desenhos, ensinamentos sociais,
datiloscopias.
Nas latrinas sujas as meninas passam o minuto de alegria roubada ao
trabalho escravo. (19–21)[13]

In the first place, this paragraph exemplifies one of the scandalous dimensions of *Parque industrial* mentioned by the author's son, Geraldo Galvão Ferraz, in his "Prefácio" to the recent reissue of *Parque industrial:* "Como alguém se atrevia a estampar a linguagem das ruas? Finalmente, como alguém podia querer exaltar daquela forma a condição feminina?" (13).[14] Street language in its feminine register is present in two ways. In the first place, the novelist has no qualms, in recording the worker's justification for requesting authorization to go to the bathroom, about having her state forthrightly that it is because she is taking a laxative. Not only is this an unambiguous reference to bodily functions quite contrary to prevailing norms of literary decorum (except, of course, scatological language in lesser genres such as satire or parody), but it involves a woman explaining bodily functions openly to a man. This she must do in order to obtain his permission, as her overseer, to absent herself from her position, and it underscores the humiliating subjugation not just of the worker, but of the *female* worker, a specific detail of that subjugation which one could hardly expect to find in other contemporary Brazilian proletarian writing. Galvão's discourse of social denunciation allowed her to focus on such a synecdochic incident

though she surely must have known it would be distasteful to her readers—
indeed, she likely chose it precisely for that reason.

Moreover, as the narrative description moves into the realm of the latrine, two other details of the gross reality of proletarian experience emerge.
The first is the fact that the latrine was first a men's room and is now set aside
for the women's use: this lack of concern for the different hygienic needs of
men and women constitutes yet another cause for the workers' indignation
at being treated miserably. The text refers to the fact that the walls "gravam
os desabafos dos operários" (19), making it clear that the bathroom has been
used by both men and women. Additionally, the text goes on to refer to (although, admittedly, not to transcribe) the salacious graffiti directed against
the workers' supervisors. Unquestionably, the semantic scope of the word
impropérios—insults—would include material both sexual and scatological.
The sort of "women's talk" represented by the allusion to bathroom graffiti
is likely a transcription of how these women might actually speak in public among themselves. One woman does call specific attention to the graffiti, and thus it becomes clear that the insults are part of the consciousness
of these women. Another observes that they should be covered over, but
no one seconds this suggestion. The fact that the workers are reading the
impropérios becomes clear when there is a brief interchange with reference
to one of them, although in this case the graffiti alludes to politics, "—O
que quer dizer esta palavra 'fascismo'?" (20).[15] So, while we do not actually
hear the women reading the graffiti aloud or themselves using the sort of
language written on the walls, it is evident that they are reading the graffiti
but do not understand its political allusions. In calling the writing *porcaria*
(dirty word) and using the word *versinho* (jingle), the women demonstrate
that they know at least the dirty meaning of the scrawled words.

But the latrine has a different importance in the feminization of social
space in the novel. If, in a first instance, it is a realm where women can acknowledge dirty street language among themselves, even if we do not actually hear them uttering it (I would underscore again the fact that Galvão's
novel is significantly audacious just in acknowledging the existence of bathroom graffiti which is read by women), the latrine is not only a refuge from
the enslavement of the factory floor, but it is an exception to the masculine
dominance of their world. Since this was once a men's room, as represented
presumably by the male perspective of the dirty writing on the walls, it is
evident that these women cannot ever really free themselves from masculine domination. Yet, for the brief and precarious minutes they are able

to escape into the latrine, they are able to converse among themselves as women. This conversation functions on two levels. The first is that it takes place in a minimal space removed almost entirely from male scrutiny, although one might maintain that, to the extent that the graffiti may have been mostly written by men, that scrutiny in some sense follows them into the bathroom. The second is that conversation among them takes place at all; that is, escaping into the bathroom empowers these women to speak.

In the preceding segment, the reader has seen how the male voice of the patriarchy as embodied in the exploitative functioning of the factory scolds the female workers for even exchanging a well-meaning warning: not only is casual speech banned, but meaningful speech as well. It is not clear whether the overseer knows that the latter rather than the former is involved. The simple fact is that one of his responsibilities is to suppress any speech among the female workers under his supervision in order to enhance production. The text uses a discontinuous oxymoron to capture the way in which this space reserved for women, while transitorily enabling them to meet and speak away from the scrutiny of the male overseer, is nevertheless contaminated by the masculinist world that dominates and, as figurative labor slaves, owns them. That is, their happiness stolen from the factory floor, a space continuous with the prevailing masculinist space of their world, is colored by the filthy conditions of the latrine—filthy in hygienic terms and filthy also as a consequence of the supposedly predominantly male-oriented graffiti.

Galvão contrasts the overwhelmingly male world of the factory, where women are slaves in a branch of patriarchal capitalism, with the more feminine world of the needleworkers in the following chapter of *Parque industrial*. Yet in the atelier, where the owner/supervisor is a woman ("Madame"), the women are no less enslaved by the same system, with Madame responsible to customers who are integral parts of the world of the owners:

> Madame corre de novo acompanhando a freguesa que salta para um
> automóvel com um rapaz de bigodinho [....] Uma [das costureirinhas]
> murmura, numa crispação de dedos picados de agulha, que amarrotam a
> fazenda.
> —Depois dizem que não somos escravas! (25)[16]

Although Galvão presents in this chapter a workplace consisting of women overseen by another woman, it is only a feminized space in the sense that it focuses on women's experiences in another form of labor enslavement (specifically, Madame has threatened to fire a worker if she does not "agree" to remain working until one in the morning on a rush order), one with no alternative, if precarious, refuge from the workplace. Madame even calls them "umas preguiçosas" (25),[17] the same sort of characterization of the women under his charge used previously by the male overseer.

A different form of feminized space in *Parque industrial* involves the ill fortunes of the seamstress Corina, who becomes pregnant at the hands of a careless lover. Abused by her mother's violent boyfriend, exploited by her lover, and unwilling to heed the warnings of one of her companions that her lover will abandon her and Madame will fire her when they find her to be pregnant, Corina ultimately realizes that there is no place left for her but the brothel. The figure of the seamstress "gone bad" is a legendary one that is particularly eloquent in underscoring how all women who perform menial tasks are exposed to seduction, exploitation, and abandonment by the men who dominate their world. Perhaps the eloquence of the seamstress derives from the way in which she toils in the production of refinement, but is, notwithstanding, no less subject than her sisters who work in the factory to degrading abuse.[18]

The brothel is another realm in which women obtain only a spurious escape from masculine supervision. Of course, they are at the service of the sexual demands of men, but there is a sense that the brothel is a woman's world, ruled over by the matriarchal Madame. Indeed, one of the symbolic functions of the brothel is to enshrine a particular interpretation of femininity, one that may perhaps even involve a divinization of the practice of prostitution.[19] Nevertheless, the social reality of the prostitute as alluded to by *Parque industrial* has nothing of the divine and becomes, as we see through Corina, yet one more station of the cross in her social exploitation. As if Corina's demotion to a whore were not enough for the explicit representation of the sordid in Galvão's novel, once again the author has scandalous recourse to women's language in order to highlight the unfortunate nature of her material existence. In this case, it is specifically a language uttered by women, since it is the whore's speech of seduction and arousal as utilized in the practice of her office and in the generation of profit (ultimately for her male employers in the industry of prostitution) through sexual commerce. It is a language Corina must learn: all language is a learned activity, and specific versions of language are acquired in specifically defined spaces and with reference to specifically defined occupations, with the space here being that of the brothel and the occupation defined as that of prostitution.

To be sure, human sexual activity involves a version of language characteristic of it. From one point of view, the language of prostitution might be viewed as something like an enhanced version of the common speech of human sexuality, while from another point of view (but not one in any way contradictory to the first), the language of prostitution might be viewed as supplementary of common speech. A frequent feminist postulate holds that patriarchal sexuality fundamentally constitutes the sexual exploitation of women, and that women are prostituted by patriarchal matrimony and obligated to represent themselves as whores, one dimension of which involves a woman talking dirty to arouse her partner sexually. Such a particularly tendentious view of conventional heterosexual matrimony would, if Galvão were to have subscribed to it (and the outrageous details of her personal life as regards bourgeois matrimony certainly could be seen as her endorsement of some version of this interpretation; again, Bengell's film is useful here), indicate how the woman as prostitute is defined exclusively in terms of her sexual trade, which means that we are witnessing a language that exclusively defines her being.

Thus, Corina's violent and, one assumes, humiliating introduction into the realm of the brothel is accompanied by her process of initiation into its particular language, a language which is hers as a female prostitute and which will be part of her new exploitation by yet one more facet of patriarchal capitalism:

No dia seguinte, um sujeito lustroso a leva para um bordel do Brás.
—Vestida assim, ninguém te quer.
Abre-lhe a blusa, rasga-lhe o soutien e a empurra para as vitrines da porta.
Nas vinte e cinco casas iguais, nas vinte e cinco portas iguais, estão vinte e cinco desgraçadas iguais.
Ela se lembra que com as outras costureirinhas caçoava das mulheres da rua Ipiranga. Sente uma repugnância, mas se acovarda. Faz entre lágrimas, como as outras.
—Psiu, benzinho. Vem cá. Te dou o botão . . .
Aumenta pouco a pouco o vocabulário erótico. (49)[20]

It is worth noting that this passage contrasts two instances of discourse: that of the women in the dress shop and their women's talk about prostitutes, on the one hand, and the actual vocabulary of the prostitute as one of the dressmakers moves laterally from one form of enslavement to another.

What is significant about this detail of the passage is how *Parque industrial* captures the diversity of women's experiences as social subjects in the industrial heart of São Paulo, as well as the way in which it shows iteratively their utter subjugation to the exploitative dynamic of enterprise.

Female sexuality reappears in the novel when the narrative returns to Eleonora and Matilde, whom Eleonora, despite announcing that she is going to marry a rich man, kisses at the beginning of the school day at the Escola Normal. This school, by the way, is another pseudo-woman's space, in that it has a female student body being prepared for an exclusively female occupation (the teaching of primary school). Nevertheless, the faculty and administration are male, and there can be little doubt that this is yet another institution integral to the patriarchy. While Eleonora does marry well, Matilde is reduced to living in a tenement:

> A entrada de um automóvel de luxo anima a vila coletiva. Eleonora desce, elegante, contrafeita.
> Matilde! Recebi o seu endereço. Que horror, você morando aqui!
> —O que você quer? Mamãe perdeu o emprego. Está envelhecendo.
> —Continua linda, sua tonta! Se quisesse morar comigo! (61)[21]

Eleonora's invitation might appear innocent on the surface, but it is, like the prostitute's, a language of seduction with which one woman, with an economic power and privilege afforded by her union within the bourgeoisie, undertakes to exploit another:

> Matilde chega, pálida, no tailleur modetíssimo. A boina rusa esconde os olhos ternos [...].
> Ming serve aperitivos.
> O risinho infantil desaparece pouco a pouco nos beijos. O almoço foi curto. Ming sai. Matilde foi despida e amada. (62)[22]

Despite the lesbian interludes in Galvão's own bohemian life (Bengell's film falls just short of explicitly portraying Galvão's amorous relationship with the famous artist of Modernismo, Tarsila do Amaral, a woman with whom Galvão also shared the affections of the poet Oswald de Andrade and Elsie Houston, a famous songstress played in the film by Bengell herself),[23] *Parque industrial* hardly provides a benevolent image of same-sex female love. Once again, the lesbian boudoir is a spurious female space, not only because Eleonora shares it with her husband Alfredo, who acquiesces to her demands that he disappear because Matilde is coming, and not only because Eleonora is shown taking advantage of Matilde's poverty (she buys Matilde's affections and thereby prostitutes the woman to her own sexual needs), but more because it is clear that Eleonora is only able to indulge her particular sexuality thanks to the privilege marrying into the haute bourgeoisie has provided her: Matilde confesses to enjoying the luxury Eleonora provides her and says that she was not interested in her sexually when they were schoolmates, but only now, because, as she says to Eleonora, "—Não tinhas este apartamento nem estas bebidas gostosas . . ." (63).[24]

Repeatedly, *Parque industrial* focuses on women's experiences as subjects in their world, but in circumstance after circumstance, what appears to be a feminized space is so only because it is a precarious realm inhabited by women—one in which any form of empowerment, any form of effective feminization of that space, is undermined by the fact that it is dominated by an implacable masculinist universe in which the dynamic of industrial exploitation ensures that women can never really speak in their own voice, never really control the spheres in which they move. Consider one final example: that of the Lithuanian immigrant Rosinha. The novel returns to the factory and to a worker uprising:

A voz pequenina da revolucionária surge nas faces vermelhas da agitação.
—Camaradas! Não podemos ficar quietas no meio desta luta! Devemos estar ao lado dos nossos companheiros na rua, como estamos quando trabalhamos na fábrica. Temos que lutar juntos contra a burguesia que tira a nossa saúde e nos transforma em trapos humanos! Tiram do nosso seio a última gota de leite que pertence a nossos filhos para viver no champanhe e no parasitismo! (77)[25]

What is marked as feminine about this speech is not the speech itself, although note the lovely feminine metaphor of taking away a woman's last drop of milk. Indeed, Rosinha uses the grammatical masculine that subsumes the real-world feminine within it, and she asserts the need to "estar ao lado dos nossos companheiros" and "lutar juntos." But what *is* distinctly feminine here is the fact that a woman addresses other women, a woman with a "voz pequenina," but a woman's voice nevertheless. When the strike is repressed by the police, the narrator presents the figure of a broken Rosinha:

A polícia surge, carrega. Uma mulher pequena fica no chão, gritando com a perna triturada. Os seus cabelos loiros, lituanos, escorrem lisos pela testa suada. Parecida com Rosinha. (94)[26]

In this fashion, Galvão, historically accurate in her narrative mosaic of the industrial district of Brás (which she unquestionably sees as emblematic of a universal capitalist oppression: "Brás do Brasil. Brás de todo o mundo" [83]),[27] is willing to show the record of women's lives and their experiences as social subjects in the home, in the street, in the factory, in other workplaces, and even in the brothel and the lesbian boudoir. She is willing to capture their women's talk and their acquisition of the vocabularies necessary for survival. And she is willing to portray those precarious moments, described as "stolen," in which they are able to engage in women's talk against but never really free of masculinist scrutiny. But what we are left with in the end is the screaming of a severely wounded Rosinha, or someone just like Rosinha, a scream unheeded—at least by the charging agents of exploitative capitalism—as the only definitive feminine voice.[28] To be sure, Galvão makes use of the privilege of literature, a privilege that is hers because of her own bourgeois upbringing, to articulate a feminist voice that was not/is not yet possible for her characters. But still, Galvão's own silencing by the Communist Party—which obliged her to publish under a pseudonym and then essentially forced her to renounce her membership—as well as the fact that the Brazilian academic establishment has yet to make an adequate place for Parque industrial in the national literary canon are alternative ways of silencing women's speech.

3

Appendix: Patrícia Galvão

The Private Autobiography of a Brazilian Feminist Writer

porque não poderei contar as gargalhadas

que já estou ensaiando.

☀ Patrícia Galvão, *Paixão Pagu* (128)

Only two women's names have routinely been attached to the momentous Semana de Arte Moderna. Both of the women mentioned were painters: Anita Malfati (1889–1963), who saw the equally important Armory Show New York in 1913 and was inspired to spearhead a similar show in São Paulo; and Tarsila do Amaral (1886–1973), whose impressive canvases have gone on to become, in the visual arts, veritable monuments of the Semana.

However, there was a third woman, Patrícia Galvão.

Galvão is mentioned on the margins of the subsequent cultural flourishing in the 1930s that flowed from the Semana.[1] It was not until Norma Bengell's film *Eternamente Pagu* (1987), however, that Galvão began to enjoy something like a general cultural recognition. I wish I could say that the efforts of feminist literary scholarship in Brazil (whose existence is somewhat debatable, certainly at least on institutional academic terms) have served to confirm Galvão's importance in the bibliography of research on the Semana and, as a consequence, in Brazilian cultural history, but just look under the entry "Pagu" in the *Dicionário de mulheres do Brasil*.[2] However, this work of documenting Galvão's importance has been taken on by the Brazilian poet Augusto de Campos, whose biography and anthology of Galvão constituted the first major bibliographic entry. In addition, we have the editorial work of Geraldo Galvão Ferraz, Galvão's second son, the criticism of the American David K. Jackson, as well as the translation, along with his wife, Elizabeth, of Galvão's novel, *Parque industrial*; as such there is now a growing second-wave bibliography on Galvão, but as yet little of it has been published in Brazil, where the writer remains absent from major historiographic works.[3]

Yet, when Ferraz published in 2005 a document of his mother's that he titled *Paixão Pagu; a autobiografia precoce de Patrícia Galvão* (Pagu's Passion: The Precocious Autobiography of Patrícia Galvão), it was something of a best seller, promptly becoming difficult to obtain even at major booksellers in São Paulo such as the FNAC, a vast cultural supermarket with various outlets in the city and, now, in other places in the country. If Galvão remains uninteresting for Brazilian scholarship, which is not known for its comprehensive dedication to modern writers anyways, she now seems to at least have some cachet in the general Brazilian cultural imaginary.

Paixão Pagu was written in 1940 as a private letter to Geraldo Ferraz, with whom Galvão was entering into the long relationship that would last until her death in 1962. Ferraz was a writer and journalist, and they collaborated well together, though Galvão was unsuccessful in her bid for political office in 1950. Galvão had been involved first in a sham marriage (to the poet Waldemar Belisário) in order to escape the rather stultifying paternal abode in Santos. Her real matrimonial goal was the poet and major spokesperson for the Semana de Arte Moderna, Oswald de Andrade. Since he was already involved with Tarsila do Amaral, Galvão knew her parents would never approve; hence the sham marriage.[4] Galvão's marriage to Oswald de Andrade was a stormy one: she both had a son with him (Rudá, who has cooperated with Ferraz in providing material about their shared mother) and engaged fully in the radical politics that made her the first female political prisoner in Brazilian history during the infamous fascist-like Estado Novo (New State) of Getúlio Vargas in the late 1930s and 1940s. Not only was Galvão imprisoned, but she published *Parque industrial*, became directly involved with the Brazilian Communist Party (which insisted on the pseudonym for the novel, considering it a serious personalist breach on Galvão's part to publish it under her own name), and, for a period in 1932, lived and worked in the area of the fabric mills east of the central core of São Paulo. This experience gave her some of the practical information contained in her novel; *Parque industrial* remains a singular publication event as it is the only social realist novel written (if pseudonymously) by a Brazilian woman.

The text published as *Paixão Pagu* is, as I have stated, a private accounting of her life and feelings that Galvão addressed to Ferraz at his request. Necessarily, it is tinged with disillusionment about her relationship with the Communist Party, the sense of exploitation over the notoriety she gained for her political imprisonment, and, most of all it would seem, bitterness over her failed marriage to Oswald de Andrade. As a letter addressed to her new lover, it is intensely confidential. Curiously, it does create the sense that in Galvão's eyes Ferraz legitimately requested such an accounting— through both the features of the profoundly self-probing apologia characteristic of the confessional mode of Catholic culture and the self-critical reflections that Galvão had engaged in on at least one occasion. On this occasion, she was acceding to the demands of the Communist Party hierarchy to explain her allegedly willful personalism. Self-denunciation, confessional apologia, ideological and sentimental positioning upon demand by a new lover: these are features that make *Paixão Pagu* an important feminist cultural document. I will return below to the question, however, of the legitimacy of son Ferraz's publication of this most private correspondence.

I would like now to focus on four semantic nuclei in *Paixão Pagu*. Let me say first, however, that *Paixão Pagu* is a somewhat chaotic document. That is, it does not follow a strict narratological structure nor is the chronology always evident, except, perhaps, for someone who has all of the details of her story at hand. For this reason, I have concluded that the most interesting mode of entrance into the text is via semantic nuclei. I understand this to mean particular themes that emerge as recurring motifs in the document. The insistent articulation reveals the major concerns of Galvão in the personal transition from Andrade to Ferraz and from the more bohemian existence the former charted for the two, to the more structured and creative relationship Galvão came to enjoy with Ferraz. Indeed, Andrade's frequent affairs with other women and Galvão's own intense revolutionary activity, her travels in 1933–34 in Europe and Asia (where she wrote journalistic dispatches and participated in political militancy), and her two imprisonments between 1935 and 1940 for political activities against the Vargas regime are signs of what turned out to be a very erratic and irregular interaction with Andrade—starkly opposed to the more mature and sustained involvement with Ferraz. Their relationship is perhaps best characterized by their collaboration on a work of fiction, *A famosa revista* (The Famous Review; 1945). There are two salient features of this novel: Galvão is given first credit, and the novel, at least in its first edition, borders on the inaccessible.[5]

The first thematic nucleus regards the degree to which Galvão always felt alone in the world: "Andava então sozinha" (53).[6] This is, to be sure, the common contemporary existential topos of alienation, and it would not be remarkable as anything other than part of a rhetoric of negotiating recognition from a new sexual partner if it were not for the fact that the comment is actually a coda—hence the conclusive tag "então"—to a more significant self-assessment, which is that she failed to understand why others saw her as ill behaved when she saw herself as so good:

> Naquele tempo eu é que não compreendia o ambiente. Eu me lembro que me considerava muito boa e todos me achavam ruim. As mães das outras crianças não queriam que eu brincasse com suas filhas e fui expulsa até um dia da casa de Álvaro George, da livraria, porque não queriam que eu tivesse contato com as suas crianças. Só consentiam ali minhas irmãs. Eu nunca consegui perceber minha perversidade. Tinham me feito assim e jogado em paredes estranhas. Andava então sozinha. (53)[7]

Although Galvão does not tell us what the signs of "minha perversidade" might have been, it is important to note that this passage, in turn, is appositive to the bald statement: "O primeiro fato distintamente consciente da minha vida foi a entrega do meu corpo" (53).[8] Although she informs Ferraz that she was twelve at the time, she does not enter into details. It is not clear if the subsequent reference to perversity is sexual in nature as a consequence of her precocious sexuality or even the degree to which she was fully conscious of her actions. Thus, I would argue, the controlling nucleus here is her alleged perversity and the way in which she may have been branded a "bad girl" among decent families in Brazil in the early 1920s. Those reasons would not have been limited to sexual misconduct or the perceived harbingers of it, but would surely have included anything that could be perceived as indecorous or unladylike: in Bengell's film this involves cheating on a school exam and smoking. Galvão goes on to assert: "Não tive precocidade sexual" (53),[9] and that a sexual awakening for her took place much later, underscoring how her perversity must, therefore, have been perceived as a much more free-floating signifier than its more restrictive sexual sense. In this way, the first nucleus is grounded on an existential loneliness resulting from repeatedly being considered the so-called bad seed and therefore socially unacceptable. There may be a certain amount of disingenuousness on Galvão's part here, given the circumstances of her self-characterization to Ferraz.

Much in the record indicates that Galvão wished to construct herself as a "bad girl" and a "wild woman" and tried to upset the world of bourgeois decency, beginning with her own family and the expectation it would have wished to enforce concerning the silent self-subjugation of women, including the unquestioned acceptance of the heterosexist marriage contract. In this regard, it is important to bear in mind that Brazil in the early twentieth century was exceptionally conservative regarding marriage contracts, with enormous sanctions meted out to those who failed, or were perceived to fail, to comply. Indeed, the world of bohemianism in which Galvão sought refuge from the bourgeois expectations of her family provides one grimly eloquent measure of the intractable nature of the heterosexist contract (for information concerning the interrelationship between conventional female sexuality in São Paulo—city and province—and the lure of bohemian life for women during this period, see Rago). Yet by 1940, having put the bohemian world of Oswald de Andrade and the rigors of the Communist Party behind her, Galvão apparently wished to rescind the bases of her notoriety.

The second nucleus revolves around the nature of Galvão's erotic relationship with Andrade. It is important to keep in mind that Galvão left Andrade, justly or unjustly, as the reasonable consequence of his matrimonial unfaithfulness or, at least, that she used his infidelity as a pretext for the essentially irrational loss of physical attraction between partners. It is unsurprising, albeit perhaps here rather remarkably conventional, given Galvão's public persona, that part of the justification of her attraction to a new lover is the intense repugnance experienced in recalling the relations she engaged in with the ex-lover. Yet Galvão's characterization here is particularly vigorous and represents a crude bluntness hitherto unfound, I would wager, in the discourse of any other Brazilian writer of the period, male or female. First of all, Galvão establishes a certain loathing for the sexual act, at least as she experiences it with Andrade. Rarely in *Paixão* does she address Ferraz directly, but she does so here, in a calculated appeal to one man in the negotiation of her feelings with regard to his predecessor:

Não sei, Geraldo, se você pode compreender o que senti naquela noite [em que Oswald procurou meu corpo pela primeira vez depois do nascimento de Rudá]. Oswald mostrou-se demais. E tive-lhe nojo. Nojo e ódio pela decepção que me feria. Senti o ato sexual repousado numa repugnância eterna. Nunca mais poderia suportar Oswald e julguei nunca mais poder suportar o contato masculino [.... E pensei] naquele homem ao meu lado, auxiliando o coito sórdido com oferta de machos. (68)[10]

This passage would seem to belie the assumption that there is an uncomplicated relationship between Galvão's frenetic involvement with São Paulo bohemian life and the adherence to some version of the principles of free love that were part of the bohemian culture of the day. To be sure, this statement is driven by Galvão's description of her sense of betrayal by Oswald, who may have been solidly heterosexual, with few scruples about the women he bedded, some apparently virtually in his wife's face. Moreover, as I have already stated, an essential organizing principle of the text is Galvão's categoric rejection of Andrade as part of explaining her interest in Ferraz, which was certainly strong enough for her to write what others might consider a rather abject account of her feelings. However, a certain lesbian undercurrent is one of the issues in Galvão's writing that must eventually be dealt with in detail.

I have referred to this lesbian undercurrent in my previous discussion of the almost totally female world of her novel *Parque industrial*, and I have also noted how Bengell insinuates Galvão's lesbian liaisons in her film *Eternamente Pagu*. However, at the same time, it would be foolish to fall into the sexist trap of avowing that the expression of repugnance for sexual intercourse with a man necessarily connotes lesbianism, especially when that repugnance coincides with what feminism will identify as the legitimate disgust on the part of a woman in the face of sexual intercourse with a man who is characterized with the terms that Galvão uses here to describe Oswald de Andrade's sexuality.[11]

After discussing the dynamics of a family based on the love for her son Rudá and the repugnance induced by his father (113), Galvão characterizes her physical loathing for Oswald in a manner that is truly jolting:

Senti os braços se apertarem, mas senti tambem que tudo era inútil. Havia obscenidade em seu contato. Eu ainda cedia muito nesse contato, mas não escondia a repugnância. Oswald continuava colecionando sexos. A sua boca lembrava-me continuamente um sexo feminino que eu fosse obrigada a beijar. (114.)[12]

One must leave aside the sexist segue implied here by converting the purportedly virile bearded masculine mouth into the female genitals, with the latter being presumedly repugnant in a way that the man's mouth is not.[13] What Galvão is rejecting here is the long-standing patriarchal confirmation of the presence of facial hair, still often prominent in the formal portraits of powerful men and aspirants to that status during the early third of the twentieth century. It is, concomitantly, important to note that the pictures of Ferraz, such as the ones reproduced in *Paixão Pagu*, all depict him as clean-shaven. Thus, rather than a casual example of a woman's unquestioning use of sexist figures, what Galvão is essentially doing here is finding a useful metonymy for underscoring quite emphatically her repudiation of Oswald's sexuality in favor, if only implicitly, of what Ferraz will now have to offer her.[14]

The third semantic nucleus of *Paixão Pagu* involves Galvão's relationship with the Communist Party, which, after the publication in 1933 of *Parque industrial* under an imposed pseudonym and her prison terms in 1935 and 1938, deteriorated to the point of her renouncing membership in 1940. There is no need to reiterate here how notoriously sexist the Party was during the period in question, with little consideration for the differences of women's history, except to mention its subservience to vertical mandates emanating from the U.S.S.R. and Stalin's firm grip on the various national embodiments of communism. A key issue in Bengell's film is the impossibility of accommodating Galvão's independence of spirit and the way in which Party officials repeatedly accused her of "personalism" (acts of personal initiative beyond the strict adherence to hierarchical orders), forcing her at one point to compose a document of self-denunciation. *Paixão Pagu* captures this with the evocation of an exchange evidently intended to expose her insufficient commitment as a woman:

> Foi com um tom de infinito desprezo que R. atacou o que designava como aviltante sentimentalismo. E com toda a vontade de atingir arranjou essas palavras:
> —E se seu filho morresse hoje?
> Senti apenas que estava muito quente e pude responder:
> —Os filhos dos trabalhadores estão morrendo de fome todos os dias. O importante é a nossa tarefa de agora.

Porque falei assim? Senti como falseados os meus sentimentos. Estava
também principiando a formar atitudes. Odiei-me pela cretinice e desones-
tidade comigo mesma. (83)[15]

Galvão goes on to complain about the use and manipulation of her status as
the first woman communist to be imprisoned and the way in which she was
expected to use her "feminine wiles" to extract information from a source
(91). But she protests emphatically, "eu acho que é exigir demais das mulheres revolucionárias. Eu não sou uma prostituta" (126).[16] However, it was
exactly this sort of personal opinion about the dominance of the higher
predicate "Eu acho" that led to many of Galvão's woes with the masculinist
structure of the Party, which at one point she designates sarcastically as "o
meu Partido" (91).

Galvão devotes several pages at this point to discussing her views of the
Party and its treatment of women, concluding with the explicit reference,
avant la lettre, to the Cixousian laugh of the Medusa which I have placed
as an epigraph to this chapter. When one considers the importance of this
laugh, coupled with Galvão's interest here and in her writing in general on
the female body (something that certainly must have been repugnant to the
male-centric and sexist consciousness of the Communist Party in Brazil), it
is difficult to underestimate the singularly iconoclastic nature of her autho-
rial voice at this time.

The fourth and final semantic nucleus is less a question of the Galvão's
actual words than it is an issue of the very publication of the document at
hand. An author's letters are always a tricky affair, and it is for this reason
that literary heirs usually exercise a very strict control over physical access
to them and their publication, often redacting them before allowing even
the most qualified scholar's viewing rights. *Paixão Pagu* was written more
than sixty years ago, and published more than forty years after Galvão's
death in 1962. As her son makes clear from the outset of his prefatory note,
it is his father who turns the document over to him: "Um tesouro familiar
que o filho deve futuramente passar para seu filho e assim por diante" (8).[17]
This would appear to be a legitimating sign for its publication, although one
cannot help but note that, either by virtue of conscious sonly privilege or as
a consequence of the masculine bias of the Portuguese language, the document is destined to be transmitted specifically from *filho* to *filho*.

Yet the way that *Paixão Pagu* is published—essentially in violation
of confidence and privacy—leaves the reader wondering what Rudá de

Andrade might have had to say regarding the way his mother categorically and grossly characterizes his father's body and sexuality. Galvão may not have cared what Rudá would think about her feelings for Andrade, and a necessary constituent of feminist writing is disdain for the womanly principle of decorum, a disdain captured in bywords like "speaking out," "talking back," "her side of the story," "last laughs," and Hélène Cixous's ur-trope, "the laugh of the Medusa." Concomitantly, Rudá may be untroubled by what was essentially a matter that concerned his parents' interpersonal relations; indeed, he collaborates on the publication of *Paixão Pagu* by providing a selection of family photographs (see the verso of the title page). However, there is no escaping the fact that publication of *Paixão Pagu* involved the exposure of confidential correspondence between Galvão and Ferraz whose revelation could be seen by some as a masculinist appropriation of Galvão's nonpublic writings.[18]

This text, then, raises some intriguing questions about a woman's relationship to her own textual production. However, those questions have less to do with Galvão's feminist writing, in which she was able to assert an independent voice, than they do with the strategic necessities of her desire to cement a relationship with Ferraz. The author's feminist voice is strong in her previous writing, particularly in *Parque industrial*, where, at great personal cost, she defied the Communist Party to speak as a woman, and where she forges, for the first time in Brazilian literature, a narrative text almost totally dominated by women's voices. Consequently, one might ask why Galvão was suddenly willing to submit her personal voice to a man's management, as would seem to have been the case with the preparation of this private letter at Ferraz's request, a letter whose now-public existence bears a title that she did not attribute to it: private letters do not bear descriptive titles assigned by their authors (although others may title specific texts), while openly published texts do.

Galvão's subsequent life with Ferraz reveals that she was hardly dominated by any masculinist imposition on his part, as she continued to have her own public voice and ran (unsuccessfully) for public office. Also, the fact that the Library of Congress's record for the 1945 first edition of *A famosa revista* records only her name indicates that some early copies of the novel (bearing a cataloging error) gave her principal credit; in all other editions, her name appears first, before Ferraz's.

In the apparent absence of subsequent commentary on this letter by Galvão herself, one would need to engage in a large measure of psychoanalytic speculation to determine why a woman with such a strong feminist voice would, so to speak, fall back on a formula of textual production in which the woman's discourse is framed by some measure of subservient address to a male recipient, who legitimates that discourse by virtue of having requested (ordered, demanded, made a condition of) it. Whether or not Galvão's acquiescence to Ferraz's request (the exact terms of which are also unknown) detracts from the feminist nature of her discourse remains an open matter. However, the fierce nature of many of the comments in *Paixão* with respect to other men and patriarchal institutions hardly means that the letter evinces the voice of a (now) subjugated woman. The more important issue is, I would insist, what Ferraz and their son understand to be the legitimate use of Galvão's private text, one that she did not publish in her lifetime.

In the end, if there is anything like a betrayal involved in the publication of *Paixão Pagu*, it is a necessary one, since no writer can expect—nor can one expect for any writer—that even the most intimate and private of his or her writings can forever remain kept from public view . . . and scholarly analysis. Galvão has for too long remained a mostly unknown gem of twentieth-century Brazilian literature. Her growing public recognition and the increasing scholarly study devoted to her is important not only because her work merits such recognition and study, but because it is an imperative supplement to the masculinism of Brazilian literary history. And moreover, it is indeed ironic that her emergence from oblivion references Oswald de Andrade, one of the literary giants of the official record.[19]

4

Downtown in São Paulo
with Hildegard Rosenthal's Camera

> Por diversas circunstâncias, o acervo de fotografias
> de Hildegard Rosenthal constitui-se num instru-
> mento utilíssimo para pesquisadores preocupados em
> conhecer a forma com que a cidade de São Paulo era
> utilizada por seus protagonistas, os cidadãos comuns.
>
> ☼ Benedito Lima de Toledo, "Um olhar" (13)

One of the best known images created by Hildegard Rosenthal (1913–90), the Swiss-born (but registered as a German national) photographer who produced some three thousand images in São Paulo in the ten-year period beginning with her arrival in Brazil in the late 1930s, is that of the *camarão*, the shrimp-colored tram that carried passengers in and out of the financial and commercial center of São Paulo. Tosta has examined the recurring image of the tram in the poetry of São Paulo—although he does not pick up the reference specifically to the camarão in the 1933 proletarian novel by Patrícia Galvão, *Parque industrial*. In the 1920s, São Paulo began to undergo a process of enormous expansion that converted it from the modest seat of the coffee and other agricultural interests of the beginning of the century into the financial and industrial center, first of Brazil, and then of all Latin America. By the time of the much-fabled Semana de Arte Moderna in early 1922, which provided the ab quo for an assertively national and cosmopolitan cultural production,[1] and the arrival of foreign intellectuals who provided an impetus for the emerging sophistication of the city (the most famous was Claude Lévi-Strauss, who arrived in 1934 and began in Brazil the work that became so important for the development of contemporary anthropology; see chapter 5), São Paulo had undergone many significant transformations.

Certainly, the most representative was the emergence of a central urban core that anchored the growth of the city, with industrialization to the east, the concentration of immigrant masses to the north and east, and the construction of elegant residential satellites to the west and south. The development of the Universidade de São Paulo, which was crucial to the modernization of the city (and as part of which project Lévi-Strauss arrived in Brazil, although his relationship with the administration was not amiable and he accordingly did not long remain on the faculty), was first developed out of facilities of the preexisting Faculdade de Direito (Law School) in the downtown area, then moved in 1949 to a large and quite sumptuous site southwest of the urban center. The urban center of the city has historically been identified as the Praça da Sé (Cathedral Plaza), where the metropolitan cathedral is situated, although other points, such as the Praça da República (Plaza of the Republic), the Viaduto do Chá (The Tea Viaduct, one of the symbols of the city), and the Avenida Paulista (site of branches of over fifty international banking houses) are equally predominant in the urban imaginary of São Paulo. It is in and out of this central core that the trams function, among them the colorful camarão that Rosenthal so notably photographed. Indeed, the tram or trolley car—and the motorized bus—appear in nine of the forty-six images gathered in the 1998 catalog of Rosenthal's photography, *Cenas urbanas* (Urban Scenes), published by São Paulo's Instituto Moreia Salles, which is now the repository of her monumental work.

But what is particularly noteworthy about this image is the way in which it captures the utilization of this vehicle of modern transportation to enhance its urban iconicity by having it serve as the billboard for a slogan of São Paulo's urban growth. Long before such public forms of transportation were converted into dense texts of commercial and public service

Figure 4.1. *Trasportes públicos—bonde na Praça do Correio* (c. 1940) by Hildegard Rosenthal. Reproduced courtesy of Acervo Instituto Moreira Salles.

information, with advertisements and announcements plastered all over the vehicle's exterior, interior, and strategically at the stops and stations of its run, such that passengers can often read only a portion of these texts at each step in their itinerary, the São Paulo camarão prominently displayed the slogan reflecting the city's self-consciousness regarding its important growth. The slogan reads: "SÃO PAULO É O MAIOR CENTRO INDUSTRIAL DA AMÉRICA LATINA." The capital letters of the text run almost the full length of the car, and they are, one might say, enclosed in the quotation marks of the front and rear doors through which pass the hundreds of passengers who read any one vehicle each day, all preponderantly involved in some financial or commercial way with supporting the assertion made by the slogan. The slogan appears as a banner in what seems to be a specially designed space whose height is exactly that of the capital letters and which occurs between the slight overhang of the curved exterior roof of the vehicle and a small overhang of the top of the vehicle that runs all the way around the vehicle above the front cab, the rows of windows, the two doors on the right side and the rear compartment.

This latter overhang constitutes a very emphatic underlining of the capitalized text. Since the banner runs along the side of the bus where passengers mount and dismount, they cannot help but contemplate an assertion which their travel is likely reinforcing. This is a slogan that announces its text as much to the casual pedestrian of the city as it does to a large sector of the agents of the social text within which the slogan acquires its meaning. The indirect object of the implied predicate of assertion—"I say to YOU that . . ."—is as much the casual observer who needs to be told this truth, as it is the individual who suspects it is true because of his or her daily toil within the industrial apparatus.[2]

Rosenthal's photograph is brilliant in the way that it focuses on the trolley. The vehicle is one of a line of trolleys parked at the major stop of the Praça de Correio (Post Office Plaza; the imposing post office building may be seen in the upper right-hand background), and the body of the vehicle fills the central portion of the photo in a swath that reaches from border to border, although the focus is made more interesting by bleeding the rear of the vehicle outside the left-hand margin and by including a portion, bleeding out the right-hand border, of a second vehicle. Positioning the line of sight as such underscores the way in which this vehicle is part of a presumably large fleet of such cars, itself an index of the mass movement of the population going about its business; to adapt Warren Harding's famous phrase, "the business of São Paulo is business."[3] The clean line of the trolley—which is accentuated by the horizontal banner of the slogan, itself parallel to the set of four safety bars that run the length of the windows—is repeated by a series of horizontally drawn spaces that run down the lower portion of the photograph and bleed off outside the bottom margin. These spatial bands include the file of passengers waiting to board the vehicle. The single file is discernible among the jumble of some fifty individuals (mostly men and all appropriately uniformed, in the best British fashion, for their occupation in the city)[4] moving around the open space recorded by the bottom half of the photograph: the strip of the passenger island, itself bordered by a curb, the bricked channel along which other vehicles might pass (this transit surface antedates the massive paving that universally characterizes the city today), and, finally, another pedestrian area, either an access sidewalk or a passenger island associated with yet another set of vehicles (a larger image of the important set of bus stops in the Praça da Sé, along with parking areas for cars, may be studied in image number nine of *Cenas urbanas*). This sort of parallel geometry, so characteristic of the formalist designs of modernism, certainly augments Rosenthal's representation of the bustling city. And note the appropriate use of verbs here: the premodern marketplace teams with individuals, but the modern commercial cityscape bustles with its denizens.

As an assertion, the slogan implies the need to establish São Paulo's ranking among the industrial cities of Latin America. Not only does it presuppose the possibility of employing the absolute adjective *a maior*, but it also presupposes an inventory of cities among which to establish São Paulo's ranking. This assumption is problematical at best, since one can only wonder what the level of industrialization was in Latin America in the late 1920s and early 1930s. Proletarian novels are scarce in Latin American literature from this period, which is that of the high point of a social realism denouncing the exploited factory worker of capitalism. Argentine literature involves a modest bibliography of narratives on proletarian lives, a presence that will be addressed by the first Peronista government (1946–52), with its roots in the urban labor movement.[5]

However, in Latin America generally, a cultural production protesting the exploitation of the worker typically means the menial wage earner of agriculture or mining—that is, nonurban enterprises. This is equally true in Brazil, where texts by Rachel de Queiroz, Graciliano Ramos, and José Lins do Rego all involve rural settings.[6] This explains the importance of Galvão's *Parque industrial*, not only as a feminist text, but as a singular example of urban proletarian fiction. The simple fact is that, aside from industrialization in Argentina (meatpacking enjoying a historical prominence), it is questionable whether one can reasonably speak much of this process occurring anywhere else in Latin America before projects of industrialization (along with economic theories of import substitution) such as those promoted by Juan Domingo Perón in Argentina in the 1940s and Fidel Castro in Cuba in the 1960s.[7] Brazil has had such a long history of comprehensive industrialization that its neighbor, Argentina, has at times spoken of the bane of Brazilian overproduction being dumped on the Argentine market.

As a consequence, the assertion that São Paulo was the major industrial center of Latin America cannot have been seen as occurring in the context of a contentious debate, except perhaps vis-à-vis Brazil's traditional rival, Argentina (sometimes, it seems, a rival in all things, from borders to soccer, from filmmaking to sin . . .), but certainly not in the face of any competition from its neighbors (Uruguay, Paraguay, and Bolivia, among them) or from any other Latin American economy. In the 1920s, Mexico, for example, the other great economic power in Latin America, was just beginning to recover from the devastation of the barbarous decade of the 1910 revolution, and prosperity only came after World War II, in which, like Brazil, Mexico was a close ally of the United States and benefited accordingly. So to assert the primacy of São Paulo's industrial base serves, perhaps, more to inspire the pride of the bustling bees of the industrial hive than to sort out economic realities. Perhaps, for Rosenthal, there was a certain measure of ironic glance to be associated with such an assertion, in the jejuneness of it all, especially for someone who had arrived in Brazil evading the horrors of Nazism, a movement founded in large measure on Germany's industrial capitalism.

Although Rosenthal was not herself Jewish, she left Germany during the early years of the Hitler regime because she had the temerity to marry a Jew (see biographical notes, De Franchesci). In Brazil, she was always accepted as something like an honorary Jew, and such an important intellectual and photographic historian as Boris Kossoy acknowledges her contribution to the realm of Jewish cultural production in Brazil that he eminently represents (16). Certainly, Rosenthal is very much a part of Brazilian photography, appearing in standard reference works (for example, Fernandez Junior), featured in prominent expositions, and accorded unique status by cultural foundations such as the Instituto de Moreira Salles, which houses her negatives, on which it based a one-person show (the show's exhibit catalog inspired this chapter); Rosenthal was also featured in a program by São Paulo's TV Unicsul/Canal Universitário do Sul, of the Universidade Cruzeiro do Sul. Although Rosenthal's work was essentially concentrated in the 1930s, her negatives run into the thousands, providing a pretty much untapped documentary source for historians of this crucial period in Brazilian history, which corresponds with the tail end of the halcyon years of cultural production that followed the Semana de Arte Moderna, the aftermath of the Great Depression, and the rise of Getúlio Vargas, who came to power by coup in 1930 and imposed the semi-fascist Estado Novo in 1937. While Rosenthal's photographs are not directly political in nature, they can be important to understand this period of intense social change in the country's major demographic, commercial, and financial center.[8]

Most commentators have underscored Rosenthal's primary interest in photographing human beings in public spaces. This is especially evident in the case of the photograph I have commented on at length above: rather than only framing the camarão, as it might be found in a holding area after hours, she captures it in full service, surrounded by the bustling Paulistanos whose workday is facilitated by this colorful vehicle, with its upbeat, gung ho message regarding the preeminence of São Paulo's industrial base. Another famous work of Rosenthal's is a self-portrait. Photographers are famous for their self-portraits, and this one is equally interested in the photographer as another human being, as another participant in the social commerce she is capturing; it is, therefore, intriguing to speculate as to the reasons when a photographer chooses not to include a self-portrait.[9] Dating 1940, this image shows a petite and very formally dressed woman. Her gaze is that of a worldly aristocrat, and one can imagine her roaming the downtown streets of São Paulo (not all of her images are from the central core of the city, but an impressive number are), lugging one of the almost unwieldy top-scale cameras of the day.

Rosenthal had an assistant whom she was not above posing in her shots.[10] Although none of her photos are stagy and she appeared not to have had an interest in photomontage,[11] unlike her contemporary German colleague Grete Stern, who was beginning to work at the same time in Argentina (Foster, "Dreaming in Feminine"; Stern), this fact means that it would not be quite accurate to represent these images as altogether spontaneous and unplanned. That is, although there is much of the random in Rosenthal's collection, it is not simply a portfolio of images belonging to someone who went out on the street and shot only whatever struck her fancy; in addition, as any artist might, to select important images of the Paulistano workaday world, she also planned images to enrich, one might say, the human presence in them. This is especially intriguing from the point of view of a photography that focuses on the built human environment, the urban cityscape, rather than on the circumstantial human inhabitants of it, as in the case of Lévi-Strauss's photography of São Paulo. It is important to note that Lévi-Strauss's images, published under the heading of Saudades de São Paulo (Nostalgia for São Paulo), belong to the same period in which Rosenthal worked. Of course, Lévi-Strauss did photograph human beings (there is a particularly nice image of his father, who pioneered the use of photography in painting), and Rosenthal did photograph some urban spaces in which human beings are absent. Yet there is an essential contrast between these two foreign photographers working in São Paulo in the 1930s.

Unsurprisingly, given the synechdochic nature for Rosenthal's photography of the image of the camarão, she seemed particularly taken by unpretentious urban laborers, young and old, men and women. The latter inclusion is an important one because, while one cannot merely assume that Rosenthal was a feminist, her gaze as a woman (in addition to her gaze as a foreigner) is important, insofar as it necessarily cannot have reduplicated the masculinist gaze on the female body: feminism is not inevitable for a female cultural producer, but masculinism is not either, and the text at least offers the possibility of encountering a negotiation of the concepts of gender.

For example, there are two connected images of a woman burdened by her load. She wears the dress that, in Rosenthal's own European vocabulary, would likely identify her as a peasant, although she appears to be a small truck farmer: rough-cut blouses over a long skirt, with cloth stockings and heavy shoes, touched off with the sort of long apron down the front typical of country folk. In the first image, she is carrying a large, obviously tightly packed burlap bag on her head, and she clutches a great squash in the crook of her left arm. In the second image, although she still bears the burlap bag on her head, the squash is on the ground, resting against two other equally full bags and a small market basket containing what appear to be potatoes or other similar vegetables. In the first image, she is standing beside a trolley, a more modest one than the camarão. The trolley's posted run is to São Caetano, a suburb to the southeast of downtown São Paulo. It would have been an extremely outlying area in the 1930s; indeed, São Caetano is the patron saint of laborers, unmistakably an indication of its population.

The background of both images appears to be the central market, which is located north of downtown and is today considered a historical landmark. The fact that it is quite small indicates the limited population base of São Paulo at the time. One can compare it to the vast Buenos Aires Abasto; built in the early 1900s and located in the heart of the old immigrant quarter to the west of downtown, the Abasto, a Les Halles–like structure, befitted the enormous growth of São Paulo in the late nineteenth century (Berjman-Fiszelew). Thus, Rosenthal's image is that of a woman who has come to sell her produce at market, a fact that is confirmed in the second image by a depth shot in which we see the life around the market: other sellers, some customers, produce, a couple of horse-drawn carts that would have been used to transport the produce itself, and the city in the background, extending beyond the facade of the market. Receding into the background is what would have been the trolley that appears in the first image: if the woman

Figure 4.2. *À espera do bonde na Zona Cerealista. À esquerda, o Mercado Munici-pal* (c. 1940) by Hildegard Rosenthal. Reproduced courtesy of Acervo Instituto Moreira Salles.

has not been let off the trolley with her produce, she has crossed paths with it, in a conjunction of the modern, male-chauffeured device of transporta-tion, and the traditional, premodern female produce vendor. Significantly, one can make out in the farthest reaches of the photograph the modern downtown commercial and financial buildings, and the cars parked along the street (contrasting with the horse-drawn carts) and other buildings be-side them attest to urban modernity. Indeed, as ancient as truck farming is, the urban marketplace is an imposing fin-de-siècle edifice, well in keeping with the other traces of modernity in the city. Such a building—part of the masculine modernity of the city—constitutes a way of disciplining, orga-nizing, and regulating the farm-based economy that has traditionally come into the city through the chaotic open-air market, which has always, signifi-cantly, been dominated by women.

There is, then, a measure of feminism that attaches to these two pho-tographs, both in terms of a woman photographer studying a female pro-duce vendor and in the sense of capturing the juxtaposition between this traditional form of woman's work and the modern male-driven metropolis. But there are a couple of interesting ancillary details as well. For example, the camera never shows the woman's face, only her left profile in the first image and her back in the second. Indeed, we see her head bent over in the first image from the weight of the burlap bag she carries upon it, as though fulfilling her role as a beast of burden obstructs her face. This does not necessarily signify the humiliation of women: Graciela Iturbide's photographs of the working women of Juchitán, Mexico, amply demonstrate peasant women in full, joyfully fulfilled by their work.[12] In contrast with the anonymity of the faceless produce seller—who becomes something of a figure representative of all such sellers by her under-individuation—we have a female onlooker who stares at the camera as it does its work in recording this scene.[13] That is, there is a triangulation between three women: the produce seller, the photographer, and the female onlooker. Moreover, this onlooker is dressed in more modern fashion than the produce vendor. Although her garb is not definitively elegant—and, therefore, the woman could be a housewife or the housekeeper of a wealthy residence—this woman, assumedly a market customer, mediates between the photographer and the farm woman, since she is part of the economy represented by the public market: if she were not there to purchase the farmer's produce, the latter would not be there to sell it, and hence there would be no basic economy worker for the photographer to study in her two images. Note also that we are speaking of two images: it is unusual in this series for one subject to appear in two images, and the fact that the produce seller does only underscores Rosenthal's interest in this photographic study.

One final detail: a man in the second photograph, conventionally dressed in business garb, looks away from the camera, as though singularly uninterested in this photographic interchange between women. Yet a fourth woman, who appears also to be a market vendor, *does* contemplate the photographic transaction. This fourth woman is seated beside another person, who also witnesses the scene: it appears to be a male child, probably her own, since young children typically work alongside their mothers in the marketplace.[14]

Other of Rosenthal's images reveal, however, the dominance of public space by men—men of all ages, as in the case of the ragamuffin with his shoe-shine box and the nicely dressed newspaper boy: long socks, short pants, clean white shirt, 1930s-style work cap, and a smiling face, offering a newspaper whose headline regards German troops massed on the Swiss

Figure 4.3. *O leiteiro—Praça Marechal Deodoro* (c. 1940) by Hildegard Rosenthal. Reproduced courtesy of Acervo Instituto Moreira Salles.

border; this would date the photograph from the end of the 1930s, and the news would be of particular interest to Swiss-born Rosenthal. In another photograph, an equally well-dressed ticket taker on a sleek modern bus tends a client, and one of Rosenthal's best-known images is that of a milk-man removing a crate of bottles from his equally sleekly modern delivery van. Modernity is signaled by not just the van and its carefully uniformed driver, or the note of modern medicine in the brand name of the milk, Leite Vigor, and the announcement that it is *pasteurisado*,[15] but also by the landscaped apartment buildings in the background and the overhead telephone/power lines; this is very much the image of a modern, "vigorous" São Paulo in its daily routine.

However, from the point of view of a feminist perspective on the city, in addition to the potpourri of images of the male-dominated streets, one photograph in particular attests to the overwhelming male presence. Nine men and a preadolescent male child are captured in this photograph (in addition, we see part of the shoulder of an eleventh male subject). They are gathered outside of a commercial establishment, perhaps a clothes store, that advertises wholesale and retail transactions (it is common in Brazil to find both in the same business), and the legend down one of the support columns of the facade announces the availability of *tintas* (dyes/paints). All of the men are dressed in conventional business attire: suits, white shirts, ties, and hats; at least one is wearing a vest, and the boy is also formally dressed in a white shirt and pants. At least half of the men are watching something transpiring on the sidewalk to their left: perhaps a newspaper headline being called out by a vendor, a street-side pitchman, an altercation—in sum, any of a number of options that would constitute part of the paradigm that might be called the street theater of daily life in the modern metropolis.

Of special interest in this photograph, in addition to the display of formality in these men dressed for the street—the particular formality of São Paulo is often commented upon in comparison to the more informal Rio de Janeiro[16]—is that the men here constitute a range of ages, such that there is a generational continuity in the combined masculine presence they effect. For example, to the far right stands the young boy. He appears at the back of a man in his late fifties or sixties, while alongside the latter is a young man in his twenties, and next to him a man in his late thirties or forties. While these are very rough approximations, one is struck by how the four male figures clearly discerned in the foreground represent four different age groups: this undoubtedly spontaneous assemblage attests to how men of all ages dominate the street, and the boy included in the photograph is surely learning to become a man by hanging around his seniors.[17] Moreover, this scene takes place on the sidewalk, which, while the men stand outside of one establishment, serves to connect an array of commercial enterprises, carrying the lifeblood of modern São Paulo (one will recall the historical development of São Paulo from an agricultural distribution hub to a world-class financial center; all cities are about business, but the business of São Paulo is unquestionably Business).[18]

The sidewalk is, additionally, a very broad space; probably even one of the pedestrian malls that emerge as part of the commercial center between the Praça da República northward to the Viaduto do Chá. These pedestrian malls, beyond contributing to pedestrian protection from vehicular traffic and allowing intensely circulating foot traffic, are veritable stages of urban life. Today, they often provide space for performance art and musicians, but they have also become additional commercial spaces where small-business operations that cannot afford a permanent location line both sides of the

Figure 4.4. *Pontos de encontro—Rua Líbero Badaró, esquina con Avenida São João* (c. 1940) by Hildegard Rosenthal. Reproduced courtesy of Acervo Instituto Moreira Salles.

mall and often even the center with stalls, tables, mats, and cloths displaying wares in the form of a large open-air bazaar, thereby providing the spectator—and the photographic spectator like Rosenthal—with a geometrically greater inventory of subjects and circumstances. Although Rosenthal may have been primarily interested in studying individuals in the urban landscape, easily a dozen of the photographs appearing in *Cenas urbanas* concern large multitudes, many of them adequately characterized by the cliché "teeming," while a goodly number of other images focus on the built—and building—environment of central São Paulo.

In one semi-staged photo, Rosenthal effectively captures her assistant eating a piece of watermelon purchased from a fruit cart in the street. This is also a photograph dominated by men: to the left the fruit vendor is surrounded on three sides by four male customers, all dressed in typical business garb. To the right, a group of three equally formally dressed men are engaged in conversation, while a fourth man can be seen beyond, though he is not participating in the conversation. The latter are standing outside the door of a haberdashery, so once again commerce is an important detail in the photo, permitting the juxtaposition of the informal economy of a street vendor versus the more modern clothes store. The woman is looking somewhat askance, and closer examination shows part of the body of another woman who is talking to her, although she is mostly hidden—blocked out—by one of the men in the conversational group. Certainly, the women are outnumbered by the masculine presence on the street, as though they were interlopers in this all-male universe. What is quite humorous—and, surely, serendipitous, since Rosenthal's images are not elsewhere marked by any irony of detail—is the fact that the woman is standing directly below a street sign reading *CONTRA-MÃO*, "wrong way," which the playful viewer might want to read as suggesting—as signing—that the woman is out of place in this street scene.

I do not wish to argue that Rosenthal had a feminist artistic agenda. Rather, the amount of space in this chapter devoted to the first image—her most famous—underscores that her principal fascination lay with the intense movement of the modern capitalist cityscape that was fast becoming definitive in São Paulo seventy years ago. Although as photographs they are static, this image of the trolley and the preponderance of images of cars and commercial vehicles stress the movement of the streets, as do those of the pedestrians. But there is no escaping the fact that the streets belong to the men of this world of commerce and finance,[19] and the vehicles are their business instruments as well. One of the images confirms this by showing an elegantly dressed woman paying a taxi driver his fare. Just as other images of buses, trolleys, and carts all show male chauffeurs, this photograph stresses how women, if they travel by vehicular conveyance, are transported by men. In this way, an inevitable consequence of Rosenthal's examination of the Paulistano streets of the 1930s is that a woman studied what was still very much a public masculinist realm.[20]

5

Saudades do Brasil

Claude Lévi-Strauss's Photographic Gaze on the City of São Paulo

Cheguei portanto a São Paulo preparado para encontrar bem mais do que um novo quadro de vida: uma daquelas experiências em tempo e em dimensão reais geralmente vedadas às ciências humanas por causa da lentidão com que se modificam os fenômenos e da impossibilidade material e moral de agir sobre eles.

❂ Claude Lévi-Strauss, *Saudades de São Paulo* (14)

Tristão bought maps of São Paulo but no two agreed; the bus routes wound about like tortured snakes, and when he emerged, sick from the twisting and swaying, he walked south when he meant to walk north.

❂ John Updike, *Brazil* (59)

In 1934 the young French anthropologist Claude Lévi-Strauss (1908–2009) set out from the French port of Marseilles to assume a position in sociology at the newly formed Universidade de São Paulo. Unlike Spanish-speaking Latin America, which had universities from early in the sixteenth century, Brazil did not have a university tradition properly speaking (although it did have professional schools, called *Faculdades*) until the twentieth century, as the landed oligarchy preferred to remand its sons, as it had for centuries, to fabled Coimbra in the motherland of Portugal. However, by the early twentieth century there were enough immigrant families without ties to Portugal to move for the founding of local universities, and (although there is some dispute over who was first) the German community sponsored the founding in 1910 of what is today the Universidade Federal do Paraná in Curitiba. By the 1930s, the new financial barons, through the newspaper *O estado de São Paulo*, were in a position to move for the formation of a university in what they considered to be the dynamic center of twentieth-century modernity; after all, the 1922 Semana de Arte Moderna did much to establish categorically modern Brazilian culture, drawing a line in the sand with respect to the traditionalists whom they associated with the predominantly Portuguese-identified capital—first of the Empire and then of the Republic—of Rio de Janeiro. Thus, it came as no surprise that the founding impulse of the Universidade de São Paulo, the USP, originated from French culture, whose vanguard influence was so evident in the Semana de Arte Moderna and the many subsequent faces of the Modernismo movement it helped generate (for a history of the USP, see Cardoso; also see chapter 20, "Modernism," in Morse for the insertion of this artistic movement into the context of the socioeconomic history of São Paulo). The French government was instrumental in the formation of the new university, undoubtedly seeing the possibility for expanding their sphere of influence in Latin America, and to this day the USP is known, with as much disdain as affection, as the Brazilian *aldeia gaulesa* (Costa, passim).[1] Not everyone would agree that the USP is Latin America's premier university, especially in terms of its research faculty, but there can be no question that it ranks among the region's top-tier institutions of higher learning.

Lévi-Strauss's tenure at the USP was relatively short lived, and by 1941, Lévi-Strauss was teaching at the New School for Social Research in New York City, having left Brazil in 1937. However, it was during his tenure in Brazil that Lévi-Strauss "discovered" the indigenous cultures of the region, as he so eloquently relates in his 1955 masterpiece *Tristes tropiques*, and during the 1938–39 period he conducted the extensive investigations, financed by the French government, among indigenous populations in central Brazil that would comprise part of his groundbreaking *Anthropologie structurale (Structural Anthropology)*, published in 1958. There are many gaps in the accounts of Lévi-Strauss's tenure in Brazil: [2] I personally have always been struck by Lévi-Strauss's lack of interest, as a Jew, in addressing anti-Semitism under the early Getúlio Vargas regime (Carneiro; Williams 225),[3] prior to the shrewd commitment by the extra-constitutional president, who was not without his fascist leanings, to the cause of the Allies in 1941. Except for the rather brief remarks about São Paulo recording his initial impressions in the first chapters of *Tristes tropiques*, which are more in the vein of a travelogue than a sociopolitical commentary, Lévi-Strauss appears never to have devoted much thought to Brazil as a modern country. Though he recognized its suitability as a laboratory for anthropological research, it is only with his invitation to visit Brazil in 1985 that he recalls his experiences, observing that in his youth anthropology meant studying the Other, while today it includes the examination of one's own society (*Tristes tropiques*, "Prologue" 18–19).

Along with Lévi-Strauss's invitation to Brazil on the fiftieth anniversary of his original voyage to that country, there came the publication, in French in 1994 and in English in 1995, of a dossier of Lévi-Strauss's own photography from the period of his original research in the country. *Saudades do Brasil: A Photographic Memoir*,[4] to cite the English translation, quite reasonably includes a large number of photographs that relate to the anthropological research conducted among the Nabikwara and Tupi-Kawahib in the central interior of the country.[5] But the one hundred and eighty photographs also include sixteen images from Lévi-Strauss's stay in São Paulo, along with an introductory commentary that records his recollections of a city undergoing the rapid transformation from an outpost village to a modern metropolis that has allowed São Paulo to become the largest city in Brazil, the second largest (after Mexico City) in Latin America, and the financial capital of the continent. In 1996, *Saudades de São Paulo* appeared in Brazil, and it includes exclusively Lévi-Strauss's photography from *Saudades do Brasil* relating to that city: a bit more than fifty images repeat the former, including different angles of the same subject, but a number that were not included in *Saudades do Brasil* also make their way in.

The purpose of this essay is to examine Lévi-Strauss's key photographs of the São Paulo that he saw in the 1930s.[6] I am not particularly interested in contrasting the São Paulo of the period with the contemporary mega-lopolis, nor is it pertinent here to compare the French anthropologist's images with those of Brazilians (of which there is a goodly amount) or other foreigners (of which there is little: São Paulo has never been considered much of a tourist destination and, therefore, not an especially photogenic one). What I am interested in is the organization of Lévi-Strauss's gaze: what spaces of the city caught his attention and how he captured them. It is worth noting that, by contrast with his photographs in the field, the images of São Paulo are not characterized by the record of human subjects.

Understandably, as the anthropologist made use of the camera to record the development of his research, he would focus insistently on human subjects, since part of his disciplinary interest lay both with the way in which the subjects of his research related to their physical environment, to their "natural" settings, and the way in which their bodies constituted cultural texts in terms of dress (and relative undress), ornaments and adornments, instruments of daily occupations, tattoos, and passive and active interactions between individuals.

Underlying all of Lévi-Strauss's images is the inevitable question of what the Parisian intellectual must have thought of the still-raw cityscape of the Brazilian provincial capital.[7] I do not mean to imply that he may have had any condescending attitude toward São Paulo, since he remained there to teach several years and went on to use Brazil as the foundation of his life-long scientific work. Yet a certain measure of "disconnect" was to be expected, as a country like Brazil was still far away from the thoroughly modernized early twentieth-century France: indeed, one of the issues presented by these photographs is the degree to which one can deduce from them any sustained interest in the ways in which modernizing São Paulo was still/already markedly different from Paris. On the one hand, the analytical eye of the photographer may seek to understand all of the material contexts of the urban project that São Paulo had embarked upon; on the other hand, one cannot be surprised to find an emphasis on those details of the built environment that, when framed with relative autonomy, reveal various degrees of felicitous accomplishment in imposing European modernity on the tropics. Subsequently this will mean the emergence of Brazil's own national forms of modernity, especially as regards the built environment, in architecture and design. But this particular modernity cannot have been much in evidence in the mid-1930s.[8]

All of the images in Lévi-Strauss's dossier are accompanied by brief commentaries. The first one is singularly noteworthy for the way in which it inaugurates, so to speak, the anthropologist's view of the city: "The city also had a singular beauty, due to break in rhythm, architectural paradoxes, contrasting shapes and colors. Despite, or perhaps because of, lack of planning, the urban landscape could be lyrical" (*Saudades de São Paulo* 27).[9] What is particularly striking about this observation in the context of the photograph it accompanies is the way in which it so perfectly captures the binarism that is one of the founding principles of Lévi-Strauss's anthropological thought (see Leach's extensive explanations). Lévi-Strauss grounded himself on the principles of early structural linguistics, which say that the distinctive features of language—first phonology, and then, by extension, the ever-larger realms of, successively, morphology, syntax, and (only sketchily examined) lexicon—organize themselves along binary lines: a feature was either x or non-x. That is, a consonant was either voiced or non-voiced (voiceless), a tense morpheme was either past or non-past (present), a syntagm was either subjunctive or non-subjunctive (indicative). In Lévi-Strauss's theorizing, the principle of the binary organization of the human mind—that is, the brain's conception of the universe as binary leads to a binary organization of lived human experience, and the social structures we create in turn reaffirm the brain's binary conception of the universe in an unending cycle of perceptual feedback—is most famously evident in his understanding of the configuration of clans or moieties (a word that explicitly captures the binary division of social life [*Les Structures élémentaires de la parenté*; 1949]) and, providing a phrase, "the raw and the cooked," that has become virtually a byword of contemporary culture, his understanding of the symbolic function of the permissible and the taboo within a cultural unit (*Le Cru et le cuit*; 1964, volume I of the series *Mythologies*).

The photograph in question is virtually the embodiment of the principle of the raw and the cooked. By capturing a view of the burgeoning architecture of São Paulo in its juxtaposition to the preexisting landscape, Lévi-Strauss in effect creates a binary opposition between the "rawness" of the landscape and the "cooked" city. Although there is a simultaneity about this juxtaposition, there is also a historical dimension. Binary structuralism is paradigmatically synchronic, asking what distinctive feature oppositions exist that are, at the moment of analytical scrutiny, operant; diachronic before-after changes in the structure of the language are irrelevant and mean only that there have been, and will continue to be, successive diachronic stages as identified by the same number of analytical scrutinies. In the case of the photograph, however, the binary oppositions are double: there is, first of all, the patently evident juxtaposition between the city and nature; and there is the juxtaposition between preexisting nature, which is being encroached upon by the exuberantly expanding city. In constructing this juxtaposition, Lévi-Strauss was notably prescient, since São Paulo, seventy years later, continues to mushroom in an apparently unstoppable fashion, such that, with the exception of some marvelous green spaces maintained within the city, the preexisting foliage has been systematically uprooted, and what remains is seriously threatened by the heavy pall of pollution that perpetually hangs over the city.[10]

By foregrounding a remaining swath of downtown foliage—probably part of the Anhangabaú strip park that lies just east of the Praça da República, anchor of the city—the aforementioned photograph underscores the "natural" that is being displaced by the "cultural" or "social" in the form of the built environment, which here includes several high-rises, one of at least twenty stories. These edifices emerge from among the trees as, quite literally, alternatives to them, in the sense that it would be inconceivable for them to be built without trees being removed: subsequent landscaping might replant trees and other foliage as part of the amenities of the property. Indeed, high-rise residential buildings in São Paulo today are noted for their lovely gardens, typically part of the ground floor planning, and often provide a buffer between the street and the building and between one building and another—a significant alternative to the row house–style New York high-rises.

In this way, the historical dimension of first the trees and then the buildings is also the synchronic binary of the raw and the cooked, as nature and built environment must coexist in a difficult tension in the modern city, with the real possibility that the latter will encroach unremittingly on the former, such that the landscape background of the built environment will ultimately disappear in favor of an unbroken vista of jumbled buildings that are all that make up the metropolitan environment. Although the binary between the raw foliage and the cooked architecture is very evident in this photography, Lévi-Strauss's commentary, while observing that the urban landscape could be lyrical, nevertheless seems to perceive that a "lack of planning" will mean that the foreground is bound to disappear. Indeed, in a reversal of the motif of Dunsinane Wood, the city is marching into the

Figure 5.1. *Vale de Itororó, a partir da rua Xavier de Toledo* (c. 1937) by Claude Lévi-Strauss. Reproduced courtesy of Acervo Instituto Moreira Salles.

foreground, and a suggestion of the built environment can be seen in the lower left-hand corner in the form of what appear to be rooftops emerging from among the leaves of the trees.

Enhancing the contrast between nature and the built environment in the photograph is the texture of geometry. The round trunks of the trees and limbs contrast with the essentially boxy nature of the buildings, whether old (whitewashed nineteenth-century constructions) or new (the cement skyscrapers). Yet the one high-rise that dominates the center of the background, the very midpoint of the photograph, appears to have rounded corners in the sort of art deco patterning that combines different geometrical shapes. Also, there is a round or oblong building next to it, although it is hard to tell whether this is a rounded part of another building or a standalone structure in that shape. These and a few other non-square features of other buildings, such as cupolas or what may be a smokestack, are exceptions that only serve to underscore the rectangular regularity of the buildings as the constructed mass of the present. Moreover, when the viewer's eye returns to the foliage, its jutting irregularity—the morass of branches, fronds, and leaves—contrasts with the easily discernible patterns of the buildings: for example, if the second floor has seven windows facing the camera, the fifth floor is likely to have seven windows, and all are equally distributed on every floor. Even when a building begins to have fewer windows as it rises, it requires little effort to discern the pattern in the change of their distribution; these are all constructions of modernity, wherein a guiding principle is to correct the irregularity, chance, and, in general, the "imperfections" of nature in the transformation of space by culture.

Of course, the São Paulo skyline looks considerably different today, seventy years later. Most of the original nature disappeared, to be replaced, where there is greenery, with the near regularity of human design. This is even the case at one of my favorite green spots in the city, the Parque Trianon on the Avenida Paulista, across from the MASP, the Museu de Arte de São Paulo, one of the premier examples of high modernity in the city. The Trianon is a semitropical forest in miniature, but there is no question that it is well planned. Moreover, the Paulistano skyline today provides many examples of postmodern architecture and its recovery, so to speak, of the irregular patterns that transcend the binary mindset. If Lévi-Strauss's intention, with this photographic image, was to capture the bursting energy of a city in the throes of one of the most dynamic processes of modernization in Latin America in the early twentieth century, he has done so admirably.

Lévi-Strauss's second photograph is of the Viaduct (Viaduto do Chá) and a modern office building under construction. While the east end of the Viaduct is still part of the original downtown business and commercial district, it is no longer the anchor it once was: in true postmodern fashion, such operations in São Paulo are now conducted in many clusters throughout the city, the most important being the Avenida Paulistana, where the major international banks are concentrated (I mentioned above the MASP and the Parque Trianon, which are located along its trajectory of approximately fifteen long blocks). Yet the west end of the Viaduct, as seen in this image, still is anchored by the Teatro Municipal (officially "Theatro Municipal"), one of the great opera houses of Latin America, and one of several magnificent installations in Brazil that are major examples of nineteenth-century prosperity (as, of course, also exist in other countries like Argentina and Mexico).[11]

Indeed, the juxtaposition between the very early twentieth-century opera house (the Teatro Municipal was inaugurated in 1911) and the trappings of near mid-century modernity is remarkable. Although cars must have been scarce in Brazil when the Teatro first opened, the stately Packards of the Paulistano moneyed class are very much in evidence. Almost uniformly black (and certainly uniformly sober, despite a couple of sports coupes), the cars are martially lined up both around the Teatro and along the edge of the elegant entrance to the park across the street. This image of exceptional order (one will recall that the motto on the Brazilian flag is "*Ordem e Progresso*" [Order and Progress]) is explained by the presence of uniformed guards who not only provide security for these expensive vehicles, but direct their drivers' maneuvers in order to ensure orderly and respectable parking (and, to be sure, the economic utilization of space that is always such a critical issue in major city centers).

What is particularly remarkable about the photograph is the way in which, almost as though they were geological layers, one can compare the urban growths of the city. In the first instance, there is the Teatro Municipal, undoubtedly built at a time when, on that side of the Viaduct, there would have been stately mansions to complement the elegant park entrance and make the Teatro convenient to its wealthy patrons. Although the Teatro Municipal of Rio de Janeiro is a gorgeous building—its crowning touch is the Crypt of Aida in the basement that functions as preperformance and entr'acte bar, done up in Brazilian emerald marble with gold-flake touches—it is, nevertheless, a relatively small performance space. The quite vast expanse of the São Paulo equivalent (and my sense is that it is every bit as large, if not perhaps a bit more so, than the Teatro Colon in Buenos Aires which, with the decadence of Manaus, is the premier opera house on the continent) is an imposing affirmation of the wealth of the city at the time of its construction, and its successive refurbishing and its current packed-programming utilization attest to its stature as regards the self-image of great prosperity and intense sophistication that the city holds. By the time of Lévi-Strauss's photograph, the Teatro was already in its third decade of existence, regularly hosting, in addition to more traditional European-style programs, Brazilian urban cultural events.

The building to the left, along the border of the small plaza that leads to the Parque Anhangabaú under the Viaduct and diagonally across the street from the Teatro Municipal, which puts it on the southeast corner of the intersection, is a noble, six-story, neoclassic-style building that could perhaps have been constructed originally to house commercial and professional offices, or maybe private apartments. With high, arched windows, colonnaded galleries and balustrades, cornice work, and large awnings, it is the perfect complement to the Teatro, probably having been built in the decade following the latter's inauguration, and next to the elegant entrance to the park. The style of the building, with its awnings, overhangs, and recessed galleries, speaks to the semitropical climate of the state of São Paulo, an environment evoked by the palm trees in evidence in the park. Lévi-Strauss's photograph captures in this detail a moment when the architecture of São Paulo still had to take into account the local climate and provide for some structural relief from summer heat. Moreover, the varying geometry of the building captures well the uneven terrain of the locale, thereby providing a sense of harmony between nature and the built environment that differs from the tension of the first image analyzed.[12]

The importance of the relationship between the building and the park becomes evident when one examines the third building, chronologically, in the image, which shows the beginning of the rigid, boxy constructions that will dominate the full assertion of architectural modernity in the city in successive decades. This building is across the street to the south from the Teatro and across the street to the east of the building I have just commented on. It is more than twice the height of the latter, and the smaller boxes atop the building at both ends may be water towers for the first type of air-conditioning that is introduced in the 1930s, allowing buildings to be designed with unmediated exposure to the sun and with small windows that, while they may open, do not provide the ventilation made possible by the enormous floor-to-ceiling windows of the previously discussed building. What Lévi-Strauss's camera is capturing here is an example of the full burgeoning of modern capitalism in São Paulo. If the previous buildings—the Teatro and the Belle Époque palace, along with the park that they border—exemplify the seigniorial elegance of a ruling oligarchy, this third building, with nothing to recommend it in aesthetic terms, attests to the bland, if not downright ugly, functionalism that accompanies the implantation of early and mid-twentieth-century capitalism in a city like São Paulo.

Finally, beyond this third building and to the south of it lies a building under construction. I do not know if official figures are available for the rate of construction in São Paulo in the 1930s, but to judge from the empirical experience provided by walking the streets of the city, especially in the central core Lévi-Strauss's photographs concentrate on, and on the basis of the distribution of architectural styles, the 1930s saw the beginning of

Figure 5.2. *Edifício Alexandre Mackenzie, Mappin Stores e Teatro Municipal* (c. 1937) by Claude Lévi-Strauss. Reproduced courtesy of Acervo Instituto Moreira Salles.

the extensive physical development of the city in for business, commercial, and financial purposes.[13] Although São Paulo has a certain number of elegant Belle Époque edifices such as the second building commented on, it has nowhere the impressive concentration to be found in Buenos Aires, a center of capitalist enterprise that preceded São Paulo by almost fifty years. And although there is now a considerable amount of very creative architecture to be found in São Paulo, the central core that Lévi-Strauss knew continues to be dominated by the definitively drab boxes of an early utilitarianism.[14] Thus, what Lévi-Strauss captures in this image is a juxtaposition of styles—often very isolated examples rather than the large concentrations characteristic of major European capitals—that exhibit different periods of economic growth in the city, with the evident beginning of an imposition of highly functional and repetitively boxy structures that accompanied capitalist prosperity.

A third photograph from *Saudades do Brasil* (the fifth in the series) also exemplifies architectural development during the period. Its legend reads: "From one corner of the Triangle [the old commercial center] started the Avenida São-João [sic] (photographed on a carnival day) dominated by the pink mass of the then incomplete Predio [sic] Martinelli. In 1985 I saw it again in its completed state, hemmed in on all sides by other office towers" (31). If Lévi-Strauss's photograph is from the mid-1930s and official history asserts that the Martinelli building was inaugurated in 1929 (see note 6), this means that it must have been inaugurated while still under construction; indeed, perhaps construction was affected by the worldwide depression that began that year. Part of the bustle in the street is due to Carnival, but the area's commercial status is well in evidence by the buildings devoted to business that already exist in the area, from the Belle Époque mass to the left to the very interestingly turreted building to the right, which also manifests design details to combat the semitropical sun, such as large recessed windows and colonnaded balconies. The men on the street (notice that there are no women) appear dressed for business in the very conservative Paulistano style of the period. Several other photographs focus on the fringes of the city (see pages 30 and 32), where all sense of cosmopolitan industry and elegance is lost, and one looks behind the emerging tall business buildings to recover the small shop-oriented daily life of those Paulistanos who cannot participate in the exuberance of international capitalism then changing the city (33).

Lévi-Strauss is undoubtedly bemused by the backwater street scene he captures in this legend: "In midtown, cattle compete for the road with the trolley car, always jammed during rush hour" (*Saudades do Brasil* 34). I do not know if Lévi-Strauss had in mind what must have already been widely reproduced images of sacred cows sharing the streets with both primitive vehicles and modern cars in Indian cities like New Delhi and Calcutta, but anyone seeing this image is bound to make the association. Today there are no more cattle in the streets of São Paulo, and the trolley has given way to (equally overflowing) buses and a magnificent subway system. However, what is significant about this photograph is the way in which Lévi-Strauss zeros in on one of the most important elements of São Paulo modernity, the trolley car. Tosta has provided an excellent survey of the trolley car, the *bonde,* in Brazilian literature in the twentieth century, and I have mentioned elsewhere how the trolley car figures in Patrícia Galvão's 1933 novel *Parque industrial* and in Rosenthal's photography; interestingly, Galvão's novel dates precisely from the period of the French professor's first visit to Brazil. With the increase in commercial operations in the downtown area and the growth of industrial zones to the east (the focus of Galvão's novel), the trolley becomes an essential component of city life. Indeed, workday transportation remains one of São Paulo's worst urban nightmares, and, in addition to successive forms possessing a value for the city—the ultramodern subway is today every bit as much a part of dynamic São Paulo as the *bonde* was seventy years ago—transportation is an index, in its presence and in its utilization, of the enormous growth of the city.[15] Lévi-Strauss may only have been bemused by the juxtaposition, but in passing, the eye of the European visitor captured an essential component of the city (note once again the predominance of conservatively dressed male passengers).

Lévi-Strauss did not produce many photographs dealing with São Paulo: some of the same photographs in *Saudades do Brasil*, plus a number of additional ones, are contained in the separate publication in Portuguese, *Saudades de São Paulo*. I have preferred to work with the ones included in the former volume precisely because of the fascinating juxtaposition between the photographer's experienced urban eye and his nascent anthropological one.[16] Lévi-Strauss was, however, definitely taken by the city. Another of his images depicts his father, who in turn is taking his own photograph of the city, standing at the doorway of the comfortable chalet they occupied at the time (*Saudades do Brasil* 35). Lévi-Strauss comments on the car we see parked outside the house: "For me, the not too outdated Ford was a symbol of social success, since in France I had owned a mere Citroën 5 CV three-seater, also acquired second hand." Obviously, the prosperity of the São Paulo that Lévi-Strauss photographed in passing, before recording the extensive images that would provide him one set of research materials for his innovative anthropological thinking, was directly favorable to the young visiting scholar.[17]

6

Films by Day and Films by Night in São Paulo

> Carros avançam em nossa direção: eis o épico contem-
> porâneo. Ítaca na esquina, Odisseu o mendigo lendo um
> anúncio travado no chão [. . . .] Pense em agora e toda
> uma rede se instala em seu cérebro. Este perfume vindo
> da vitrine lembra uma Idoia, se se estilhaça no instante
> necesario para que o tempo pare.
>
> ❁ Rodrigo Garcia Lopes, "Cityscape" (130)

It is impossible to determine, of the approximately eighteen thousand films that have been produced in Brazil in one hundred and ten years of filmmaking, how many are devoted to São Paulo. But it is safe to say that, because of its greater profile in national and international imaginaries, Rio de Janeiro far surpasses São Paulo in filmic representations, especially if one insists on a direct correlation between the city and the plot of the film and not just its presence as a circumstantial locale.[1] São Paulo is an important venue for Brazilian filmmaking, and it is also the site of many respected film festivals, including the São Paulo International Film Festival, which dates from 1990. Yet it is undeniable that the presence of São Paulo in Brazilian fiction is not matched—at least in terms of the central core of Brazilian cinema—by an equal degree of interest from filmmakers.

However, that does not mean that there have not been some remarkable films that incorporate a significant interpretive interest in the city. This chapter will examine four of those films, but by no means is this selection intended as a sampler. Rather, I would insist that these are four particularly outstanding texts that might be complemented by a few more, but they should not be understood to constitute a random sampling, with each film representing some major aspect of the city. I do not know what a series of dominant themes for the city might be, and thus no attempt is made to attach these films to such a series.

São Paulo, S.A. (1965)

Luís Sérgio Person (1936–67) is one of the names most associated with a Brazilian filmmaking rooted in the social realities of São Paulo. Although Person died young and left only a handful of feature-length films, São Paulo, S.A. (1965) is considered one of the key films associated with the city,[2] revealing the considerable influence of Italian neorealism and anticipating the social concerns of the Cinema Novo, whose first manifestations are very much associated with the year 1965.[3] Critics are in agreement that São Paulo is thematically important because of the representation it affords, through the main character, Carlos, of the development of the automotive industry in that city between 1957–61 (Bernardet; Catani), a period in which the capitalistic development of Brazil, centered in São Paulo, expands enormously,[4] in part because of Brazil's alliance with the United States during World War II. This is, in short, a period involving considerable Americanization in Brazil, and the automobile is (despite the fact that German imports also figure into the film) an essential symbol of U.S. postwar dominance.[5]

The setting of Person's film is, consequently, firmly anchored in the Brazilian professional class—at least that segment of it relating to industrialization in the country. In an exceptionally neorealist fashion, Person correlates the psychological vicissitudes of Carlos's life—his perennial restlessness, his inability to relate emotionally, his dissatisfaction with the model of bourgeois life he has attained—with the alienation, viewed very much in Marxian terms, that industrial capitalism exacts from the individual who supinely accepts participation in the system. Carlos is something like a Brazilian "man in the gray flannel suit,"[6] someone for whom a fully emotional and sentient human existence is incompatible with the depersonalizing routine of corporate life.

Carlos is portrayed in unsympathetic terms in the film, and on no occasion is the viewer invited to see him as a tragic victim of the system. Indeed, his determined, although apparently unconscious, mistreatment of those around him, including his long-suffering wife, is shown as a character failing on his part, and *São Paulo* is driven by a voluntaristic notion of human experience whereby the central problem is Carlos's inability to take charge of his own life and overcome his debilitating alienation. Jean-Claude Bernardet sees Carlos as illustrating a "failure to choose" (286). Moreover, "Carlos, who is guided only by the opportunities that society offers him, who chooses neither for himself nor for others, who has neither idea or action with which to oppose the situation, who is capable only of flight, is ripe for fascism" (288). It might be inaccurate to describe as fascistic the unquestionably authoritarian and tyrannical military governments—any one of them or all of them collectively—that held power in Brazil between 1964 and 1985. Thus, there is little question that Person's film, released the year after the military seized political power, can sustain an interpretation of a Brazilian bourgeoisie that ensured the military's imposition of a dictatorship grounded in large measure on the promises of an enduring capitalism, industrialization, and the status quo.

If Carlos develops his investment in the status quo and by the end of the film has consolidated a life of bourgeois alienation, the film turns in part on his attempt to revolt, though he ultimately reintegrates himself within the system. Although São Paulo is constantly present as part of the backdrop of the film—as much in terms of the material reality of the cityscape as in terms of the texture of the everyday life of the social class to which Carlos belongs—it is the occasion of his brief and frustrated revolt against his chosen destiny that provides for the greatest incursion of the city into the film. It is as though when Carlos goes about the routine of his alienated life, the city, in all of its successful dimensions, is only there as an incidental arena for the tribulations of his personal story. But when Carlos assumes, no matter how briefly, a sense of inconformity that leads to a fleeting rebellion against the path he has chosen, the city looms large, not as part of an allegorical representation of the forces of modern capitalism that Carlos might resist, but rather as a directly experienced social environment that he now inhabits dialectically.

Especially effective in this regard is the opening scene of the film, in which Carlos is seen engaged in a violent fight with his wife. They argue, and he ends smashing the contents of a dining table upon the floor. As they struggle—he eventually slapping her and throwing her to the ground—the camera captures the fray through the sliding glass door leading to the balcony of their well-appointed high-rise apartment. Their voices are muffled, but the surrounding buildings of the city are deftly mirrored in the glass door and, as Carlos stalks out of the room and out of the apartment while the credits roll, the camera swings to record the buildings near and far—signs of São Paulo capitalism—that hem the apartment in. At other moments in the film, the camera will dwell on the industrial establishments of the city, of which the automotive industry is only a part, in the context, as Carlos's employer at one point says, of how "São Paulo is the engine of Brazil [. . . .] São Paulo is growing and will not cease to continue to grow."

The foregounding of the city's presence is nowhere more evident than on those occasions when Carlos wanders the streets of the city, a form of physical contact no matter how disconnected from it he may be. Moving through the city in a routine, and therefore automatized fashion (his face is usually characterized by a vacant stare and he rarely looks at those around him), Carlos's random *derivés* oblige him to negotiate his physical surroundings, some of which he may be experiencing for the first time. Needless to say, one will immediately recall how the culture of the car frees the individual from the imperative to negotiate the city in a directly physical sense: it is one thing to experience the city on the sidewalk through the soles of your feet and shoes; it is quite another to do so in the privileged space of the street, your contact mediated by the automotive machine.

The opening scene of the film is repeated at the end, and this time we hear Carlos explain his decision to "dar o fora," to flee. And once again we see the buildings of the city reflected in the glass windows of the apartment, although this time the camera will pan to those buildings as silent, monumental witnesses to Carlos's impetuous attempt to renounce the system in which he is enmeshed. Rejecting the humble Volkswagen that he has been accustomed to driving in the city, Carlos steals an upscale Karmann-Ghia.[7] As he speeds off through the streets of the city toward the coast, he energetically declares good-bye to the city. Yet his escape to freedom is short-lived. As he awakens in the car parked atop a bluff and realizes what happened, he suddenly bolts away, abandoning the car with the door open, and hitches a ride with a trucker on his way to São Paulo. As the truck passes through the industrial outskirts of the city, Carlos enters into a sort of trance in which he mumbles repeatedly that one must start all over again, all over again a thousand times. As we hear him utter this statement, in a tone of despair, the camera focuses on successive waves of individuals that wash over one another as they rush across one of the symbols of modernity in capitalist São Paulo, the Viaduto do Chá (the Tea Viaduct), which was originally constructed to connect the northern outskirts of the city to the central core, the working class to the financial class. The implication is that Carlos will once again submit to the crushing dynamic of the city.

O puritano da Rua Augusta (The Puritan of Augusta Street; 1965)

It is difficult to argue that Amácio Mazzaropi (1912–81),[8] who made over thirty films between 1952 and 1980, should be denied a secure place in Brazilian film history. Yet this seems, with notable exceptions, to be the case. Perhaps it was because Mazzaropi's comedies, with their broad parodies and slapstick situations, went against the committed leftist and Italian neo-realist–inspired grain of Brazil's Cinema Novo, an auteur movement that brought indisputable prestige to Brazilian culture and its film industry. The simple fact, however, is that Mazzaropi figures only sporadically in registries of Latin American and Brazilian cinema.[9] Eva Paulino Bueno has published an important monograph in which she sets out to demonstrate that Mazzaropi—especially with his hick persona, in the character of Jeca Tatu[10]—more realistically captures the social tensions of São Paulo at mid-century than do the often-pretentious texts of Cinema Novo.[11] When Cinema Novo filmmaking does turn to the city, it tends to focus on Rio de Janeiro anyway, although one first thinks of its treatment of rural themes concerning destitute and starving peasants; Rio and the legendary Northeast (Brazil's hardscrabble equivalent of the old U.S. South, its impoverished Italian Mezzogiorno) are part of a cinematographic imaginary that leaves little room for the issues, at once immigrant and international, of São Paulo.[12]

For reasons having to do with internal immigration in the province of São Paulo and the movement from unhappy rural sectors to the promising metropolis/megalopolis, Mazzaropi's Jeca Tatu is an unending source of the pathos of adjustment to the city, the conflict between traditionalism and modernity, the travails of attempting to make it in a hostile urban environment in many cases more daunting than the relentless misery of the countryside, and the struggle to make sense of a city life that often seems essentially incomprehensible. As Bueno demonstrates quite well, taken as a whole, Mazzaropi's Jeca Tatu films are invaluable in understanding the internal migration that accompanied the emergence of modern São Paulo: as in the case of other major urban centers in the Americas, there continues to be a proportional relationship between the degree of commercial, financial, and industrial importance of the city and the degree to which it draws in—sucks in, many would insist—the rural poor, both from the immediately surrounding province and from the country as a whole. It is an internal migration that directly complements the history of foreign immigration into the city, and Mazzaropi's films address the overwhelming confusion and disorientation of the new urban dweller.

As important as the Jeca Tatu films are in depicting the transformation of the country mouse into the city rat, I wish here to focus on a somewhat exceptional text in the Mazzaropi filmography, *O puritano da Rua Augusta* (1965), a film that falls almost exactly at the midpoint of the director's career.[13]

First of all, it is important to characterize the Rua Augusta, a major street that traverses the Jardins residential district of southwest-central São Paulo as it descends approximately twenty blocks from the dominant ridge (and dominant financial locus) that is the Avenida Paulista, one of the major thoroughfares of the central core of the city. In its day, the Rua Augusta was both a major commercial avenue of the area and the site of solid middle-class residences. Today, although the Jardins remain a privileged residential area of the city, the Rua Augusta has become a tacky—and often tawdry—commercial strip along which businesses of some social standing (such as a branch of the famous Brazilian perfumerie O Boticário) are more the exception than the rule: one of the more notorious current businesses along the street is a shop that specializes in the wares of the city's large sex trade.

However, during the mid-sixties when Mazzaropi's film takes place, the Rua Augusta is a major manifestation of the city's modernity, and the commercial and residential addresses there were inhabited by those who felt at home in and an integral part of the city. Thus, in *O puritano da Rua Augusta*, the plot turns on the degree to which Punduroso (a play on *pundonoroso*, which means: "characterized by dignity, honor, and discretion") is able to convince his family to return to traditional Catholic moral beliefs to which the careless exposition of the body, the pursuit of sensual pleasure, and the repudiation of whatever might be considered old-fashioned is inimical. Punduroso's young-adult children, in short, are committed to the frenetic modernity and the sexual liberation of the 1960s as it arrives in São Paulo. The latter live in São Paulo, while Punduroso lives outside the city, where he administers the family's interests and provides the wealth that enables the urban lifestyle of his wife and children. In addition, Punduroso owns a factory in the city, which his sons are nominally in charge of. The juxtaposition here is a familiar one for certain Latin American families of wealth: the source of that wealth may lie outside the city, typically in the vast ranches of Argentina and the agricultural installations of Brazil, but in this case also the suburban industrial sector, the so-called ABC, of São Paulo. It is this wealth that moves through the financial center and that allows the family to either have a permanent residence commensurate with its economic, and therefore social, standing or, at least, an in-town pied-à-terre where they can partake of the trappings of modernity that their wealth fuels and is fueled by, in the reciprocal fashion of capitalism. Three decades after Hildegard Rosenthal captured the aforementioned announcement on the side of a São Paulo trolley, to the effect that the city was the major industrial center of Latin America (see page 57–58), Punduroso's family situation testifies to the sustained expansion of that assertion.

O puritano opens with an extensive traveling shot, as Punduroso and his family are chauffeured through the central core of the city in their American car. As they descend the Rua Augusta and arrive at their comfortable abode—the modern appointments of the city are much in evidence in this sequence—the first thing that Punduroso spies is a classical nude statue in the entranceway to his house: herein begins a series of unpleasant discoveries by Punduroso of the extent to which his own family has strayed from honorable domestic dignity into the São Paulo of rock and roll.[14] Mazzaropi plays his main character both as a man of conventional dignity (equipped with suit, overcoat, fedora, and rolled umbrella) and as a hopelessly disjointed hick—literally, his character stumbles all over the place, apparently ill at ease in the refined urban environment.[15] After pulling one of his mother-in-law's housedresses over the naked statue, he returns to contemplate the maid (both maid and chauffer are played by Afro-Brazilians), who is decked out in skintight pants that Punduroso insists must be glued on. When he orders her to return to her customary servant's uniform, she reacts huffily. As he announces to his children that he has decided to take up residence in São Paulo, the unpleasant surprises multiply before Punduroso's appalled eyes, until the culminating moment of a house party organized by his children and their friends in the best "rock-around-the-clock" fashion.

Punduroso's opposition to modernity is not merely a disgruntled and passive one, and the title of the film refers to his active involvement with a group of religious zealots who preach their moral Puritanism in public. One

Figure 6.1. Still from *O puritano da Rua Augusta*, featuring, from left to right, Adalberto Pena, João Batista de Souza, and Mazzaropi.

of the delightful aspects of this film is the specific counterpoint between two value systems that occurs not just in a limited domestic space, but in the public sphere, where both the lived environment of the city and its citizens are materially represented. This counterpoint extends to the presence of music in the film: the religious hymns of Punduroso's companions in moral decency and the rock and roll and other contemporary enthusiasms of his children, who always seem to be carrying LP's around with them.

After a series of setbacks in his puritanical campaign against modernity, Punduroso attempts the ruse of seeming to join his children because he cannot beat them. He promises to no longer scold them for their tastes and begins to imitate them, even affecting a hippy look. This whole setup is as preposterous as his original efforts at restoring decency, but it does provide the film with a full array of Mazzaropi's typically quirky slapstick that is carried over from one film to another, such that the film is less about its ostensible theme than it is a vehicle for the main character's comic persona. The confusion Punduroso's charade provokes, including the near breakup of his marriage to a young wife who seems closer in age to his children than to him, his confinement in an insane asylum, and his daughter's incarceration in a convent, requires no extensive discussion here, in part because it is more comically situational than narratively coherent. Suffice it to say that, in the end, some sort of social equilibrium is established based on the principle that all fanaticism and excesses are bad for cohesive social existence (Bueno [3–4] underscores the social equilibrium espoused by the film; a strongly endorsed social equilibrium—a live-and-let-live attitude—is often touted as a Brazilian national trait). This may not constitute any brilliant ethical discovery on Mazzaropi's part, but in moving his slapstick comedy toward a resolution needed to conclude the film, *O puritano da Rua Augusta* provides some excellent snapshots of São Paulo in the mid-sixties, ones that are less off-putting than the images of the dour film *São Paulo, S.A.*

O invasor (2002)[16]

Brazilian films of social violence have been typically associated with Rio de Janeiro, a city that, because of its enormous importance as a tourist center, is particularly conscious about public security. Recent films like *Cidade de Deus* (*City of God*; 2002; directed by Fernando de Meirelles and Kátia Lund), *Ônibus 174* (*Bus 174*; 2002; directed by José Padilha and Felipe Lacerda), and *Tropa de elite* (2007; directed by José Padilha)[17] are fairly routine examples that have provoked as much controversy over the aestheticizing of violence (that is, the way in which filmed violence panders to a certain range of spectator desire) as they have for "selling" a particular vision of Brazil (and, by extension, Latin American and other so-called Third World societies) as uniquely violent and therefore irremediably resistant to civilized life. *Cidade de Deus* focuses on the violence generated in Rio's slums by drug trafficking and is singular for inscribing within the filmic text the question of the aestheticizing of violence through the development of the photographic career of the main character, a career based on recording the violence of his surroundings. *Ônibus 174* depicts a bus hijacking gone awry, with the major emphasis falling on the take-no-hostages approach of the police, who are more of a threat to public safety than the hijackers themselves; a moral point of the true-life documentary film is that the police will ensure that no suspect taken into captivity will arrive at the stationhouse alive.[18] *Tropa de elite* also deals with police brutality and the indiscriminate violence the police bring to bystanders. If the elite troop is intended to counter the corruption of the regular police, it becomes in turn an even more efficient instrument of corruption, enhancing exponentially, so to speak, the violence of the regular police. In turn, this culture of violence extrapolated to a higher degree was met by many audiences with enthusiasm, as the rhetoric of the film was designed to ensure approval of the activities and conduct of the elite squad, whose struggle, glorified by the film, for survival against the double threat they must confront (from drug dealers and from the regular police) mutes interest in the ways in which they duplicate the barbarism of their dual foes.

The filmic emphasis on Rio is unquestionably tied to the greater visibility of Brazil's former capital, which enjoys a fully rounded imaginary both within Brazil and internationally. It would be difficult to believe that there is any lesser level of social violence in São Paulo, including the benchmark phenomenon of the drug trade, and there is certainly an immense bibliography of fictional writing and dramatic production that focuses on issues of marginalization and criminality in that city and concomitant police corruption. What have not been prominent are filmic representations equivalent to those focused on Rio. São Paulo holds few attractions for casual tourists, and the large international financial and commercial community that frequents the city moves in a security bubble efficient enough to mask the everyday issues of the city from their attention.[19] Since São Paulo lacks any notable role in an international imaginary regarding Brazil, a Brazilian film production that inevitably must aspire to an international market in order to survive usually chooses to ignore São Paulo.

Beto Brant's (1965–) *O invasor* is a remarkable exception, and it is important to note from the outset that it does not focus on the slums, does not follow the activities of drug dealers, and does not showcase the blood and gore of police brutality (the police only appear briefly at the end of the film). Rather—as befits São Paulo's national and international role— the film tells the story of a business operation, one that is firmly linked to the huckster developmental mentality of the city which is characterized by financial overextension, blatant displays of consumerism, and a modus operandi that is deeply complicitous with the corruption and corner-cutting that grease Brazilian business. Specifically, two members of a business partnership (they run a construction firm, the signature enterprise in a city driven by the need to reduplicate itself ceaselessly in urban monoliths) decide to do away with their third partner in order to assume his assets and cover their own shoddy dealings. They hire a hit man, who successfully carries out his assignment. But Brant's assassination thriller becomes a horror flick when the hit man, Anísio (played with eerie efficiency by rock-band musician Paulo Miklos), decides not only that he wants to pursue a relationship with the punk-rock daughter of his victim (probably more out of erotic desire than as a means to her wealth), but that he also wants, as a corollary of his active "participation" in the partnership, to take over the business. The two remaining partners, understandably, do not desire his further association.

The "rightful order" of the universe is restored at the conclusion of the film, but it is clear that Anísio will now play some role in it. The horror of what should have been, thanks to the resources of the social system on which São Paulo is grounded (easy access to hit men and the assurance of police indifference),[20] a straightforward narrative of a routine partnership restructuring arises when Anísio blatantly asserts his decision to violate the social structure and to challenge the financial (and, therefore, social) security of his one-time employers. And there is the adjunct horror for the spectator in the assertion that someone like Anísio can, in fact, lay a viable claim to the system that he has, according to the euphemism used in the film, "serviced." Part of the texture of the film involves the astonishment and, initially, the immobility of the surviving partners in view of the hit man's demand. It is as though he were speaking a foreign language, since the former are simply bereft of any horizon of intelligibility to grasp what he is getting at. There is a grim humor in all this, even when the spectator has no reason to believe that the reigning social dynamic of São Paulo is any less resistant to assault than the dense array of urban monoliths that are its signs.

The title of the film is critically ironic with respect to the functioning of the São Paulo social dynamic. In the majority of the film, the designation refers to the fashion in which Anísio invades or trespasses in the realms of the social order that should be closed to him. Yet the film opens with an invasion of his social space by the two partners seeking a hit man. Significantly, the film withholds the on-screen appearance of the potential hit man. Indeed, we do not see his face until almost a third of the film has elapsed, once he completes his "service" and arrives at the partners' office to begin new negotiations with them. Before this appearance, we first see the incursion of the two prosperously dressed businessmen, in their expensive car, into the marginal urban space in which Anísio customarily dwells. Throughout the film, there is an eloquent juxtaposition between the exterior spaces of São Paulo—predominantly characterized by a vertiginous jumble of people, vehicles, and street life in general (including screeching traffic)—and the double cocoon that the prosperous create for themselves in their workplaces, residences, and associated refuges, such as fancy restaurants, clubs, boutiques, and the like; for instance, as soon as the two accomplices forward the hit man the money he demands in the ratty bar where they meet, the partners go off to celebrate at an exclusive gentleman's club. This sort of unsubtle juxtaposition sets the film's narrative up in terms of the customary expectations of the social dynamic, which will subsequently be challenged by the outrageous demands Anísio wishes to enforce.

If Anísio encounters resistance in his invasion of the construction company, he receives a ready reception from the daughter of his murder victims (it turns out he has also killed the third businessman's wife), Marina, whose nonchalant ennui leaves her open to the hit man's feral advances. As part of this success, Marina accompanies Anísio in his tour through a city that he is beginning to feel might have something to offer him. As he confesses to her, he always thought the talk of palaces was "so much bullshit," but now he readily makes himself comfortable in her palatial life. This process allows the camera to portray the details of the life of the privileged in São Paulo, while at the same time it juxtaposes scenes of the marginal spaces Anísio had been consigned to. For Marina, these spaces represent just so much slumming, a world that she cannot be forced to inhabit, but one that is interesting for a change. It is Anísio's São Paulo, but one he has every intention of renouncing in favor of the social ascendance he thinks lies before him. What is of particular interest in this sequence is the use of nonprofessional actors drawn from the social milieu Anísio is attempting to abandon, in contrast with the polished professional actors of the world to which he aspires. Filmically, this renders the difference between the worlds in stark contrast that reinforces the obvious material differences the camera can capture so well. Moreover, such differences are highlighted by erratic camera movement and the heavy rock music that signifies the nitty-gritty of a marginal social existence.

Meanwhile, things are not working out between the two surviving partners, and one begins to betray the other with, it appears, some connivance with Anísio. The betrayed partner begins to fall apart psychologically, and we see him careening through the São Paulo nightscape as the rap music of the soundtrack speaks of "suicide capitalism."[21] As the film draws to an unresolved close, he goes to the police, but they only turn him over to his other partner, who is in the company of Anísio. One assumes that the latter two will kill the informer, but it is not completely clear whether Anísio will retain his newfound place in the palace or will disappear in a second, impending administrative readjustment. In the course of expounding in detail on the dirty dealings, abetted by police, of the São Paulo financial and commercial establishment, Brant makes effective use of the backdrop of the city itself, deftly paralleling, juxtaposing, and intersecting the realms of the privileged and the realms of their servants, with the latter ever ready to make use of the arms of the privileged in order to usurp them.

Anjos da noite (Angels of the Night; 1987)

Brazil's Rio de Janeiro–based Cinema Novo, which emerged at the end of the 1950s and came to fruition in the early 1960s, was unquestionably part of the radical populism that was, in turn, integral to the political and social culture of the day. Although very much inspired by leftist politics and left-wing cinematographic movements in Europe (especially those that opposed the unrelenting commercialism of Hollywood and its foreign imitators), Cinema Novo was able to continue to have a measure of continuity after the right-wing military coup of 1964, perhaps because it never much appealed to the masses, remaining a program of filmmaking by and for intellectuals, and perhaps also because it brought much international attention (and presumably some foreign earnings) to Brazilian culture.[22] As antidemocratic tyranny began to wane in Brazil beginning in the late 1970s, with an institutional transition to democracy in 1985, the major names of the Cinema Novo and a subsequent generation they inspired became integral components in the more universally appealing yet strongly socially committed filmmaking that has attracted so much international attention in the past twenty-five years. The filmography of Cinema Novo is often associated with rural themes—the misery of life in many parts of the countryside and the ensuing migration of peasants to Brazil's major cities—as abiding cultural motifs. But there is an important inventory of urban-focused titles as well.

Although Cinema Novo in its original form had little interest in the city of São Paulo, Person's *São Paulo, S.A.*, released in 1965 and discussed above, has been considered part of a "second wave" of Cinema Novo that includes representations of the country's largest city. However, it was not until the return to democracy and the sort of social-analysis film that comes with it that major films set in São Paulo and dealing with social issues were released. These films represent an analysis that is far more politically and thematically varied than the films of Cinema Novo, and they are not above reifying social types and leaving political implications untouched, or, for that matter, even having happy endings of a sort. In this sense, they are more interested in portraying the complexities of urban life, including the full array of details of the marginal and the voiceless, than they are in contributing to dogmatic positions.

Anjos da noite (1985) by Wilson Barros (1948–92)[23] shows vividly the break with the conventions of Cinema Novo through the carnivalesque and pastiche nature of its plot, the many instances of meta-cinematographic self-reflexivity, and the inclusion of abundant U.S. popular-culture references (including a Fred Astaire and Cyd Charisse–style dance sequence under the nighttime glare of downtown lights from buildings, cars, and streetlamps;[24] at the end the camera pulls back in a moment of self-reference to include the image of the banks of powerful lights set up to film the sequence).[25] Yet what is most striking about *Anjos* is that it is essentially a queer film,[26] not just due to the inclusion of references to homosexuals and transvestites and the depiction of homoerotic desire, but in the way in which identities, sexual and otherwise, are unstable and situational. One of the two best sex scenes in the film (the other is passionately interracial) involves the interest of the has-been film star Marta Brum, played brilliantly by Marília Pêra, who won an award for her performance,[27] in having sex with a gay escort, as she diverts his affections from his sometime male partner.[28]

Except for the ending of the film, which takes place early in the morning of the next day, *Anjos* is a braided series of images of the city nightscape. Moving in and out of various plot threads, the film literally pans the city repeatedly as the approximately dozen important characters move through private spaces (residences, cabarets, back rooms) and the street, taking part in the travel about the city demanded by their pursuit of pleasure and a livelihood built on the sins of the night. The only significant extended take on the city at night is the aforementioned dance sequence and its buildup, as the actress and the taxi boy negotiate the encounter of their bodies.[29] The action of the film takes place on the all-important Avenida Paulista, the city's (and the continent's) financial center—the dance sequence was filmed in the patio beneath the MASP (Museo de Arte de São Paulo), which is located on the Paulista—and in the side streets of the Paulista, which enter into the chic and fast-paced environs of the Jardins area.

If there is a unifying motif in the film, aside from the gay escort, who interacts with all of the other characters, a fact that underscores the importance to Barros of capturing the prominence of gay/queer culture in the city, it is a young sociologist who is ostensibly engaged in a research project that involves some of the characters. Sociologist and escort come together at the end of the film, meeting on a park bench in the early sunlight. After agreeing that it is all very hard but worth it (life in the big city, one assumes), they separate after having only shared their first names. As the escort says, they will find each other again because the city is "so small." As the film closes, we see the sociologist walking along the Avenida Paulista, caught in the hustle and bustle of the city as it awakens to present its sober daytime face.

Barros's ending is "happy" only in the sense that it underscores the necessary continuity of life and the way in which the individual will, in the end, likely find some way to survive. There is no socially or politically anchored message in *Anjos* because the director's primary interest lies fundamentally with constructing a panorama of lives in the city at night. The various forms of self-reflexivity in the film, aside from providing some transient moments of humor,[30] stand in juxtaposition to the controlled and distancing cinematographic voice of the Cinema Novo paradigm, where viewers are encouraged to understand that what they are viewing is life in the process of being lived, and that they are witnessing it through the privileged eye of the camera.[31] This was reinforced by the documentary nature of many filmed sequences and the use of nonprofessional actors. Barros could well have filmed São Paulo at night in the same manner, taking his viewer into usually closed or limited realms of the denizens of the night and dwelling on the morbid and the scabrous, all with the idea of denouncing the essentially perverse nature of the nighttime aspect of a city whose much-touted daytime atmosphere is that of the aggressive enterprise of modernity.

Barros's lack of interest in denouncing the nocturnal culture that takes place in the same spaces as the enterprise of the city's daytime constitutes, therefore, the eschewal of the superior moralistic tone of so much previous Brazilian filmmaking about social situations. To be sure, the representation of many of the events of the night, such as sexual exploitation and police brutality, is not naive or jejune. Barros's point, rather, seems to be an adaptation to São Paulo of one of the famous apothegms of Nelson Rodrigues, who antedated him in describing a full range of the social life of Rio de Janeiro: "A vida como ela é" ("life as it is").[32] In the process, Barros has given us one of the most intriguing and playful films ever made in Brazil about São Paulo.

Concluding Remarks

The history of São Paulo in Brazilian film begins with Adalberto Kemeny's and Rudolf Rex Lustig's 1929 *São Paulo, sinfonia da metrópole* (São Paulo,

Symphony of the Metropolis), modeled after Walter Ruttman's legendary *Berlin: die Sinfonie der Großstadt* (Berlin: The Symphony of the Metropolis; 1927).[33] The Brazilian film is much more than a propaganda paean to the monuments of the commercial, financial, and industrial progress that had become the order of the day in 1920s São Paulo. Along with what one would expect in terms of the most dynamic and positive images of the city, are those that allude to its underbelly, including the prison population. But Kemeny and Lustig established the basis for scrutinizing the city visually and for correlating the unique material phenomena associated with it with lived human experience.

Such a correlation is immediately apparent in the first film dealt with here, Luís Sérgio Person's *São Paulo, S.A.*, although by 1965 it was possible to refer to the alienated mechanization of individual life imposed by the city's structures of modernity.

Amácio Mazzaropi's *O puritano da Rua Augusta* (also 1965) takes place along one of the major commercial and residential thoroughfares of the period, and this comedy turns on the inevitable social conflicts provoked by the internal migration into the city from the countryside, the demands of industrialization, and the inevitable commitments to new forms of social life that modernity brought with it.

If alienation and social conflict are integral parts of modernity, corruption and cynical human relations are seen by a film like Beto Brant's *O invasor* (2002) as unquestionable correlatives of life in the fast lane as it is modeled by the privileged rich of the city.

Finally, Wilson Barros's *Anjos da noite* (1987), coming as part of a return to institutional democracy and a commitment to the social panorama of the city, stands aside from the rhetoric of the city as a destructive monster, to assume a more benevolent, but nevertheless unflinchingly honest, discourse on the human topology of the city by night. The night is crucially present in *O invasor*, but in *Anjos* it becomes fully invested as something like the alternative universe of São Paulo by day, when it operates as the business center of Latin America.

Let me repeat that this is not a sample of films on São Paulo, but rather some of the best filmic texts to analyze in order to understand how that megalopolis functions as a laboratory for Brazilian urban life.

7

Madalena Schwartz

A Jewish Brazilian Photographer

Madalena Schwartz (1922–93) belonged to a generation of European photographers, in large part Jewish or Jewish-identified, who ended up working
in Argentina and Brazil after fleeing Nazi persecution. Grete Stern (1904–
99) is unquestionably the most famous of the group (see Foster, "Dreaming"), although Annemarie Heinrich (1912–2005) is also considered a fundamental figure in the history of Argentine photography, partially because
she was something like an official photographer for Eva Duarte de Perón,
whom she had first photographed as the ingénue, Evita Duarte. Heinrich,
unlike the other persons mentioned here, was not Jewish: in fact, she was
often accused of holding pro-Nazi sympathies because of her father's military past (see Foster, "Annemarie Heinrich"). Giselle Freund (1908–2000)
spent relatively little time in Argentina (1939–45), but she created a solid
niche for herself as the consequence of her own images of Eva Duarte de
Perón, which she placed in a splashy spread in the famous North American
photo magazine *Life*. All three of these women were so well connected with
the development of European photography that their names constitute
signposts in the enormous importance Argentine photography assumes in
the mid and early decades of the twentieth century, when it became one of
that country's most significant categories of cultural production.

Madalena Schwartz resided in Argentina between 1934 and 1960 before establishing definitive residence in São Paulo, which is where she exclusively pursued her photographic career. Schwartz's success was something of a phenomenon, for she began her photography in middle age and quite by happenstance, then went on to become the most famous photographic portraitist of her generation, leaving an archive of more than sixteen thousand images. Schwartz appears to have had a very firm understanding of one of the controlling principles of Brazilian society, which sees national social subjects as an enormous jumble of diversity including both the high and the low in every possible formulation of these basic terms, and as a result her work extends from political figures of the stature of Jânio Quadros and Lula to the world of transvestite performers, the latter images constituting one of the most recognized dimensions of her work. Although Schwartz apparently never concerned herself with Jewish community life as such, it is important to see her photography as highly significant and yet one more example of the enthusiasm with which a Jewish exile can unhesitatingly enter into the rhythm of his or her new society, going on to make impressive, original contributions to it. Twentieth-century Brazilian society may have had very conflicted opinions about the presence of Jews, but it would be difficult to construct a reasonable cultural history beginning with the 1922 Semana de Arte Moderna without reference to them, no matter how "Jewish" or "non-Jewish" one might wish to characterize the texture, thematics, vision, and language of their contributions.

Hildegard Rosenthal concerned herself with photographing the public spaces of São Paulo, capturing with admirable precision the transformation of what had been the center of the Brazilian coffee industry into the major financial center of Latin America. Her images represent urban development in general terms as well as the emergence of the fascistic interests of Getulio Vargas, such as the imposing Pacaembu Stadium. In the process of creating her extensive dossier of urban images, Rosenthal could not help but provide an account of the degree to which these São Paulo public spaces were unquestionably masculine in design and occupation. In this way, the critical eye of the foreign photographer engaged in a decidedly ironic commentary on how the increasingly categorical modernity of São Paulo still suffered from the sexist legacy of Lusitian feudalism.

In contrast to Rosenthal's interest in the urban cityscape, Schwartz opted for portrait photography. People, to be sure, appear in Rosenthal's photographs, but they are part of the scenery of the great city that she was undertaking to represent. In general, Schwartz shows no specific interest in scenery and landscapes, but rather focuses her eye on the human figure whose context serves fundamentally as an extension of the subject under study; for someone like Rosenthal, if there is an intervention of the individual, it is as a functional detail of the inter-human frame. Schwartz set about to do portraits of a broad swath of Brazilians from many sectors of public life, something that one takes for granted in the day-to-day work of the portrait-ist: few have the luxury of choosing only to photograph, say, adolescents or society women or political candidates. As a consequence, the dossier of a professional photographer will have a diverse range of the "human gallery." At the same time, if Brazil can take pride—either as a reality or more as a dimension of its nationalistic self-image—in being the most demographi-cally diverse country of Latin America, in being the melting pot of races where all live side by side in cordial harmony, one would expect to find a confirmation of such proposals in the work of the portraitist. Schwartz took such proposals seriously, because one can perceive among her most famous images examples of the presumed broad diversity of the largest country on the Latin American continent. Thus, at this juncture I would like to turn to the analysis of some of the photographs that most characterize Schwartz's dossier.

One of Schwartz's most beloved images portrays the singer Clementina de Jesus (1902–87; the photograph appears to date from 1978). Clementina (I will adhere to the Brazilian practice of identifying individuals by their given name) is considered one of the most important artists of Brazilian song in the twentieth century. She stands as a symbol of the musical syn-cretism of the 1960s, during which there was a conjugation of materials of the most diverse ethnic and racial origin, with a strong emphasis on the re-covery of Afro-Brazilian roots. From the state of Rio de Janeiro, Clemen-tina was also a paradigm of abiding privilege of the Afro-Brazilian cultural sector. By the time that Schwartz did Clementina's portrait, the singer had become an artistic phenomenon and, as is the case of the "formal" portrait, the photographer's goal was to capture the importance, the public reso-nance, of her semblance. Schwartz worked preferentially in black and white, which allowed her to carefully and skillfully manage shades of black and the gradations of shadow.

Although, obviously, the skin of those called "blacks" is not truly black, its transformation via the photographic format of black and white—espe-cially against a black backdrop, which is what Schwartz used in this image—causes the subject, on the one hand, to fade away against the backdrop, while also reflecting, in a way that is both subtle and intense, the glow of the study lights. In this way, the image of Clementina tends to fuse with the unlighted background (this can be seen in particular in the lower right angle), while the area of her raised face (the upper right angle), which exists in a cross-angle relationship with the lights, allows for a varied distribution of light in conformance with the complexly varied physiognomy of her face. There is much truth in the statement that the face of a person of age maps the experiences and mishaps of their life, and Clementina's gaze—somewhere between languid, absent, and suffering—demands to be interpreted as a faithful reflection of the complicated sentiments and stories that her songs recount. Since the mouth is the principal—almost exclusive—instrument of the singer, Clementina's is the center of focus, especially in terms of her fleshy and slightly pressed-together lips.

Figure 7.1. *Clementina de Jesus* (c. 1978) by Madalena Schwartz. Reproduced courtesy of Acervo Instituto Moreira Salles.

Portrait photography is usually commissioned for a specific publicity or commercial purpose, such as to accompany a given publication or interview (an enormous array of such work by Schwartz is to be found in the dossier *Personae*). Schwartz worked for a number of publishing houses (Editora Abril, Editora Três), and she contributed to a host of fashion and news magazines (*Vogue, Planeta, Status*), as well as the paradigm of commercial media venues in Brazil, Rede Globo de Televisão. As a consequence, the portrait remains tied to a determined publicity end, and the simple fact is that the portrait fulfills, as a basic supposition, the goal of providing a positive interpretive representation, not to mention one that might be directly flattering, of the person being photographed. Although there are substantial parameters for artistic creation, it is reasonable to assume as a guiding principle that the person being photographed within this context is going to be favored by the camera's gaze. This is amply evident, for example, in the work of great Argentine portraitists such as Annemarie Heinrich and Sara Facio (see the chapter on Facio in Foster, *Buenos Aires*), to continue to speak preferentially of women photographers.

It is only when no tie of any commercial nature exists between the photographer and his or her subject that the portrait can begin to lend itself to a free interpretation, which is what, for example, happens when a highly commercial photographer like Silvio Fabrykant moves from his "formal" work in the areas of advertising and political publicity to a study such as the series *Hombres argentinos* (Argentine Men), which includes naked busts of his subjects, a characteristic that is hardly associated with formal photographic portraiture (as much as it may be with sculpture) and which is accentuated in a so-far unshown second series. One can refer also to Eduardo Gil's show, *Paisajes humanos*, which is made up exclusively of the naked busts of men and women with their eyes shut. It would be difficult to imagine one of these portraits meeting the publicity purposes or professional advancement goals associated with *Vogue* or album art. It is for this reason that the photograph by Fabrykant of Juan José Sebreli, included on the overleaf of the cover of the latter's book, *Escritos sobre escritos, ciudades bajo ciudades, 1950–97*, is really quite exceptional: the writer is represented with an aspect that is frankly cadaveric, if not vampiric. Nevertheless, the human portrait, in conventional circumstances, only lends itself to a zero-degree photographic interpretation either when the subject is unaware that they are being recorded by the camera or when they agree to participate in the creation of an image with a no-holds-barred photographic approach.

Schwartz's image of Clementina de Jesus is, one might say with little fear of contradiction, eminently flattering and sustained by a sincere desire to capture the human depth with which the singer views the world, a depth one assumes animates her art and confirms her importance as unstintingly recognized by fans and critics alike. Given the manner in which Clementina's face seems to surge forth from the black background of the frame, rather than being sharply differentiated from it, the photo gives her an appearance that is almost ethereal, which is in accord with the music of the Tropicália movement and similar projects in the way that there is the suggestion of profound autochthonous roots that the singers are privileged in their ability to channel.[1] The same artistic characteristic is present in another well-known Schwartz photograph, that of Mãe Menininha do Gantois, which dates from 1981. The granddaughter of slaves, Maria Escolástica Conceição Nazaré was born in Bahia in 1894 and was designated by the saints of *candomblé*, while still in her infancy, as a *madre de santo* of the temple founded by her grandmother. Until her death in 1986, Mãe Menininha exemplified for many Brazilians the transcendence of *candomblé* and the importance of religious syncretism by the way she brought together Afro-Brazilian practices and the clear devotion to Catholicism. Schwartz's image captures her in a pose worthy of a prince of the Church in which the juxtaposition between patriarchal hierarchy and feminine ascendance—the latter signaled by the artistic quality of the woman's clothing—could not be more eloquent,[2] and the gaze of the camera could not be more benevolent or reverential. Mãe Menininha's trajectory within the history of *candomblé* runs the course from social marginalization—with sometimes outright public persecution by citizens, the police, and the political system—to definitive incorporation in the final decades of the last century into the fabric of the religious and cultural life of Brazil. Thus, it is quite evident that any gaze upon her that was not as benevolent as it was reverential would go unspeakably against the grain of national values.

Far different is the social grounding of Schwartz's famous sequence on transvestites. No matter how much reference one might make to the many shadings of Brazilian sexual life, in which bisexuality appears as something graceful and where homosexuality constitutes a running thread of Carnival,[3] the transvestite is not always a welcome figure on the national stage beyond being tolerated in the context of cabaret performance. It is unquestionable, however, that the transvestite in all his/her glory is accepted and valued as a part of Carnival (without ignoring the parodic transvestite as a facet of the public manifestations of the entrance into Lent) and that he/ she serves as a pièce de résistance in cabaret programs for international consumption, functioning as the sanitized image of a practice that contravenes patriarchal decency and that many sectors of Brazilian society would wish to shore up. And it is precisely because of the dominant discourse of those sectors that Schwartz's photographic subjects possess an undoubted marginality that places them squarely in a social realm alien to subjects such as Clementina de Jesus and Mãe Menininha.

Perhaps the most fascinating photographs by Schwartz of the world of the transvestite are those that relate to the performance group Dzi Croquettes, which was formed in the early sixties as a response to the 1964 military coup and the sociocultural repression imposed by the governments that it legitimated.[4] In contrast to the transvestite of the tourist-oriented cabaret, Dzi Croquettes, who were openly gay men (which, to be sure, is not necessarily the identity of the professional transvestite, although it is customarily assumed to be the case), put on shows that were essentially parodies in which transvestitism was an integral part of the denunciation by spectacle of the reigning power system. Fulfilling an inevitable artistic circuit for the best of Latin American cultural production, Dzi Croquettes consolidated their fame thanks to triumphs in Paris and other metropolitan venues. The publicity images of Dzi Croquettes tend to emphasize the exuberant colorfulness of the group, but Schwartz, adhering to her practice of working exclusively in black and white, chooses to focus on the intimacy of their life behind the scenes and in their dressing rooms, where we see the members of the group engaged in the complex work of creating their public personas. These are photographs of bodies under construction, bodies of a certain sexual identity that is problematical for the average spectator,[5] an identity that becomes even more complicated when it involves a spectacle veering categorically away from the superficial gaiety of the tourist cabaret, with the goal of achieving harsh and implacable criticism of the military regime and the entire realm of social control that it represents. The fact that their performance involves the construction of a social body resistant to the dictates of the regime increases appreciably the way in which Schwartz focuses on the intimacy of the process of creation. The spectator on the other side of the stage sees the performance in the living color of the bodies of the cast, which at that point are fully constructed, while Schwartz's camera provides the audience of her photographs the privilege of seeing, in black and white, the process of construction, inviting us to rise above the

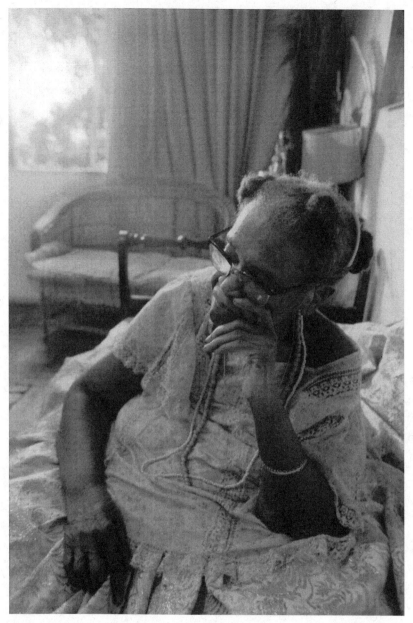

Figure 7.2. *Māe Menininha do Gantois* (1981) by Madalena Schwartz. Reproduced courtesy of Acervo Instituto Moreira Salles.

inevitable habit of our bourgeois social formation of dwelling on the grotesque dimension of the constructive process.[6] It is therefore evident that
neither I nor much less Schwartz could possibly wish for these artists to be
seen as grotesque. Rather, the point is that the images created by the camera play necessarily with the tendency of conventional society (to which we
all more or less belong, grounded in patriarchal heteronormativity) to see
the transvestite as grotesque, a tendency heightened by seeing him "under
construction," still more so in black and white, when his makeup kit has not
yet attained in full the glorious miracle of his artistic transformation.

What I have been characterizing is particularly evident in the image of
Cláudio Tovar, wherein both the bisection of his face between the presence
and absence of makeup and his markedly masculine torso barely covered
by a very feminine chemise would appear to call for an analytical gaze on
the part of the spectator as regards the construction of sexual identity—in
fact, of the very material way in which sexual identity is always a construction and a performance. Although the photograph of Cláudio captures him
clearly, we see represented fuzzily in the right background of the image all
the paraphernalia necessary for his artistic elaboration.[7] Certainly the inclusion of such elements in Schwartz's photograph, even when they are part of
the unfocused backdrop, underscores, as does Cláudio's half-painted face,
that we are witnessing an identity that is, so to speak, always painted on,
as much in the world of the theater as in the so-called real life that theater
helps us to comprehend.

There is another equally eloquent photograph of the actors—in this
case, already completely transformed into (transvestite) actresses—that is
simply identified with the general title "Dzi Croquettes." Like the previous
one, it is dated from 1974, the period of the group's greatest triumphs in Brazil and right before the two years of their highly successful European tour.
In the case of this image, the two faces of the actors are completely made
up and they are already fully dressed in their corresponding costumes; we
are witness to their extravagant outfits and the necklaces that bedeck one
of them. All that is lacking is the application of lipstick on one of them, and
this is the action that the photographer captures: the puckered lips of one
and the careful application of this finishing touch being executed by the
other.

This foregrounded image helps us appreciate the degree of construction
involved for the actors. It also highlights, as I have been stressing with regard to the privileged access that this sequence of photographs provides us

Figure 7.3. *Dzi Croquettes—Cláudio Tovar* (c. 1974) by Madalena Schwartz. Reproduced courtesy of Acervo Instituto Moreira Salles.

to the transvestite's dressing room, the construction of identity. But there is more to it than this, as we see how Dzi Croquettes engage in a parodic stance concerning sexual and gender identity as part of their outright defiance, still within the context of the military dictatorship in the early 1970s, of the social hygiene that the government strove to impose. Although it is customary to assert that masculine transvestitism is a sexist mockery of the feminine, such an accusation is grounded on the same heteronormative postulate that the military moralists defend: there is a degree of womanliness that needs to be defended and protected as a frozen, timeless given.

If it is possible to concede the urgency in questioning such a heteronormative model, parodic transformism, which is often aggressively androgynous, as practiced by Dzi Croquettes constituted a deconstructive criticism of the imperative to be/seem to be in a fixed masculine or feminine role. And in the process, it questions the imperative to sustain distinctions of male/female, man/woman, masculine/feminine.[8] These images, where it is possible to identify what conventionally distinguishes men—the hair on Cláudio's chest, the mouth and hands of one of the two actors in the second photograph (even though these are not quite as categorically masculine as body hair)—do not show the transexual process of "turning into" women, but rather the engagement with making up the body in such a way that the criterion of being—of having to be—a man in any schematic and systematic way is challenged.

My comments here have nothing that is theoretically original to contribute to the practice of transvestitism and limit themselves to introducing essentially axiomatic affirmations regarding transformism in the context of the particular theatrical mode of Dzi Croquettes that Schwartz captured. In this case the camera was not in the service of an advertising gaze, oriented from the point of view of the sort of public that amuses itself with witnessing the performance of the actors, but rather from the perspective of the actors themselves as they go about their sociopolitically grounded project of creating themselves as signs of a critical activity that was still quite dangerous ten years out from the military coup of 1964. The axis of this difference in perspective is emphatically captured in the distinction, as far as a photographic discourse is involved, between the publicity images in full color focused from the point of view of the spectator and Schwartz's black-and-white images seen from the perspective of the backstage theatrical signs under construction.[9]

Schwartz did not limit herself, in the examination of the world of transvestites, to Dzi Croquettes—images of Meise and Tony are not related to the group's performance (they might have been part of the group, but there is no way to determine this from the information provided in the catalog of the show on which I am basing my comments, although the photographs date from the same period as the others I have been analyzing). The transvestite image is very different in the latter photographs. Meise's, for example, also involves an extravagant construction, although in terms of sexual identity, as grounded in conventional markers, we are dealing with a woman "of a certain age." What is particularly charming about the photograph is that the woman stares at the camera, in a manner as defying as it is weary, as though saying, "I've been there and done it all." This detail, concentrated in Meise's eyes, is reinforced by the bags under them and her accumulation of

Figure 7.4. *Dzi Croquettes* (c. 1974) by Madalena Schwartz. Reproduced courtesy of Acervo Instituto Moreira Salles.

adornments, as though each one of them indexed a particular experience—that is, they represent trophies of particular adventures. Meise holds in her left hand the requisite cigarette of sophistication, striking the knowing pose of a worldly woman. She also holds in her right arm some sort of toy dog that stares at the camera with half-closed eyes, but with what looks like the same sort of defiance as its mistress; and indeed, both glaring looks are cast along the same angle of sight.

The same kind of photographic play with the eyes of master and animal dominates in the image of Tony, although in this case the animal is a cat: Tony's look is melancholic, while that of the cat is more startled, something that one can associate especially with the details its cocked ears. If the other transvestites, including Meise, undertake to project a body that is constructed adequately for the occasion—whether for a spectacle built on sociopolitical criticism or as a society matron who asserts her place in the world—the image of Tony focuses on the "imperfections" of his construction. His is not a semi-constructed body as in Cláudio's case, but rather a body which, it seems, the gaze of the camera wishes to show as lacking compliance with the norms of transvestitism, as least as far as the codes of the cabaret are concerned.

For example, the man places in the foreground, in a conventionally feminine pose, his muscular and unshaven legs. He is wearing over his hairy legs women's silk or nylon hose, but with an absolutely unacceptable hole in the left foot, at least for the woman properly *haibillée*. It is difficult to discern what kind of clothes he is wearing, but it seems to be some sort of bathing suit, because he is also wearing, as a drape over his left shoulder, the square piece of cloth called a *tanga* which a woman will throw over herself when emerging from the water or when it begins to cool off on the beach. It is equally difficult to tell what sort of hairdo is involved here, but a disorderly ponytail is what stands out. However, what most calls one's attention is the asymmetry of the eyes: the right one evinces a shadow beneath the mascara line, which perhaps has run for one reason or another, while the left eye shows no such accompanying shadow, although there is something like a teardrop painted there. One can also make out how the glitter applied between the eyebrows and the eyes is not equally distributed on the two sides of the face.

In sum, the portrait of Tony, moving away from the exuberant transvestites of Dzi Croquettes and Meise's accumulated extravagance, is one of enormous melancholy, which may well be as much the pathos with which heteronormative society marks the life—and the body—of the sexual Other as the general dynamic of heteronormativity. It is important to remember that social cleansing with respect to sexual matters was one of the primary imperatives of the military regime in Brazil, enacted as part of an overriding defense of all facets of the controlling patriarchy, as much in the political sector as in the private one. It is fine for a theater group such as Dzi Croquettes to be successful in finding a formula for spectacle that will allow for an artistic response in the face of tyranny, but transvestites like Meise and Tony bear witness to what remains systematically marginalized.

Schwartz left Argentina (for reasons that are never made clear in the scant bibliographical material available) at a time when there was a certain opening up between the fall of Perón in 1955 and the military coup of 1966. She ended up in a Brazil that was undergoing the events that would lead inexorably to the 1964 military overthrow of democracy, which in turn triggered other coups in Latin America that led toward the unquestioned neofascism of the 1970s. Other Jewish immigrants to the country—who could never put far from their minds the suicide of the Jewish Austrian intellectual Stefan Zweig in Petrópolis during Carnival in 1942 following his humiliation, as a Jew, at the hands of fascistic President Getúlio Vargas— would find new ways of confronting the enormous ideological contradictions of Brazil.

Although it is customary to recall that Schwartz worked mainly as a journalistic photographer, carrying out assignments from important publishing houses and from what would emerge as the most powerful media conglomerate in South America, it is important to note that the archive she created contained a considerable amount of artistic work dealing with marginalized Brazilians.[10] While it is true that Schwartz's photographs of women of color with a certain symbolic power adopt a reverent and benevolent gaze, the simple fact is that no other female photographer concerned herself with these social subjects, people who were not always assimilated unquestionably in the hegemonic cultural discourse of their country (for example, there are no blacks in the readily available work of Hildegard Rosenthal). When, on the other hand, Schwartz turned the gaze of her camera on the world of transvestites, especially during the first phase of a dictatorship lasting more than twenty years, her photographic discourse became much more complex, inviting the viewer to enter into one of the worlds that a markedly discriminatory and persecutory dictatorship wished to conceal.

In both the case of the attention given by Schwartz to Afro-Brazilian culture and her particular interest in the transvestite world of Dzi Croquettes, the photographer demonstrates a particular Jewish commitment to the Other and—to the degree that at least Brazilian *candomblé* and the world of transvestites were subject to the persecutions of the military regimes of the 1960s and 1970s in Brazil—an equally Jewish interest in the marginalized Other as a reflex of one's own historical experience in a hostile social world.

8

Days and Nights at the Copan

Regina Rheda's *Arca sem Noé*

—O Copan é mais freqüentado que rabo de piranha

[....] Obra daquela anta do Niemeyer. Como tudo

o que ele fez, é bom para ser fotografado mas ruim

para se viver.

⚙ Regina Rheda, *Arca sem Noé* (23)

For those who may have always felt that Oscar Niemeyer's modernist architecture is highly overrated, the thirty-six-story Edifício Copan in downtown
São Paulo can serve as a convenient—although for some, a negative—reminder to this effect.[1] Commissioned for the Fourth Centennial of the city
of São Paulo (1954), construction was finally inaugurated in 1957 after several financial setbacks and significant structural alterations. For reasons that
have never been clear, Niemeyer abandoned the project at one point, and
thus it is a toss-up whether he should be credited with the dramatic exterior
lines of the building, but not with its internal failures, or whether it is fair to
allege that the latter are the consequence of the basic structural conception
of the building, beginning with the very notion of the building as a city,[2]

and the possibility of sustaining close to five thousand inhabitants distributed among approximately twelve hundred apartments of differing size and
amenities.[3] Work on the building was completed in 1966. The Copan may
remain the largest reinforced concrete edifice in Brazil, but after forty years
of wear and tear, its infrastructure is noticeably deteriorated, with many of
the originally planned features either never realized (for example, a luxury
hotel in one of the five administrative blocks that make up the building)
or subsequently abandoned (for example, the cultural performance space).[4]

Moreover, the area surrounding the Copan, the old central core of the
city which consists of the nearby Praça da República and the nearby Praça
da Sé (site of the metropolitan cathedral), has decayed implacably in recent years, as the concept of the heart of the city has, in good postmodern
fashion, dissolved into a proliferation of commercial, financial, and cultural
centers that draw all but the bereft and the destitute away from the downtown and into remote urban satellites. While major edifices of the historic
downtown remain (the Banco do Brasil, the Teatro Municipal, the Edifício
Martinelli [dating from 1929, the Martinelli holds the honor of being Latin
America's first skyscraper], the Edifício Itália [still one of Latin America's
tallest buildings], among quite a few others), it is now possible to live one's
entire life in São Paulo without ever venturing into this lost central core.
However, the closing a few years ago of the Hilton Hotel, located across the
street from the Copan and figuring prominently in one of Rheda's stories
("A voyeuse"), constituted something like a definitive statement with regard to any lingering importance the downtown sector may have had com-
mercially and financially.[5]

Regina Rheda was born in 1957 in Santa Cruz do Rio Pardo, in the state of
São Paulo, and *Arca sem Noé*, her first book, was published in 1994, winning
the prestigious Jabuti prize in 1995, with a second edition issued in 2002.[6]
A general characterization of Rheda's writing must include reference to a
strong feminist voice tinged with ample echoes of the Cixousian laugh of
the Medusa; an implacable attention to the metonymies and synecdoches
of outrageous human behavior directed equally against men and women,
for whom Rheda understands that the outrageous, despite the prevailing
boredom of daily existence, is integral to humankind in both its individual
and collective instances; a sense of the free-floating despair, and often un-
bridled terror, that nags at the hearts of men and women as they face the
anonymous indignities of urban life, especially in its Brazilian versions and,
most certainly, in its São Paulo ones; the often yawning abyss that separates

the unreflective behavior of her characters and the omniscient, all-seeing, and never-daunted (and, equally, never-excusing) narrative perspective of Rheda's third-person narrator; a sense of the urban experience as paradigmatic of the daily life of late capitalism;[7] and, finally, the sense that urban existence is always and forever unscripted, defiant of voluntarist ordering and coherence, and random in a manner that puts a completely human face on chaos theory—even when acts of willful endeavor occur, they are never conclusive and are always susceptible to the principle of unplanned occurrences.

These features apply in great measure to all of Rheda's fiction, which above all else is hilariously entertaining, although here I will consider its amalgam as the underlying *écriture* of the eight longish stories that make up *Arca sem Noé: histórias do Edifício Copan*. Basically, I will be referring to the interweaving of two apparently contradictory narrative primes: the hoary proposition that the urban experience is a jungle, albeit that the jungle is contained within the flourish of curved lines and sharp angles of the now-certainly notorious Edifício Copan; and the proposition that, if life does not present the happy endings of childish fairy tales nor the grim denouements of gritty urban tabloids, it is mostly characterized by the insouciant contemporizing of day-by-day survival.

The temptation would be great to proceed to encompass *Arca sem Noé* within a cultural tradition in which the city is seen in Boschian terms as a figure synthesizing all of the narrative clichés of hell as the living and daily abode of human society. In terms of this figure, urban life is the absolute binary opposite of any and everything that might be considered beneficent to a decent, prosperous, dignified, and value-laden life, in both individual and collective dimensions, wherein these two dimensions abet and perhaps even synergize whatever is touted to be the best of life. In a word, urban space is the antithesis of the much-sought-after *locus amoenus* of all varieties of cultural production, with its subsets in terms of splendid realms, soothing gardens, invigorating parks, and uplifting vistas. More specifically, the inviting urban utopia, at least in its modernist versions (as opposed to the transcendent Augustinian City of God versions), holds out the promise of the built environment as a maximally efficient machine in which—in lieu of any inherent potential conflict between the animate human body and the inanimate components of that machine—the structures are designed and executed in their construction to ameliorate categorically the limitations, failings, imperfections, and foibles of the human body. An example in this regard might be the existence, in the face of the incapability of most human bodies of easily climbing the stairs of a forty-story building, of so-called smart elevators that transport people up and down, maximizing automatically the use of the equipment and never erring in delivering the user to exactly the floor requested. Like all utopias, the fulfillment of such design ideals customarily falls short in real life, but the modernist ideal for the city has been the sustained quest for the optimum in design and execution to meet such goals, along with the promise to seek a remedy for those segments of the system that are discovered to be flawed in quotidian usage. These systems encompass not just the sphere of locomotion to which elevators belong, but also those of water and sanitation, electricity and other forms of energy, communications, climate control, and the maintenance for machine-like edifices.

Having established such utopian principles, it then becomes possible to track their absence, failure, capricious functioning, entropy, and incapacitation through vandalism and incompetent maintenance, as well as the ways in which the resulting anger and frustration of their users promotes a sense of dystopia, of utopia deferred and frustrated, of, in a word, a living hell in which the individual is surprised to be at the mercy of the designed machine that cannot be controlled. Again, a pertinent sign here would be an elevator door that does not open, an indicator light that fails, and an alarm system that rings purposelessly. Suddenly the machine has become as much an escape-proof crypt as anything envisioned in the most delirious of Gothic configurations of walled-up living. The urban machine has ceased to function as an instrument in the maximization of honest human lives and becomes a monster that, if it does not directly kill the individual, serves to slowly and surely madden in its unavoidable deployment: one may know the elevator is not going to function correctly, but few will give up hopefully and vainly pushing the buttons in order to try and ascend the forty stories.

Certainly, Rheda's stories are filled with images of what does not work: what has ceased to work or what has never worked. The fact that her understanding of the dysfunctional urban machine is confined to the Copan is only a matter of efficient and eloquent narrative synthesis, since the Copan was designed to be a marvelous urban machine and has now become a decayed hulk that just happens to be associated with Brazil's reputedly greatest architect and just happens to allegedly constitute São Paulo's signature modernist edifice.[8] It requires no leap of interpretation to understand that the Copan is both a symbol of São Paulo as Brazil's largest and most complex megalopolis and a symbol of the futility of the promise of a modernist order for urban space. Thus, it would be possible to inventory the images of this failed promise as they manifest themselves in the texture of the daily frustrations of "life at the Copan." My choice of the elevator as a prime example of an urban machine is intended to echo similar references in the stories of *Arca sem Noé*, but the same is true of all the other components of the machine, and Rheda's wicked wit—buttressed by a language that delights in underscoring with judicious images the assaults on the all too "pervious" flesh of the building's inhabitants—never misses a beat in zeroing in on the worst violations of the modernist pact of trust between human body and designed machine.

For example, in the lead story, "O mau vizinho" ("The Neighbor from Hell"), which won on its own the Prêmio Maison de l'Amérique Latine, an elderly female tenant is driven to murder by the filthy personal hygiene of her male neighbor,[9] one of whose many disgusting habits is to leave the door of the common garbage chute wide open, thus allowing the stench of rotting refuse to inundate the apartments of the entire floor. It is this same inhabitant who utters the words against Niemeyer that I have placed as an epigraph to this chapter. He goes on to observe, as an example of the far-from-intelligent design of the building, that "Os banheiros deste bloco, por exemplo, não têm janelas. Se o sujeito soltar um peido lá dentro, morre asfixiado" (23).[10] The inherent truth of this pungent hyperbole is that it becomes impossible to determine whether the appalling personal hygiene of this neighbor reinforces the dysfunctional nature, in this instance, of the ventilation system, or if the incompetent design of the ventilation system, working in tandem with a garbage disposal unit that does not take into account inevitable human slovenliness (for example, it might have been designed with a tamper-proof spring system that would prevent its ever being left open), is part of an integrated system that promotes human filth. The elderly woman of the story strives vainly to overcome the inevitable indignities visited upon her equally by the building and its occupants, one in particular, and in the end her murderous reaction is a gesture of futility:

> Nos dias que se seguiram, Dona Adelaide não se ocupou de limpezas. Ficou tranqüila dentro de casa, o nariz atento a cada movimento no ar, ansioso por captar o fodor que estava por emanar da carne que apodrecia no apartamento do vizinho. (30)[11]

Thus, in the end, Dona Adelaide herself becomes an agent of the multilayered effluvium generated by the building.

The accumulated weight of Rheda's depiction of the indignities of urban life in São Paulo as exemplified by the details of the Copan could readily generate a sensation of intransigent frustration, of the stymieing of any attempt to pursue a human existence of substantive quality; it is unimportant if one cannot provide an objective metric of what such quality might be, since it is such a safe bet that none of the characters described in the eight stories come anywhere near attaining even the most modest, humble, and unambitious quality of life. Dona Adelaide's ridiculous attempts to maintain her former comfortable bourgeois existence—marked most impressively by the absolute norms of cleanliness to which she aspires—as she moves, first from the mansion of her marriage to one of the privileged spacious apartments of the Copan and then, as her life becomes narrower, to the efficiency unit next door to the famous playwright, synthesize by implication the rock-bottom standard of living that is all that the Copan—a horizontal, entropy-cursed, favela in-the-making—will allow for.[12]

The Copan, as a model of postmodern urban life in São Paulo, is reflected in the title of Rheda's collection, *Arca sem Noé*. If the ark is a microcosm that will provide continuity to existence beyond environmental disasters, its efficacy insured by the delegate of the Lord, then Noah, who complies with precise instructions in order to guarantee the well-being of his charges, has in the case of the Copan disappeared from the scene.[13] Brazilian society may remain hierarchical, patriarchal, and authoritarian, but no one, ultimately, is in charge of the world of the Copan: the service personnel and the managerial staff are simply incapable of keeping the building running or—to move away from my guiding metaphor of the edifice as a machine and to adhere to Rheda's allusion to Noah—to keep the building afloat. The eight stories of *Arca sem Noé* are a veritable catalog of the disasters that high-rise condominium dwellers may be subject to.

Yet, despite the reader's expectations, Rheda's stories are not a catalog of despair: that is, while the multiple recurring and overlapping system failures of the Copan may induce anger, they do not breed despair. There may be a certain measure of resignation in having to accommodate one's life to one more inconvenience—and there is much about these stories that has to do with the molding of body and spirit within the unyielding constraints of life at the Copan—but Rheda, ever the good-natured Brazilian, is never willing to subscribe to the inevitable destruction of the human spirit. Since her narrative tone is neither pathetic nor tragic—tones that have long characterized accounts regarding life on the margins of human society, the literature of the poverty-stricken Brazilian Northeast being of paradigmatic importance here—but rather carnivalesque, Rheda portrays the denizens of the Copan as survivors of urban life. While *Arca sem Noé* is not precisely a handbook of urban survival—and the question as to what to do when suddenly faced with a weekend without water is not a trivial one—it is a gallery of urban inhabitants who somehow manage to get by, despite all the odds ranged against them.

Such a narrative stance constitutes an important dimension of urban writing: the advancement of an image of survival that defies accepted popular wisdom about city life in general and so-called Third World megalopolitan life in particular. To be sure, all of the clichés regarding urban life are confirmed here, from the alienation of the lonely crowd to the numbing quality of hours spent futilely attempting to conduct the simplest task of daily life, from the aggressive interpersonal commerce of packed living conditions to the inevitable, ever-present erosion of the manmade landscape, from the downward spiral of recycling space to the eventual abandonment of it. If one of the icons of modernity in the collection is the Hilton Hotel across the street from the Copan, reader knowledge about its current abandonment might well occasion a reflection on what it will mean—symbolically in terms of the São Paulo cityscape and personally in terms of its thousands of inhabitants—when the time comes to decommission the Copan. Forty years is ancient for a building that could never be adequately maintained from the start, and within the universe of the stories themselves, the abandonment and recycling of the commercial spaces that occupy what is now the dingy ground floor of the building is, for the casual passerby, the visible face of the invisible living spaces above ground level. There is a passing reference to the conversion of the much-touted cultural space, here identified both as the Cine Copan and the Cine Teatro Copan, into a Pentecostal meeting place, but such a transformation failed to rid the area of its smell of musty decay (100–01).

And yet, and yet, they survive. . . . Well, some kill each other, as the elderly lady does her noxious neighbor in "O mau vizinho," and Leonor falls to her death along with her friend Margarete in "As duas amigas." It appears that Margarete, although she is being shoved to her death at a spot on one of the floors where the protective railing has come loose, cannot depart this world without her friend, and she quickly grabs her blouse to carry her down to the ground with her:

> Rápida como um raio, Leonor empurrou a colega no abismo. A menina reagiu, agarrando a colega pela blusa. Ouviu-se uma gritaria no terraço e, antes que algum corpo bronzeado tivesse tempo de erguer-se da esteira, as duas já sobrevoaram a metópole em direção ao inexorável asfalto.
>
> Não se sabe se Margarete desmaiou durante a queda ou se, lúcida, teve em seu vertiginoso fluxo terminal de pensamento um lugar para o resentimento. Mas sabe-se que o psicólogo [que atendia Leonor] sofreu muito com a tragédia. Quanto a Leonor, antes de esborrachar-se no chão, perdoou-os. ("As duas amigas" 119)[14]

Rheda's carnivalesque tone is amply apparent here, as well as her nonchalant narrative omniscience.[15]

I would like to turn now to one of the most interesting stories in the collection, "A voyeuse" ("The Voyeuse"). In this story, the supremely bored housewife Vera Lúcia, who has little use for her brutish husband, discovers one day the delights of masturbating with the curtains of her bedroom open, such that she is on display to an employee of the nearby Hilton Hotel who happens to look her way as he stands at the window of one of the hotel's rooms. Subsequently, he invites other employees to share in the sight. The fact that Vera Lúcia has no particular physical charms to recommend her is immaterial to her spectators: the very fact of any female body put on erotic display in such an abandoned fashion is sufficiently unique in the panorama of the city to entice those men who watch her. However, one day her husband discovers her engaged in this routine of displayed self-pleasuring and leaves her. She is delighted to have unconsciously discovered a way of ridding herself of his loutish presence, but when he is unable to live without her (not to mention ready to reassert his masculine control), he returns to her, ready and willing to collaborate in her exhibitionist theatrics:

> Nesse momento a campainha tocou. Seu Hildebrando, o marido, o tronco em que Dona Vera enredara sua vida, o mastro em que ela içara seus sonhos, o crucifixo ao qual ela se atrelara, sua única estrada para o futuro, tinha voltado. Trazia vários pacotes embrulhados em papel de presente. Abriu-os com as próprias maos, cheio de inédita boa vontade. Eram revistas, vídeos, fotografias e baralhos pornográficos, que iam sendo espalhados pela cama com energia jovial. Dona Vera se jogou nos braços dele.

Do outro lado da avenida, à janela do hotel, um camareiro os espiava. A esposa começou a fechar as cortinas mas foi impedida pelo marido que, impetuoso, escancarou-as à curiosidade do camareiro, o qual serviu de testemunha ao amor possível, necessário e inapelável de Dona Vera e Seu Hildebrando. (138–39)[16]

What is particularly interesting about the story, in addition to the tone of jouissance in the face of a new sexual beginning for what at first appears to be a dead-end marriage, an utterly exhausted human relationship, is the apparently "incorrect" use of the term *voyeuse*. Since Vera Lúcia is the only woman in the story, the noun can only refer to her. But what is the object of her sexual gaze? She of course knows she is being watched by the hotel employee and, later, by his companions, but she is not witnessing their sexual engagements: at best she fleetingly sees their gaze directed toward her body and her erotic manipulation of it. Because of her posture—lying back on the bed with her legs spread wide—she is not really in a position to follow in detail their contemplation of her sexual theatrics, unless what she is privileged to see voyeuristically is her imagined vision of their gaze upon her. This can surely constitute a valid form of voyeurism. To the extent that the hotel employees are voyeuristically witnessing a sexual spectacle, they are, in turn, engaged themselves in a sexual act, irrespective of whether they end up masturbating themselves (or each other) as they watch her perform. In this sense, "A voyeuse" is an excellent example of my assertion that an architectural machine such as the Edifício Copan molds its inhabitants. Dona Vera is able to experience—to see—a change in her attitudes toward sexual fulfillment and, ultimately, toward the sexual fulfillment that she can now have with her (legitimate and societally sanctioned) husband because of the way in which her apartment in the Copan and its situation in such visible proximity to the Hilton Hotel allows for the conversion of her bedroom into the stage of an improvised porno theater of the sort that has come to proliferate in the surrounding area. But while she is the performer and the hotel employees are her audience, the title of the story implies that she is, in the end, and much more importantly, a spectator of her own spectacle. It is a spectacle that at first includes only her as a solo actress, but into which she draws her husband, as much grateful for his newfound sexual ardor as he is for having found a way to return to her household. In this way, the performance possibilities afforded by the Copan, rather than promoting the sort of inexorable destruction of human society envisioned by so much gritty and dirty urban realism, in fact contribute to the renewal of conjugal bliss.[17]

If the Copan, then, exemplifies the modernist concept of the building as a machine at the service of efficient living, it is both an experiential disaster and a site of human survival. Enmeshed in the structure of the building—perhaps even in a cyborg-like fashion in which there come to exist structural continuities between the animate building, with its erratically functioning structural components, and the equally erratic human inhabitants that justify its very existence—the occupants are shown in the final analysis of Rheda's *Arca sem Noé*, despite the absence of any guiding shipmaster, to navigate, with varying degrees of success, the urban flood.

9

Trekking the Urban

Eduardo Emílio Fenianos's *Expedições Urbenauta; São Paulo, uma aventura radical*

Para mí la vida en la ciudad no es tan desagradable como
se la suele pintar.

⬡ Clorindo Tosta, "Placeres del ser urbano" (n.p.)

Astronautas vão para a lua / Urbenautas vão para a rua.

⬡ Eduardo Emílio Fenianos, *Expedições* (14)

São Paulo is, by some accounts, the fifth-largest demographic concentration in the world, the second in Latin America after Mexico City, which in
most accounts is the largest in the Western hemisphere and second-largest
in the world.[1] One is, therefore, to be excused for asking a rather clichéd
question: "How does one ever grasp this sort of urban space?" Answers may
vary with regard to Mexico City, but there can be little doubt that São Paulo
is not a very user-friendly city—just read the accounts of what its citizens
go through every day in going to or from work, or experience the city as an

average tourist who might attempt to stroll the downtown, facing pollution, overcrowding, and the threat of crime.

Of course, the answer to the overwhelmed and naive tourist's question is that most people do not experience the megalopolis as a whole; rather, most individuals, in the numbing routine of their daily lives, whether as domestic servants or university professors, merely live in little more than fragments of the city, fragments that they may control with some degree of efficiency as though it were their native—or near-native—language. This includes even the individual who has a two-hour bus ride to work: the point A of their residence may be one urban reality, and the point B of their workplace another. But those points in between are only a blur, since with any kind of luck they may get a seat and be able to doze, if not sleep, during the trip from A to B, although it is more than likely they will have to transfer at least once during that commute.[2] But even the transfer points are blurs: under such transportation circumstances, could one possibly have the energy to stroll the area around the bus stop, given the crush of passengers simply trying to get on the next vehicle? Of course, some individuals do have a wide-ranging experience of the city—say policemen or real estate agents—although they may be confined to certain districts of it. Only taxi drivers and news reporters are likely to have really random access to the city on a daily basis. Even the individual who frequents cultural institutions or commercial venues exemplifies a patterned access: a series of points C, D, E, and so forth, that in short order begin to repeat themselves, with only occasionally a new institution or venue added as others are lost.

Thus, the radical urban adventure of Eduardo Emílio Fenianos, who I will hereafter refer to by his self-assigned soubriquet as the Urbenauta, involves accessing São Paulo in a manner that is decidedly artificial, and it is perhaps this aspect of it that, in the end, is the most radical: rare indeed is the individual able to assemble the resources to undertake the Urbenauta's urban expedition. Beginning on February 10, 2001, the Urbenauta—with a set of equipment every bit as complicated as the Abercrombie & Fitch kits described by Theodore Roosevelt in his famous safaris (and note that the Urbenauta's commencement falls close to the hundredth anniversary of the redoubtable explorer's South American undertaking, as recounted in *Through the Brazilian Wilderness* [1914, it describes an expedition in 1913–14])—set out to map through his personal experiences the vast city of São Paulo. This was not the Urbenauta's first such adventure: in 1997, he conducted a similar undertaking in his native city of Curitiba, the capital of the state of Paraná, which is immediately south of the state of São Paulo (the air connection between Curitiba and São Paulo is less than an hour). This expedition garnered an enormous amount of attention, and, in addition to publishing his diary, *O Urbenauta: manual de sobrevivência na selva urbana* (The Urbenaut: Survival Manual for the Urban Jungle; 1998), he released a video directed by Luciano Coelho, *O Urbenauta, uma aventura na cidade* (The Urbenaut, An Adventure in the City—it is not great, but it is useful), and a marvelous series of small books featuring his photography on the individual neighborhoods of the city.[3] Since Curitiba remains a very ethnically diverse city (it prides itself on the fact that there is a city park for every major ethnic group), these publications effectively capture that important urban dimension.

The title of the Urbenauta's original adventure is perhaps a bit inflated. Without downplaying the harsh economic and social realities experienced by those whose lives do not jive with the much-vaunted self-image of the city as one of the great garden cities of the world, Curitiba is hardly an urban jungle, and the author's designation is more a gentle spoofing of that self-image than it is an accurate sociological interpretation. Although the Urbenauta's expedition certainly brings out a portrait of the city not to be found in the boosterism emanating from City Hall or the numerous coffee-table books now available (one of which is also written by Fenianos, *Almanaque Kurytyba*), all in all, the three-month trek cannot have been all that rigorous. The image unquestionably changes when one turns to São Paulo, not only because of its sheer geographic dimensions (765 square miles according to http://www.demographia.com/rac-sao.pdf), but also because of its huge population relative to Curitiba, which is on the order of six or seven to one (twenty million versus three). Significantly, the Urbenauta does not repeat the trope of the urban jungle with reference to São Paulo, although the subtitle "uma aventura radical"[4] certainly alerts the reader to the staggering dimensions of his undertaking.

This staggering quality is quickly discernible in the prefatory material, where the Urbenauta speaks of his team of twenty-one individuals (6), a time line of eighteen months, and reproduces images of his gear (8–9), some of which looks more appropriate for a lunar voyage than meandering around the cityscape. It is evident that some of this is tongue-in-cheek. For example, the illustrated account of the Urbenave Gulliver (the name is duly explained) refers to the two garbage disposal units mounted on the spare-tire storage unit: "A urbenave tem duas lixeiras—uma para material

Figure 9.1. The Urbenauta speaks with a family of eleven. Reproduced courtesy of Eduardo Fenianos.

orgânico e outra para lixo reciclável—que podem ser utilizadas pela população, contribuindo assim, de uma maneira simples—mas educada—para a limpeza urbana" (9).[5] The spare-tire storage unit contains, above the canister, the word "*JOGUE*" (PLAY; THROW) and below the word "*LIMPO*" (CLEAN). This is a play on words frequent in advertising and, in this case, urban campaign slogans: it means both "Play Clean" and "Throw [garbage away] Neatly." This detail sets the frequently playful, ironic, self-deprecating, and simply happy-go-lucky tone of the Urbenauta's adventure and the notes he takes on it. He was out to have a great time, and, in contextualizing his undertaking, he wants the reader to share the spirit of the voyage and experience its actual fulfillment.

I have touched on how the pretext for *Expedições Urbenauta: São Paulo* (Urbenaut Expeditions: São Paulo) is the tradition of the dark continent treks exemplified by Theodore Roosevelt and others, as one can study them in, for example, Roosevelt's *Through the Brazilian Wilderness*. Whether or not Brazil was to be considered a veritable dark continent on the order of the prevailing images of sub-Saharan Africa, the use of the trope "wilderness," which presumedly applied equally to urban centers like Rio de Janeiro and São Paulo (as well as to Santiago de Chile, Montevideo, and Buenos Aires, which were also stops on the tour, despite the book's title), the Amazonian jungle, the Andean area, and the Pernambuco-Bahia coastline applies a flattening characterization that not only assimilates different physical geographic features of South America to a single image, but also equates that image with any of the many other wilderness notches that Roosevelt carved on his riding crop. Exploring the wilderness was important stuff to the bearers of the white man's burden. And note the chronology: Roosevelt visited South America immediately after completing his presidential term in 1908, and he did so at the invitation of the American Museum of Natural History, with, eventually, a whole coterie of scholars involved.[6] If something like what is described in *Through the Brazilian Wilderness* (and one cannot overlook the spatial metaphor of a radical penetration that brings the expeditionary team out on the other side) may be considered the paradigm of the imperial gaze on the primitive Other, it serves very effectively to frame the Urbenauta's personal project.

While the Urbenauta does not invoke Roosevelt (who never has anything substantive to say about São Paulo, although he does praise Republican Rio with enthusiasm [349], and has some passing praise for Buenos Aires [32]), he does invoke Gulliver, and one of the primary ways of reading Jonathan Swift's famous *Gulliver's Travels* (1726) is as an unrelenting satire on the British imperial undertaking and the primitivizing mentality it fueled (that is, in part Edward Said's trope of Orientalism). Not only does the Urbenauta eschew any sense of an imperial gaze, beginning with the image of Fenianos on the book's back jacket flap as a hip, bare-chested, smiling young man (no statuesque pose alongside a fallen beast of the jungle here), but the facts of his social subjectivity render one unlikely, even impossible. Aside from being relatively young (he was only thirty-one at the time), he is portrayed with an urbane instrument, the camera (he is taking a picture of the photographer, Dado Pimpão, who, in turn, is taking his picture), not the high-power rifle of the expeditionary force (which did take photographs, but the photographer is never pictured). Now, one is well aware of the ethical questions of photography and the fact that the camera is hardly a benign instrument of knowledge. It is frequently deployed for purposes tantamount to spying on the misery and suffering of the Other (Sontag, passim), and the controversies surrounding Sebastião Salgado's monumental portraits of human suffering, as seen in Evbaldo Mocarzeli's documentary, *À margem da imagem* (On the Margin of the Image; 2003), are a good place to begin to understand the intrusive nature of photography.

Yet, while the Urbenauta refers repeatedly to his visual documentation of the expedition, his actual book contains none of that material (except for the celebratory photo of the journey's completion). But what is more significant in the Urbenauta's case is the reversal of the axis of his gaze. The very expression "imperial gaze" means that the viewer enjoys the privilege of the more powerful—materially and symbolically—perch, from which he (the masculine pronoun is important here) contemplates what is manifestly secondary, peripheral, marginal, and even abject, to his centrality. This was the case of the American Roosevelt in Africa and South America, as it was the case of individuals too numerous to mention in the Indian subcontinent, or Lévi-Strauss in Brazil. Such a gaze does not always involve condescension, but the rhetoric of metropolitan-centered "I" versus peripheral "them" is unquestionable, as can be seen in a key Brazilian text like Euclides da Cunha's *Os sertões* (1902), in which the Rio journalist, critical though he may be of the central government, covers the exotic phenomenon of the Canudos rebellion in the Northeastern backlands in the late 1890s. But, of course, the Urbenauta is not privileged with the metropolitan-centered first-person discourse, since it is he who is from the provincial capital of Curitiba, who is acceding to the urban monolith; not like the ur-Manhattanite Woody Allen viewing Midwestern American life or the Munchkinland of Los Angeles in his film *Annie Hall* (1977), but, rather, like the Mormon mother of Tony Kushner's play *Angels in America* (1993) trying to come to grips with New York. Since the Urbenauta is from Curitiba, it would only be through an enormously complex task of assimilation to the megalopolitan gaze that he would be able to duplicate the center/periphery interplay crucial to the imperial gaze.

Yet the Urbenauta makes it quite clear that the precise purpose of his expedition is to engage the city as someone who does not know it and as someone who comes to it with a decidedly unprivileged frame of reference. He opens his "Prefácio interessantíssimo" (A Most Interesting Preface) with an assertion framed in terms of the venerable rhetorical formula "Not A, but B," in which the negated member refers to none other than two legendary urban sophisticates: "A minha São Paulo não é a de Oswald ou Mário de Andrade. A minha São Paulo é a de Cristóvão Colombo e Charles Darwin" (11).[7] His two persons in the affirmative member of the rhetorical formula are prime examples of explorers who did not have the faintest idea what they were really going to find and could not, therefore, have exemplified the masterful control (even if only retrospectively in their accounts) of the fully vested agents of the Empire. The accounts of the agents of the Empire, even though they may often contain references to horrendous dangers and stunning failures, by their very nature are characteristically triumphalist: they recount the triumph of the expedition that allows for the account to be written in the first place, and that account is a form of control, through the language and style of the master, of the content that it is reporting. To return to an example like Roosevelt's *Through the Brazilian Wilderness*, one can appreciate the stylus gravis of a concluding paragraph:

> In short, these men, and those like them everywhere on the frontier be-
> tween civilization and savagery in Brazil, are now playing the part played by
> our backwoodsmen when over a century and a quarter ago they began the
> conquest of the great basin of the Mississippi; the part played by the Boer
> farmers for over a century in South Africa, and by the Canadians when less
> than half a century ago they began to take possession of their Northwest.
> (333)

Against the implied backdrop of a long tradition of imperial travel and expedition literature, *Expedições Urbenauta* strikes a totally different discursive pose that is based on three guiding textual principles: (1) the narrator has not come to São Paulo to control a form of knowledge about it, but to give himself over fully to the unknown adventure; (2) the very tone of his narrative ensures that it is he who is constantly controlled by the nature of his undertaking, and the first-person pronoun is not that of the agentive proposition "I do," but rather that of an experiential proposition, like "I have happen to me" or "it befalls me";[8] (3) in the final analysis São Paulo cannot be known, and any account of an expedition to it, therefore, cannot be an explanation of the city but only a declaration of the (never-global) ways in which it was experienced.

In terms of the narrator's handing himself over to the unknown dimensions of the city, it is important to note that he is deviating significantly from the discourse of his academic formation as a sociologist.[9] That is, this is not the text of a sociologist. Social science protocols may inform the Urbenauta's way of initially scrutinizing urban reality, along with the questions that he has set out to ask. However, the slippage from a putatively proper sociology into a frequently and roundly criticized nonscientific

ethnography is characterized precisely by the disappearance of an articulated set of premises and research methodology and by the replacement of
the disembodied third-person who explains procedures, presents data, and
draws conclusions by a first-person voice that recounts experiences and interpersonal interactions and speculates on their meaning in ways that are
marked prominently by the affective, phatic, and poetic functions of language (Greimas 124–27). This may be observed in something like an introit
to the account of the expedition, which is the enumeration of the goals of
"Parte 1: A selva," which gives the impression that there are subsequent
parts similarly identified, without there really being any. Much in the fashion of the inventory of goals and objectives of a research project, the author
enumerates ten "Objetivos desta fase," some of which are:

> —Desbravar e fazer reconhecimento da porção da Selva da Cantareira que
> está dentro do município de São Paulo.
> —Demarcar os pontos cardeais norte e sul da cidade . . .
> Durante a navegação dos rios, buscar outros ângulos e pontos de vista para
> a cidade, ganhando o olhar do rio para a rua e não da rua para o rio, como é
> no cotidiano . . .
> —Alertar governantes e população sobre a importância da preservação
> de recursos naturais, principalmente a água, que corre sérios riscos de se
> tornar escassa ainda no século 21. (12)[10]

These objectives are prefaced by some statistics about the area and the unlikely fact that this phase's "apoio" (help) will come from the Força Aérea
Brasileira (Brazil Air Force); it is closed by a series of nine boxes giving rel-
evant information about five major rivers and a reservoir of the region. It
is not immediately clear how a flyover, courtesy of the FAB, will contribute noticeably to a consciousness-raising of governments and the citizenry
about the serious threats of water shortage in the area, and the third point
about achieving a new perspective on the city from the middle of the noxious, alarmingly polluted waters of the river in a "barco a motor" (motor
boat) sounds more like something out of João Guimarães Rosa's magical
realist story "A terceira margem do rio" ("The Third Bank of the River")
than an exercise in correcting urban perspectives. To be sure, the urban lay-
out must take into account the presence of the one river that crisscrosses
the city, the Rio Tietê, and will continue to unless the river is rechanneled
or directed underground. Moreover, one is very well aware of the presence
of the river not only because it so dramatically bisects the city from east

to west, but because its stench may be perceived well before its polluted waters may be actually espied.

Finally, the first objective gives the impression that the Selva da Cantareira, like the Tietê, is to be found in the heart of the city, when in fact it constitutes São Paulo's northern boundary. The extent to which this is more of a jocular discourse than the framing of a research project by the disembodied voice of the social scientist (disembodied, one ought to emphasize, because it contains no internal markers of subjective identity, other than existing appositionally to the name of a stipulated authority) is confirmed by the inclusion, on the following page, of one of those maps that indicates population concentration by a gradated key corresponding to heat concentration; the rivers are indicated in conventional blue, and a white dotted line outlines the official boundaries of the municipality. This map is given the title "*A selva*" (The jungle), but it is apparent that the jungle is not the surrounding surviving areas of the primeval forest, but rather the city of São Paulo itself—that is, the urban jungle. This map will be repeated throughout the book, each time modified to represent the quadrant of the city being explored, along with a key to the neighborhoods of each section.

This framing pleasantry is confirmed by the fact that, when the actual text begins on page 14, under the title "*Urbe et urbi*" ("in and by [or for] the city," a trope of the customary "*urbe et orbe*," "in the city and in the world"), the starting point of the expedition is the downtown Praça da Sé, one of the oldest anchors of the city and the location of the metropolitan cathedral. And as the Urbenauta says: "a realidade começou a se mostrar bem maior do que minha imaginação" (14).[11] The wondrous affirmation sets the tone for the way in which, as a reiterated characteristic of *Expedições Urbenauta*, the narrator will be amazed, marveled, and stunned by what befalls him. If this is, one will recall, the basic narrative tone of Swift's parody of imperial travels of exploration, in the case of the Urbenauta it serves to underscore the way in which any shred of putative scientific objectivity yields to the overwhelming experience of the lived human environment of the streets.

Indeed, most of the subsequent approximately five dozen chapters open with a humorous title, an explanation of how expectations keep changing, and a description of how the Urbenauta's journey is; rather than being propelled by an overarching experimental design, he is at the mercy of the accidentals of life. For example, about midway through the book, there is a chapter titled "*Entre a vida e a vida*" (between life and life), another title that is manifestly a trope of a common, everyday phrase. It is typical in that it opens with a description of the weariness of the narrator, his recurrent struggle against the limitations of his resources, the evocation of the amenities of his real life (hence, the juxtaposition between one "life"—what he is used to—and another one—that imposed by his expedition), and what quickly imposes itself from the start as the one ruling imperative of his day, the need to find a place to sleep that night:

> Trânsito na Marginal Tietê parado. Sexta-feira. Saudades de chegar em casa, preparar algo pra comer, tomar banho e depois sair. O real é que escolhi isto.
>
> Estou com uma dor de cabeça caprichada e muita dor no pescoço. Eu que no começo sofria pelo aperto do carro, hoje me contento em não precisar mais subir escada, abrir gaveta, abrir a porta do armário. Simplesmente viro a mão direita pra trás e pego o remédio na farmácia da urbenave. Estou mais organizado no meu novo esquema de vida.
>
> Tomei o remédio, liguei no som da urbenave a minha música da sorte e, ritualisticamente, me considerei dentro da Zona Norte. Primeiro objetivo: encontrar um lugar para dormir. Na manga, um só contato, o Manoel, um office-boy que conheci na Barra Funda, justamente no dia em que dormi na rua. Ou ele, ou a rua como cama outra vez. (172)[12]

Certainly, the intrepid explorer never knows what lies around the next bend in the river and is never fully confident that he will find an adequate and secure campsite, and undoubtedly it is only human to complain of one's unexpected circumstances. My point here is not that the Urbenauta is some sort of devalued explorer, but rather that the very sense of the city he wishes to transmit is what it imposes on the individual: the irritations of a Friday afternoon traffic jam, the assault on the body of being cooped up in a vehicle which will likely be trapped in traffic simply from being out on the street, and the fundamental uncertainties of urban life, here captured in the anxiety of finding someplace to sleep (one is always anxious about the precarious nature of every transaction in a city like São Paulo) and the need to back oneself up with ritualistic good-luck music.

Part of the key to survival in an expeditionary conquest is to struggle against being consumed by the jungle. Failure in this effort will result in what befalls the hero of the Colombian José Eustasio Rivera's 1924 novel *La vorágine* (The Vortex). "¡Los devoró la selva!" (203) are the closing words of the novel, the title of which is itself a metaphor for the jungle. Additionally, one must struggle valiantly against the indignities that accompany yielding to the temptation to "go native": part of the white man's burden is also to resist being swallowed up in this sense. But concomitant with the image in *Expedições Urbenauta* of the expeditionary agent as someone who gives himself over to the experience and is therefore buffeted by what we might call the rapidly shifting tides of the city is a self-deprecating image, one of sustained irony in the face of being overwhelmed by the city he has chosen to take on. Consider, for example, the ironic tone of the following, yet another report on the difficulties of finding a place to sleep:

> Por volta das seis horas, já partindo para Pirituba, me dei conta de não ter um lugar pra dormir. Primeiro pedi a uma senhora que me desculpou de uma forma bastante simpática de um momento em que fiquei com a urbe-nave parada, observando uma bela esquina da região, sem me dar conta de que outras pessoas deveriam seguir seu caminho e continuar levando a sua vida na maior cidade do Brasil. Não deu certo. Depois vi uns garotos jo-gando e se preparando para o Mercado Imobiliário. Joguei um pouco com eles e quando pedi pouso o corinthiano do grupo fez uma boa observação. "Nossa meu, que mendigo estranho que você é!! Te um jipão desses e não tem onde dormir." (183)[13]

In fact, the Urbenauta usually finds someone to take him in, including the claim that he was able to "fechar com chave de ouro a expedição pela Zona Norte, consegui dormir dois dias na casa de uma ex-namorada" (204).[14] His goal is to sleep in the house of people he meets along the way, and he is usually successful in doing so, leading him to participate in the lives of the people who take him in, including their domestic arrangements, their daily routine, their leisure activities, and, since this is the multifaceted *Brasil crente*, their religious observances. The narrator's deeply respectful tone toward the people with whom he stays echoes one of the most culturally useful dimensions of expeditionary writing: the careful observations about the way other people live. Such a tone mitigates the litany of ironic commentaries on the vagaries of his undertaking. This leads to what, in recounting one of the details related to the documentation of his expedition, is described as a social pact:

> Como as filmagens da expedição estão sendo feitas em sua maioria pelos próprios moradores, depois de uma certa amizade apresento meus equi-pamentos e passo a ensinar a galera a manusear câmara de vídeo e câmera fotográfica. O que faço é entregar a câmera a um daqueles que poderia querer tirá-la de mim. Ensino como manuseá-la e coloco em suas mãos a

responsabilidade de me mostrar o mundo em que vive. No lugar da descon-
fiança, a confiança total. É um pacto. (234)[15]

There is no irony here, only a tone of respect toward his saviors and the
sharing that is described here in terms of a social pact.

Nevertheless, both the Urbenauta's self-deprecating irony and his sober
respect towards his hosts, most of whom are socioeconomically quite humble, function on the same discursive level: just as the accounts of his own
limitations and setbacks serve to reduce the narrator's objective authority
as accorded by the "I" versus "They" disjunctive optic, the descriptions
of the social pact that he forges with the people he meets and the ways in
which he participates in their everyday lives function equally to erase that
optic, and over and over again there is the sense that the Urbenauta is one
with his subjects. Speaking of one of the older women with whom he finds
refuge, he closes his account with an expression of great affection: "Con-
versamos até a madrugada. Ambos dormimos de portas abertas e a rua me
deu mais uma maravilhosa e sábia avó" (154).[16]

As positive as the Urbenauta's experiences in crisscrossing the neighborhoods of São Paulo during the course of dozens and dozens of months are,
he must, in the end, make a confession that surely strikes dread into the
heart of any researcher: he cannot, in the final analysis, really grasp his object of study. The Urbenauta's voyage ends back in the Praça da Sé where it
began:

Abracei e agradeci a todos, curioso em saber o que acontecerá conosco depois. Vi cada um retornando à sua vida. E me preparando para retornar para
minha. A praça se esvaziando . . . Antes de entrar na urbenave e voltar para
casa, vi um senhor apontar o dedo para o meu lado e dizer a outro: "Ele tá
voltando de uma grande viagem. Deu a volta ao mondo e está chegando
agora.

No fundo ele estava certo. O desafio da Volta ao Mundo hoje é saber
como conviver com a solidão das multidões, não se sentir sozinho cercado
por 6 bilhões de seres humanos, ultrapassar os muros sociais, vencer a
violência, a pobreza, o desrespeito mútuo, a indiferença do ser humano
pelo próprio ser humano e pelo planeta que o abriga. O desafio da Volta
ao Mundo hoje é saber como construir cidades sem destruir o planeta e a
nós mesmos. O mundo não precisa de gente que pense somente na lua. O
planeta precisa de gente que pensa na rua . . .

Olhei mais uma vez para a Praça da Sé e pensei comigo:

"São Paulo é mesmo uma aventura radical! Quando pensamos ter alcançado o seu fim, ela nos lembra de que tudo está apenas começando!" (264)[17]

These are the closing words of *Expedições Urbenauta*, and they have all of the eloquence of the poetic closure of narrative texts, particularly when high adventures and great emotions are being recounted.[18]

But if the narrator is Odysseus redux after a successful return home from the rigors of the cement jungle, he is also Sisyphus redux, in the sense that he can never accomplish his goal of grasping the—if I may be permitted to abound in classical allusions—protean megalopolis. As an expedition that takes the pulse of a great contemporary city of the world, *Expedições Urbenauta* is a fascinating text that founds a totally new genre within an inventory of the cultural production of São Paulo: indeed, part of its excitement is derived from fantasizing over duplicating the same sort of adventure in one's own immediate *selva*: indeed, the last page of the text is the announcement "Procuram-se urbenautas" (272),[19] preceded by the "Manifesto Urbenauta: 120 razões para você viajar na cidade em que mora ou desafiar Selvas de Pedra" (265–69),[20] a veritable hortatory coda for his imagined community of readers. Yet to a great degree the book's strength lies in the way it is relentlessly personal, at least in contrast to professional sociological accounts of the city (for example, Caldeira; Maricato). This text cannot be read in the way formal sociology would envision, nor can it be read in terms of the principles of mid-brow guidebooks, such as those of someone like Frommer (who gives very short shrift to São Paulo anwyway [Uhl 191–212; Rio merits over one hundred pages]), with the implication that it is not of much interest to the sort of (imperial?) readers he has in mind. Perhaps *Expedições Urbenauta* is more comfortable in the company of the Lonely Planet guides (Selby et al.), although this ecological audience presumably will find little to interest it in São Paulo: the 1998 edition I have at hand devotes only pp. 271–91, out of a total of 713 pages, to the city; Rio, unsurprisingly, spans pp. 146–93. The Urbenauta, to be sure, convincingly articulates the sort of ecological consciousness one must bring to a Lonely Planet guide to fully appreciate its recommendations. However, where the narrator goes with that consciousness, both in the acuity of his scrutiny and the scope of his experiences, provides a truly unique adventure in the *selva de pedra*.

10

Drawing São Paulo

The Graphic Fiction of Fábio Moon
and Gabriel Bá

Big cities have a lot of layers—different buildings, different neighborhoods, different jobs, different people. All those differences create multiple story possibilities, as you are constantly in contact with all kinds of people in all kinds of situations. You can really experience the complexity of human existence and see how everyone is different.

⚙ Fábio Moon, *De:Tales: Stories from Urban Brazil* (qtd. in Shook 44)

So-called graphic fiction is intrinsically urban in nature, both in terms of the circumstances of its production and distribution and in its themes (see Smylie for basic information on the development of the graphic novel). This is because the graphic novel, like comic book art in general, relies heavily on the social and economic conditions of the city for its origins and popularity, and the narratives of graphic fiction exploit in particular the contradictions, discontinuities, and daunting complexities of negotiating survival and transcendence in the urban context. Or, to put it differently, the latter features of the urban context find in the graphic novel a particularly fertile medium of expression and interpretation. In this sense, graphic fiction is one more option for the staggering task of analyzing through art the always unresolved and confusing—and often barely perceived—issues of contemporary urban life.

Graphic fiction is derived from the far older tradition of comic book art, and if there is anything particularly distinctive about it, it is a fundamental self-image regarding the seriousness of its artistic enterprise and the complex interaction between the drawn image and the narrated story line. Whereas comic book art may often rely on image alone (but cannot rely on text alone) or be grounded in the four- or five-panel strip, graphic fiction aims, like film, for a sustained narrative via inseparable image and dialogue, with a complexity of image that may, in fact, be committed to capturing subtleties of lighting and sound which are also characteristic of film. The contrast is illustrative between the relatively simple line drawings of, say, Gary Trudeau's enormously influential subtleties of image—where the main thrust of the strip lies in its political and ideological commitments and the sophisticated humor with which the latter are pursued—and the enormously sophisticated and integrated deployment of image and text, narrative focus and point of view, ambiguity and interpretive layering found in Will Eisner's graphic novels of immigrant Jewish life in New York City,[1] Robert Crumb's quirky adventures, or Art Spiegelman's Pulitzer Prize–winning *Maus* (1986).

The distinction between comic book art and graphic fiction is tenuous at best: when do Trudeau's or Berkeley Breathed's isolated strips yield to a sustained narrative, especially when the former frequently employ narrative devices that provide some measure of continuity from one strip to another?[2] These narrative devices include not just recurring characters, principal and supporting, but also consistent plot lines, motifs, and concrete signs (such as Opus's closet of repressed memories and traumas in Breathed's eponymous strip). To be sure, all categories of cultural production are to a large extent arbitrary in nature: one recalls the comment, in the face of negative criticism about the structural nature of his novels, by 1990 Nobel Prize–winning Spanish author Camilo José Cela, that a "novel" is any text under whose title the author places in parentheses the designation "(novel)." Indeed, Spanish also has the phrase *novela gráfica* (it remains to be seen how extensively it is actually used and recognized). The term *romance gráfico* exists in Portuguese, but it is not used with much frequency, and texts that look like English-language-designated graphic novels are lumped in that language under the heading *quadrinhos*, which literally means "small pictures." The term *quadrinhos* refers first and foremost to the panels of the comic strip and, by extension, to the cartoon strip itself and isolated or interconnected manifestations of the strip (for strip, Portuguese uses *tira* or *tirinha* [*de quadrinhos*]; Cirne; Nadilson Manoel da Silva; Literatura).

Cartoon art is extensive in Brazil and, to judge by the material available in any major bookstore, such as the French-based mega-cultural centers, FNAC (pronounced "faynakey"), it is not for any lack of examples of graphic fiction that no distinguishing term has emerged in Portuguese. Antecedents in Brazil in the form of simpler comic books with a sustained narrative line—such as best sellers like *O amigo da onça* (The Jaguar's Friend), *Chiclete com banana* (Chewing Gum and Bananas), *Piratas do Tietê* (Pirates of the Tietê River), or *Asterix* in Portuguese translation and in image-based versions of classical works of fiction—[3]are to be found side by side in bookstores with the most contemporary titles of graphic fiction.

Of the practitioners of this growing field of urban art, the twin-brother team (born 1976) of Fábio Moon and Gabriel Bá has emerged as among the most creative. Their experience is now extensive and they have achieved one of the abiding goals of the Latin American writer—to be published in English.[4] *De:Tales: Stories from Urban Brazil* was published by Dark Horse Books in 2006: quite a milestone for Latin American graphic art, since the work of the most famous graphic artist in Spanish, Quino (Salvador Joaquín Lavado), creator of *Mafalda* (1966–73), which has been translated into dozens of languages, has yet to be made available in English.[5] Winners of many prizes for their extensive production (their Web site, www.uol.com.br/10paezinhos, lists twenty individual works and collaborations with others as well as their inclusion in nine anthologies of graphic fiction), the brothers have worked as a single team, both doing writing and illustrating, and each has worked separately, although, as is common with cartoon art, little of their work is available in formal library collections: OCLC's FirstSearch WorldCat contains only ten international entries for Fábio Moon and ten for Gabriel Bá; several of these entries represent their work together. As of this writing in late 2007, *De:Tales* has yet to be completely cataloged by any participating library.

For purposes of this discussion, I will be drawing from the strips written originally in English in *De:Tales: Stories from Urban Brazil* (2007), none of which are contained in the Portuguese collections I have been able to consult.

I have consulted three of the Moon-Bá collaborations in Portuguese available in São Paulo bookstores: *O girasol e a lua* (The Sunflower and the Moon; 2000); *Meu coração, não sei porque* (My Dear, I have No Idea Why; 2001); and *Mesa para dois* (Table for Two; 2006).[6] Although there is a general urban focus to these three volumes, one cannot say that they are really urban in nature. *O girasol e a lua* deals with amorous relationships and their sadistic undercurrent—for not knowing how to properly love, the protagonist, Kamarov, loses the object of his affections to an avatar of Jack the Ripper. The story is complex and often confusing, involving porous spaces, the darkness of the realm of the moon (*a lua*), and the assumed surname of one of the artists. Indeed, the authors' self-presentation at the end of the volume includes an image of Moon with a head in the shape of the moon; Bá (perhaps his chosen surname refers to the Egyptian hieroglyph that represents the human soul) is given the image of the talisman that saves the main character from death in the story; the cover of the book, however, has a man with the head of a sunflower holding the book, on whose cover appears the image of the moon: this book is supposedly Kamarov's first-person account. The story is urban in the sense that it takes place in a large city that seems to be New York—one can make out the silhouettes of the Empire State Building and the Chrysler Building on one panel (19; see also 66)—although the police cars in another read *"POLÍCIA"* (54); yet another panel has a hot dog vendor (48), and other police shields say "Police Department," while their uniforms say *"Polícia"* (55). This linguistic indeterminacy would indicate that no specific urban reality is pertinent here, and at best there is the general implication that sadistic sexual desire is urban in nature, which one has no reason to assume is necessarily the case, despite whatever urban-anchored dimension accompanies the Jack the Ripper figure.

Meu coração, não sei porque (also transcribed on the first numbered page of the narrative as *porquê*) is also about romantic love, but this time a love that triumphs. The use of children, who move in and out of adulthood, might give one the initial impression that this is children's literature. But the extensive and sophisticated deployment of the technique of narrative reversals projects the latter as objective correlatives for the difficulties of love in asserting its proper force in the lives of individuals. This makes for a very adult story, even if the postmodern reader might wish to take exception to the notion of eternal romantic love in its most elementarily heterosexist configurations.

Just as the first two volumes concern the difficulty of love, the most recent text I have been able to consult, *Mesa para dois,* also deals with a young couple who, out of timidity and mutual blindness, almost miss the chance to get together at a "table for two." There is also the utilization of a porous story within a story. Neither *Meu coração* nor *Mesa* are particularly urban, although both involve pictorial illustrations of the city as backdrop. Of minor functional interest is the breakdown of the city bus as the occasion of the chance encounter between the woman protagonist and the young man who almost does not end up sharing with her the table for two.

All three of these volumes are of considerable artistic value and contain original conceptions—if not in narrative language, in graphic representation—that include complex juxtapositions of circumstances and events. Of particular interest are lengthy dialogues broken up into chained balloons that crisscross each other and create the illusion of rapid interchanges by exchanging the position of the two character's textual balloons: A's is above B's head, and vice versa, with the balloon's tail indicating which enunciation belongs to which character.[7]

There is, however, a substantial increase in narrative sophistication between the foregoing texts and those contained in English translation in *De:Tales.* Moreover, all twelve are unquestionably urban in nature, in the sense that the material related has a direct and highly meaningful connection with the lived urban experience. I would now like to analyze in detail a selection of the strips from *De:Tales.*

One's attention is immediately drawn to the fact that, of the twelve strips in *De:Tales,* two are entitled "Reflections" and are basically duplicates of each other, with the exception that some of the graphic details are distributed differently or focused differently between them, and that the second version contains an additional detail in terms of an exchange between two men in the restroom of a bar. "Reflections" is built on the procedure of doubling a character so that we see him contemplating himself as someone else and engaging in conversation with himself over the question of whether he will engage seriously with a woman he met accidentally and caused to spill her drink.[8]

Self-contemplation, including talking with oneself either silently or openly, is likely a universal feature of human psychology. But it was the romantic notion of the doppelgänger that established as a literary technique, characteristically in poetry, but also in prose, the procedure of splitting one psychic unit—that is, one human subjectivity—into multiple voices, characters, and identities; this is not precisely the same thing as having dual/multiple personalities, although a cultural text may use this as one way of configuring the doppelgänger. Needless to say, from a typological point of view, one could construct many actual and possible variants. Perhaps the most famous example in Latin American literature of such a doubling is Jorge Luis Borges's short text "Borges y yo," which deals with the juxtaposition between the private, interior world of the writer and the public persona of that writer when he has achieved fame (from *El hacedor*; 1960)—it closes with the observation that "No sé cuál de los dos escribe esta página" (808).

Moon and Bá's strips are fairly consistent in the representation of the two artists as persons, either singly or in conjunction, in their strips. As correlated with the photograph on the back cover of the two brothers, the character with short dark hair in the strips can be identified as Moon (see page 79); the character with the longer, sometimes blond and fuller hair is Bá. Not that such identification is all that important, although it does have to do with the way in which some of the strips juxtapose two speaking characters whose graphic images are kept apart, while the strip under discussion splits one of them (the one I have identified as Bá) into two separately speaking individuals.

In this case, the character of the strip, after bumping into the woman, enters the restroom, and we see him making use of the facilities. Another man enters and installs himself in front of a neighboring urinal. Public urinals in Brazil, especially in places like bars, typically provide virtually no privacy, and male-male sociability may involve conversation between patrons, although eye contact is scrupulously avoided as a way of signalling that we are all men here but not seekers of men: it is one thing to acknowledge the other's presence, but quite another to cruise him, and restroom etiquette is quite formalized in this respect. Yet the reader is able to see what one urinating neighbor is able to see, which is the actual act of urination, penis size and configuration, and the fashion in which a man undertakes the act, including the details of his hygiene.[9] I dwell on these men's room details because the strip is built on the fact that the two men actually stare at each other (55 and 60), whereupon the first one exclaims, "You . . . You're me!" (56). The second man goes on to state, "No, I was you, but not anymore" (56 and 60). What emerges is that the second man is the first man before he bumps into the girl (this is the rather sexist word used in the text) in the bar and then apparently seeks refuge in the bathroom in order to avoid taking up with her in the sort of narrative characteristic of a chance bar encounter, where any pretext can serve to break the ice and inaugurate the narrative scheme that will result in the participants scoring with each other in any number of ways.

However, the second man goes on to state that he was the first man until the latter forewent the opportunity presented by the chance encounter and that he, the second man, represents the depression deriving from the self-contemplation of foolishly letting a hot opportunity pass. He concludes by saying, "And you have already changed. You are already other than me. Good luck" (56 and 61), implying that all the first man has to do is complete his business at the urinal, go back out to the bar, and follow through with the girl who must be waiting for him to return. Yet the first man hangs back in the bathroom, wondering what has just happened and whether he has had too much to drink. Meanwhile, the second man returns, drink in hand, a bit inebriated, but perhaps less because of the drink than because he made progress with the hot girl. When the first man exclaims, "You again?!" (57 and 62), the second man says that he must be mistaking him for someone else. This explicit disengagement between the two men, as the second man goes on to show in his comments, is based on the way in which the latter has scored the girl and shows that one must take advantage of such opportunities rather than hanging back, a radical example of which is retreating into the no-man's-land of the bathroom.

The role reversal of the doubles between one who is depressed over his timidity and one who may follow through, on the one hand, and one who has scored and one who has hung back and, as a consequence of waiting too long, lost his potential score to another, is confirmed by the way in which the second man states that he must get back to the bar before the woman moves on to another loser (58 and 62). That the second man in the second exchange accuses the first man of taking too long to urinate, wasting his time talking to others/talking to himself in the bathroom, adds another dimension to how ducking into the restroom may be a consequence of not really knowing what to do with a woman when the opportunity arises. This, in turn, is reinforced by the insinuation that talking to other men in the restroom, including watching them urinate, in fact signals a lack of sexual initiative, a crippling inability to even begin to follow through with women. This may not be a sign of (latent) homosexuality, but it is certainly a lapse in competency as regards the game of sexual encounter.[10]

Figures 10.1–10.3. Text and illustrations from *De:Tales*, © 2006 Fábio Moon and Gabriel Bá, pp. 29, 37, 52. Published by Dark Horse Comics, Inc.

Figure 10.4. "Reflections," from *De:Tales*, © 2006 Fábio Moon and Gabriel Bá, p. 56. Published by Dark Horse Comics, Inc.

Thus, "Reflections" becomes a very eloquent meditation on the so-called bar scene, which itself is often a metaphor for the difficulty, tenuousness, and potentially disastrous nature of the game of sexual encounter. The seediness of most bar scenes, even those that are ostentatiously upscale, a seediness duplicated and even augmented by the condition of the restrooms, may be read as an objective correlative of the precarious nature of human sexual commerce and, indeed, the way a chance encounter may for some be preferable to a meaningful, stable relationship. I do not think any moral judgment is intended here (either in the Moon/Bá strip or in my engagement with it), but only a neutral characterization of the realities of one sexual scene: the bar as both opportunity to quickly score and occasion for sexual timidity to quickly affirm itself. The material added to the second version involves the second man lecturing the first: "Oh no. I mean, yes I am you . . . / . . . But I didn't freak out about the whole me-before/me-now crap . . . / . . . And I went back to the party and got the girl" (62). In other words, as one says colloquially, "get on with the program and stop wasting time."

In this case, self-reflection, self-examination, and self-dialogue, rather than providing the opportunity for psychic growth—the idea examining life makes us emotionally stronger in dealing with the world—points toward a crippling weakness, at least as far as sexual commerce is concerned. In both versions, the man is alone with himself, contemplating the extent of his lost opportunity. In the first version, he looks almost longingly toward the exit from the bathroom, as though unable to cross back through it; in the second version, his face a mask of frozen surprise, he continues to engage in the act that displaces his sexual pursuit of the girl, holding (in an onanistic fashion) his penis and urinating. The stark lines of the drawings in both versions, including rapidly shifted perspectives on the characteristic space involved, contribute to a very harsh assessment of sexual incompetence.

The vast majority of the twelve narratives in *De:Tales* deal with the intertwined theme of spiritual alienation and tenuous and unstable love in the megalopolitan setting. This setting is never explicitly identified as São Paulo,[11] although to be sure, it is evidently so as a combined consequence of the identity of the authors, internal details resembling the physical appearance of that Brazilian city, and the way in which the language of signage and such is in Portuguese, rather than translated into English. São Paulo is certainly no more alienating than any other massive metropolitan area (although it is more polluted and dangerous than many others), and because of this it would be difficult to say that Moon and Bá are making any specific point grounded in the human geography of Brazil's—and South America's—largest city. Indeed, the general setting is middle class, such that no particular point is made about the texture of poverty that, in film for example, may be particularly evident in São Paulo, where in-migration from the outback contributes to a steadily expanding lumpen very much in visual evidence. The result is that the characters of the strips—recurrently Moon and Bá in the guise of their artistic alter egos—are very much the Everyman (and Everywoman) of urban (post)modernity.

One of the longest and most complex strips in the collection, "Late for Coffee," is a particularly ingenious representation of the fragility of human communication, including sexual relations (presumably the zenith of such communication), in the megalopolitan setting. Of immediate interest is the reference to coffee as the focal point for a (potentially) amorous encounter. While São Paulo is not as much a café society as Buenos Aires, the Brazilian city nevertheless does do honor to the Parisian model, where meeting for a coffee, accompanied perhaps by a dessert or a light lunch, is an integral part of the social fabric, and such a meeting between friends, lovers, and even business partners is acceptable and appropriate at any time of the day or night. Where in American culture an initial meeting might typically be for afternoon or evening drinks in a lounge catering to those seeking anonymity—a sexually encouraging environment, with a conjugation of elements propitious to such an endeavor (smoking, decor, lighting, music, a compliant barman, and other similarly disposed patrons)—the Parisian-style café is an open and often gleaming public place, where the high prices of the menu allow for the sort of lingering that meaningful conversation may require. However, one might know that in postmodern São Paulo, such cafés are typically located in shopping centers, and a good number of the customers are taking a break from shopping or waiting for a movie to begin (to be sure, there are also many traditional cafés that predate the shopping centers). But these clients do not interfere with those for whom the café is a good site for the opening moves in a tryst, even though in Vila Madalena a bar might be far more suggestive.

The title of this story has another important resonance for São Paulo society, and that is the factor of lateness. As South America's largest megalopolis, movement from point A to point B is often a staggering undertaking. It is not uncommon to hear of individuals traveling two hours to work, a trip requiring multiple transfers between train, subway, and the most common form of transportation, bus, with the last having to compete with all other vehicles on broad, modern streets that are, nevertheless, still inadequate. Since the economics of the city make it difficult for individuals to live close to where they work, the hours involved in transportation consume a good share of an individual's nonworking time. It is the pleasure of a planned meeting in a café, with all of the "time-out" possibilities that suggests, and the frustration of beating the clock in congested traffic that often assumes nightmare dimensions in São Paulo which contextualize this text, with the story by Moon and the art by Bá.

There is a certain fantastic quality about "Too Late for Coffee" that delightfully contrasts with the hard-edge material nature of life in the city, where the constant struggle for survival allows little room for flights of fancy. Yet in this strip the entire story is premised proleptically on a tardy scheduled encounter that was never programmed in the first place. The initial panels show the protagonist standing on the corner of Avenida Angélica and Avenida Higienópolis, in the upper-middle-class section of Higienópolis in the larger district of Consolação in central São Paulo, a circumstance that lends the story a particular privileged-class dimension.

As the protagonist examines his watch as though waiting for someone, an attractive young woman approaches and informs him that he is too late to fall in love with her. The protagonist reacts with some bewilderment, stating that he does not even know her and, therefore, by implication cannot be late for a scheduled appointment for love or anything else. The woman's cryptically answers, "so what?" (31). Part of the interest of the strip originates from the way in which the narrative disruption occasioned by the unexpected charge of the woman is represented by a series of images of their respective faces, as though the way they look at each other in this chance encounter is more important than the nonsensical dialogue between them. Certainly, this confirms the conventional wisdom that visual interaction may be more important than verbal in establishing intimate relationships, but it is also a correlative of the way in which the fanciful quality of their meeting is at odds with the fast clip of the city, such as we see in other stories in the collection: it is—and this is unquestionably another cliché of an intimate encounter—as if the world around them had receded (literally, for example, the street sign is less legible than it was when we first see the protagonist checking his watch).

There ensue the expected stages of negotiating a dialogue—as much physical as verbal—between them, as she invites him to share a taxi with her despite his protestations that he does not even know her name. As the protagonist grapples with how to make sense of this encounter, we see the lettering on her skimpy top, *Sein und Zeit* ("Being and Time"), the famous Heideggerian existentialist injunction about the necessary contextualization of being within a time frame, of existence as a historical proposition. This is certainly the case in "Late for Coffee." Although time in the chronological sense is here inverted, such that one is late even before an encounter has been (or could possibly have been) programmed, it is within the time frame set up by the woman's appearance that the sudden being of the two individuals, as far as their existence for each other in a reciprocal relationship, occurs. They do not exist for each other outside this chance encounter and the inverted chronology the woman sets in motion, a fact reflected in the detail that neither knows the other's name: in human societies, one's name (whether given or chosen) is the fundamental anchor of being, the mode by which one is most identified by the world.

In strips of a more romantic persuasion, the anomalies of the encounter here would work themselves out in favor of a positive relationship derived from the quirkiness of what, in retrospect, might be viewed as the woman's effective come-on toward a highly presentable man standing alone on an upscale street corner, checking his watch as though he had been stood up by someone else. In another fanciful twist, the taxi driver leaves them on a corner featuring both a café and a bar, and a conversation between them ensues as to whether it is too late in the day for a coffee or too early for a beer (37). Of course, in a Parisian-style café, either is available, but the disjunction is necessary here to represent the continued negotiation still necessary between the two. The protagonist suggests compromising by going across the street to an ice-cream parlor, and in response to the woman's question "What flavor?" responds, "ice cream comes in many flavors . . . / . . . just like life" (38). As they walk the neighborhood, eating their respective cones, the process of negotiating their relationship moves into high gear, revolving around what each is looking for. This exchange, with longer panels involving the segmented and interlocking dialogue balloons that are a Moon-Bá trademark, also allows for a suggestion of the panorama of the city: it is sustained in the garden city, the appropriate context for what may become an extended amorous idyll, rather than the hardscrabble cacophony that is the São Paulo experienced by the majority of its inhabitants.

Being, in terms of the engagement with the other, comes to a head when the woman is willing, after all, to confess that, "I'm not myself anymore. / Not without you" (42). When a black cat crosses their path, it provides the opportunity for further reflections that end, without an element of sappy sentimentality, on how the roots of trees intertwine are as though they were holding hands (45). All of this provides the authors with the opportunity to pursue the central setting of an idyll-in-the-making that would appear now to be a given fact, as the lovers kiss against the backdrop of the neighborhood (with a majestic tree prominently displayed). The movement of the graphic focus from the cityscape in general (which we briefly see when the two first sit side by side in the taxi) to privileged neighborhood streets—lined with lush vegetation in a way that is not really typical of most living spaces in São Paulo (which may, however, have the backdrop of distant green hills)—enhances the fantastic quality of the story. It is, therefore, unsurprising that the idyll cannot last, cannot be definitively forged. The physical reality of the city reemerges with the street sign announcing Rua Purpurina, in the equally upscale area to the west of Consolação, Vila Madalena. A bird perches on the street sign, and the expression on the separate faces of the would-be lovers reveals that they see it as more of a bad omen than the black cat. The woman announces she must leave, saying, "You're late. / You lost your chance to fall in love with me" (51). When he asks what she feels within her heart, she says, "A memory" (51), and walks on.

In the final panel of the strip, the protagonist is seen, his back to the reader, facing the broad panorama of the complex built environment of the cityscape: skyscrapers, phone lines, light posts, intersections, the extended descending slope of the street. Where in the opening panel we see him from the front in a circumscribed neighborhood space, he is now cast, so to speak, upon the ocean of the city. "Late for Coffee" is proleptic in the sense that the finale of the story is announced from the outset, and the narrative works towards its confirmation. A more romantic narrative would put the world back together in such a way that, whatever initial reverses may have been (and here, as has been noted, there is the literal reverse of cause-and-effect chronology), love triumphs in the end, with the entire setting devolving into a pathetic fallacy that supports the amorous denouement. But there is nothing romantic about the way in which Moon and Bá view life in São Paulo, and in this sense the privileged dimension of these two would-be lovers is ultimately quite ironic: a memory of possible love, but never its embodiment in reality, is the lot of the urban Brazilian. In this sense, "Late for Coffee" only confirms the sense of loss and despair found in other stories in the *De:Tales* collection.[12]

Conclusion

As a city fast approaching twenty million inhabitants, there are many different São Paulos, and it is unlikely that anyone today could write a comprehensive analysis of the city and its cultural production. The day is long gone
of viewing cultural production as: very much circumscribed regarding class
interests and themes; written from a masculinist (and heteronormative)
point of view; based on a homogeneous value system that, while perhaps
never specifically Catholic in a sectarian way, most assuredly assumes a
"Western" commitment that excludes as much indigenous culture as it does
non-Christian cultures such as the Jewish or the Japanese.

Two threads that can be called something like a social alignment dominate the chapters that make up this book. Against the backdrop of a culture
that is the consequence of the impressive growth of a São Paulo intransi-
gently committed to the project of political and economic modernization
(major traces of which can be seen in the photography of Claude Lévi-
Strauss), I have chosen, in the first place, to emphasize culture that promotes proletarian interests, without writing necessarily from a populist or
Marxian perspective. One major reason for this is quite clear: São Paulo is
a laboratory of immigrant culture and, while not all immigrants belonged
to the proletariat, the vast majority did, and they populated the factories
and workplaces and peopled the streets. Patrícia Galvão's transition from
bourgeois privilege to the Communist Party and her writing on the lives
of textile works (among others who move through *Parque industrial*) is
complemented by the interest in the street of an upper-class immigrant like
Hildegard Rosenthal and the interest in marginal human types of a working-class immigrant like Madalena Schwartz. Concomitantly, Mazzaropi's
films focus on the question of internal proletarian immigrants within the

province of São Paulo, depicting the enormous contrast between rural lives and those of the modern megalopolis. Fábio Moon and Gabriel Bá give an immediate feel of the complexity of urban life in their graphic fiction, where, by the end of the twentieth century, rural and citified, native-born and immigrants, marginal and privileged have melded into a continuous cityscape. Eduardo Emílio Fenianos traversed the streets of the city in a far more ambitious way than Rosenthal ever could have, while filmmakers like Luís Sérgio Person, Wilson Barros, and Beto Brant followed in the founding footsteps of the directors of the 1929 film *São Paulo, sinfonia da metrópole*, Adalberto Kemeny and Rudolf Rex Lustig, who were well aware that the most important stories of the city were to be told in the streets and based on the lives of everyday people.

The second thread that runs through this book is that of gender. While the material does not permit me enough of an opportunity to pursue questions of queer lives, they do peek through in Galvão's writing (the very fact that *Parque industrial* defies the masculinist view of the world, aside from elements of lesbianism that also appear) and in the photography of transvestites that was a major interest of Schwartz's. Director Wilson Barros's "angels of the night" have much that is queer about them, although I pass up the opportunity to investigate queer elements in *Paulicéia desvairada*, given the fact that Mário de Andrade's homosexuality is now an open fact.

Of greater interest to me has been the matter of feminist cultural production in São Paulo, and how the emergence of such a perspective is a significant component of a modernism that challenges the patriarchal culture of the city's traditions prior to the early part of the twentieth century. Patrícia Galvão is absolutely crucial here, and recent interest in her writing is recognition of her great iconic importance.

Galvão arguably had a feminist consciousness to one degree or another, unlike immigrant women such as Rosenthal or Schwartz, although their cultural interests (very much Jewish in the latter's case, while only circumstantial in the former's) led them away from the patriarchal in ways that have important connections with feminist principles. And if Niemeyer's Copan project is a monument to the masculinist city (the city of the Noah of the title of her collection of stories set in that building), Regina Rheda engages very much in a feminist deconstruction of sexist assumptions of lived space. By contrast, and let us concede in an unconscious fashion, Fenianos's journey through the streets of São Paulo is driven by sexist assumptions, a primary one of which is a man's ownership of the city. This seems equally true of the virtually all-male world of Moon's and Ba's graphic fiction. None of this production provides a reliable sociological record of the permanence of patriarchal primacy or the effective challenges of feminism as far as the history of São Paulo is concerned. But it does demonstrate important issues raised by the project of modernity in that city.

Certainly, other important issues relating to the city could be dealt with. One that intrigues me only shows through obliquely here, and that is the division of geographic space, especially the west-east divide that separates the more affluent western neighborhoods from the more proletarian ones, which absorbed humble immigrants and provided them employment in an extensive network of factories and the like.[1] Another topic that could also be foregrounded is that of the Avenida Paulista, a north-south dividing line reinforced by the Avenida's importance as the major financial locus for South America's economy. It also appears obliquely in Lévi-Strauss's photography, in Barros's film, and, in a very important way, in Andrade's poetry.

These and other meaningful lived spaces in São Paulo will provide the opportunity for much further work on the city and its cultural production. I see this text, then, as only an initial sampler.[2]

Notes

Introduction

Epigraph translations

I am not led; I lead.

When all is said and done, São Paulo was not a city of blacks, or whites, or mestizos; nor of foreigners or Brazilians; nor was it American, or European, or native; nor was it industrial, despite the growing number of factories, nor an agricultural mart, despite the crucial importance of coffee; nor was it tropical or subtropical; nor was it yet modern, although it had more of a past. That city arose suddenly and unexpectedly, like a huge mushroom after the rain, and it was an enigma for its own inhabitants, who were perplexed in their attempt to understand it as they might, while at the same time they struggle so as not to be devoured.

Author's note: All translations are my own unless otherwise noted.

1. Although there is much in the way of anecdotal material about Italians in Brazil and a smattering of research monographs, there is no comprehensive examination of the subject yet published.

2. In an enormously suggestive essay, Justin Reed, after discussing the way in which so-called Third World cities have emulated metropolitan models, details the ways in which a city like São Paulo exemplifies urban features now being emulated by so-called First World metropolitan centers. As the Brazilian philosopher Nelson Brissac Peixoto states, with particular reference to São Paulo, "The large Latin American cities have become battlefields. A war is being waged for the occupation of entire urban areas, and for control over infrastructure and public spaces." ("The Latin American Megacities" 233).

3. São Paulo's current transformation is into a "third world metropolis in a globalized economy," according to the abstract in English of Taschner and Bógus's discussion of the socio-spatial segregation of the city (87), whereby "the wealthy [are concentrated] in central rings, thus making the periphery the domain of the poor" (87).

4. São Paulo is also particularly important in this period for its architectural

developments, beginning with the Edifício Martinelli, Latin America's first skyscraper, inaugurated in 1929. Lévi-Strauss's photography, discussed in this study, shows a particular interest in capturing the architectural growth of the city. See Segawa on São Paulo on the cusp of *Modernismo*.

5. Andrade's important role in the Departamento de Cultura is examined by Dassin in her "Capítulo 6. Vida y cultura."

6. Already the important Swiss French-language vanguard poet Blaise Cendrars had spent six months in São Paulo, arriving in 1924. According to Sevcenko ("São Paulo"), Cendrars was particularly impressed with the exemplary dynamism of São Paulo, which was riding the crest of the bullish international economy of the early 1920s. In one of his several poems about São Paulo, Cendrars captures the mechanical intensity of the city:

"Klaxons Électriques"
Ici on ne connaît pas la Ligue du Silence
Comme dans tous le pays neufs
La joie de vivre et de gagner de l'argent s'exprime par la voix des klaxons et de la
    pétarde de pots d'échappement ouverts. (Cendrars, *Au Coeur du monde* 62).

7. Gabara discusses the importance of photography for the vanguard period in Brazil during the twenties and thirties: "Photography played a central role in the modernist production of both images of popular culture—the folkloric and the masses—welding together these two faces of the popular and revealing their powerful influence on the formulation of literature, art, and theory" (73). It is regrettable that Gabara does not go on to also characterize the importance of film in the same vein, although, in all fairness, one should note that the popular influence of film came about a decade later.

8. While he does not discuss in any detail the relationship between Macunaíma and São Paulo, Rosenberg provides an excellent analysis of the novel as an allegory of the contradictions of modernism and *antropofagia*, a major proposition of Brazilian modernism, whereby national culture was to be the result of the cannibalistic consumption of European culture. São Paulo is, for the anachronistic indigenous protagonist, the emblem of "forward acceleration" (85); reference is also made, in terms of the adventures of Macunaíma as he sets forth from his home "in the depths of the virgin forest" (Rosenberg's English translation of the opening line of the novel [81]), to the "tumult of São Paulo as paradigmatic of modern urban life" (77).

9. Mention might also be made of Alice Brill (1920–), a German Jew who has spent her life as a photojournalist and artistic photographer, capturing many important images of São Paulo as well. It is important to note that many photographers in São Paulo in the 1930s and 1940s were refugees from German Nazism.

10. The documentary is not actually discussed in any detail in my essay on film, since it was unavailable for viewing, although some information exists about a project to release a new edition of it. It is generally acknowledged that Kemeny and Lustig were inspired by Walter Ruttmann's *Berlin: Die Sinfonie der Großstadt* (1927). Kemeny and Lustig were likely Jews (we know that both were from Hungary), although Jews were never prominent producers and directors in Brazilian filmmaking, at least to the same

extent they were in the United States, Argentina, and Mexico. See Gatti's extensive summary of the documentary.

11. The *dérive* is a concept of urban French culture and refers to the practice of leisurely strolling through the city.

12. Lúcia Sá published in 2007 an excellent book comparing São Paulo and Mexico City as megalopolises; this she does by an examination of important culture texts. However, her approach is more nearer to sociology than cultural studies, as revealed by the lack of any extensive reference to cultural theory (except for Walter Benjamin) and the fact that the Library of Congress assigns a class number in sociology (there is extensive reference to important urban scholars like Henri Lefebvre, David Harvey, and Michel de Certeau). But Sá does examine a significant range of cultural production from the two cities, and the only important duplication is her excellent description of the Fenianos book that I examine in my chapter devoted to *Expedições Urbenauta*. Since half the book covers Mexican literature about Mexico City, barely eighty pages are devoted to São Paulo, which is placed second in her title. However, Sá provides solid discussions of cultural phenomena that I do not examine, such as fiction, contemporary poetry, rap music, and graffiti art. Few of the authors in this study are mentioned except in passing. I state this not as a criticism of Sá's excellent monograph, but to underscore that there is no duplication between the two efforts.

CHAPTER 1. Mário de Andrade

Author's note: This essay appeared originally in *Iberoamericana* 19 (2005), 27–40. It is used here with the permission of the editors.

1. The original orthography of the title was *Paulicea desvairada*.

2. Actually, Andrade had published *Há uma gota de sangue em cada poema* (There is a Drop of Blood in Each Poem) in 1917. However, this volume is considered a youthful exercise in imitation of the Parnassians and is not included, for example, in the edition of *Poesias completas* [sic] from which I am quoting. The latter, however, appears as Vol. II of the "Obras completas de Mário de Andrade," provided in a list facing the half title page; Vol. I is identified as "Obra imatura," one of whose three components is *Há uma gota*.

3. The poetry of Gregório de Matos (1636–96?), as gathered in *Crônica do viver baiano seiscentista* (Chronicle of Life in Bahia in the Seventeenth Century), is not about the city of Bahia, but rather about human society in the context of court life.

4. "My feet are lacerated by the thorns of the sidewalks . . ." (Andrade, *Hallucinated City* 69; all translations in this chapter are from this edition). The ellipses in this and subsequent quotes are part of the poetic texts; indeed, the use of ellipses is integral to the *"polifonia poética"* (poetic polyphony) Andrade champions in his "Prefácio" (paragraph 36 [69]).

5. Further page references to poems and lines of poetry are to be understood to refer to this edition unless otherwise stated.

6. The paragraphs are not numbered in the original edition nor in all critical editions, but they are in the one I am citing from.

7. In my opinion, to write modern art never means to represent modern life through its externals: automobiles, movies, asphalt. If these words frequent my book, it is not because I think that I write "modern" with them; but since my book is modern, these things have their place in it (16).

8. Paulicéia is an alternative, and evidently more poetic, name for the city of São Paulo; it may well be that Andrade uses it here in an ironic fashion, since he is doing something very different in his poems from evoking the poetic images associated with a name such as this.

9. The Brazilian language is one of the richest and most sonorous. And it possesses that really splendid sound *ão*.

10. An articulation that often results in the charming overgeneralization that "Portuguese is just like Romanian," since the latter is the only other Romance language to have developed that phone, as is represented by the circumflexed vowel (an unrounded high back vowel; unrounded [u]) in the very name of the language: rumâno. However, where [ï] is a phoneme in Romanian, it is strictly an allophone—stressed /ã/ in contact with following unstressed /o/—in Portuguese, a process of regressive dissimilation: the unrounding of /ã/ in contact with the following rounded /o/, pronounced, in any case, as [u], since progressive assimilation nasalizes the post-/ã/ vowel, which, since it is unstressed is raised from [o] to [u] (thus, this does not involve progressive assimilation to the high [ï], since it would be raised irrespective of whatever vowel or consonant proceeded it). In short, Andrade is correct in saying that this is a very distinctive—and, indeed, complex—detail of Brazilian Portuguese phonology.

11. Grammar appeared after languages were organized. It so happens that my unconscious knows nothing of the existence of grammars or of organized languages. And my unconscious, like Sir Lyricism, is a smuggler. . . . (16)

12. Pronouns? I write Brazilian. If I use Portuguese orthography, it is because it furnishes me an orthography without altering the result. (16)

13. Gomes (27–33), for example, refers to the linguistic originality of *Paulicéia desvairada*, but like most critics he devotes his attention to the analysis of *Macunaíma* as presenting the best corpus for understanding Andrade's commitment to the "gramatiquinha da fala brasileira" (Little Grammar of Brazilian Speech); see also Proença. Both are examples of microlinguistic analysis—Gomes more grammatical and syntactical features, Proença more lexical ones; neither, regrettably, gets into issues of linguistic ideology, as does Pinto in her critical edition of Andrade's *A gramatiquinha*. Interestingly enough, she dates the writer's interest in the elaboration of the *Gramatiquinha* from 1922, the same year in which *Paulicéia desvairada* was published (Pinto 33). The most extensive treatment, however, of the language of *Paulicéia desvairada* is Roig's very detailed stylistic analysis. Again, this is more in the vein of a microanalysis of a specific poetic corpus than an essay on linguistic ideology.

14. It is notable that Jack Tomlins's translation of *Paulicéia desvairada* into English states that it is "translated from the Brazilian."

15. São Paulo! tumult of my life . . . (21).

16. Harlequinate! . . . Diamond tights . . . Gray and gold . . . (21).

17. Horrid cities! (25).

18. I insult the bourgeois! (37).

19. Down and away! Boo! Away with the good bourgeois gentleman! (39).

20. My London of the fine mists! / High summer. The ten thousand million roses of São Paulo. / There is a snow of perfumes in the air. / It is cold, very cold . . . / And the irony of the little seamstresses' legs / looking like ballerinas . . . / The wind is like a razor / in the hands of a Spaniard Harlequinate! . . . / Two hours ago the Sun burned through. / Two hours from now the Sun will burn through. // A St. Boob goes by, singing beneath the plantain trees, / a tra la la . . . The city police! Jail! / Are jails necessary / to preserve civilization? / My heart feels very sad . . . / While the gray of the goose-fleshed streets / chats a lament with the wind . . . // My heart feels very glad! / This cocky little chill / makes me feel like smiling! // And I walk on. And go on feeling / with the agitated alacrity of the winter chill, / something like the taste of tears in my mouth . . . (35).

21. Lima insists that Andrade's poetry is characterized by the "anonimato da subjetividade" (the anonymity of subjectivity; 43). It is undeniable that the poet's vision of São Paulo in *Paulicéia desvairada* is markedly subjective, but this does not attenuate the often very specific material presence of the city in the collection.

22. My feet are lacerated on the thorns of the sidewalks . . . / Hygienopolis! . . . The Babylons of my base desires . . . / Houses in the noble style . . . Bonanzas in tragedies . . . / But the night is all bridal veil in the moonlight" (69).

23. that enchanted spectacle of the Avenue! (47).

24. Anthill where all bite and devour one another! (51).

25. Oh! This supreme pride in existing São Paulo-wise!!! (75). Actually, "Paissagem No. 4" is not the last text in *Paulicéia desvairada*, although it is the last free-standing poem, at least in the conventional sense of poetry. The volume closes with 254 verses of short poems representing diverse Paulista voices, framed by prose statements, all constituting "As enfibraturas do Ipiranga (oratorio profano)." The setting for this oratory is the esplanade of the Teatro Municipal, which is where the Semana de Arte Moderna took place in February 1922. Avenida Ipiranga is a major avenue that passes along the south side of the Praça da República, a few blocks away from the Teatro Municipal (see Nunes on this composition as emblematic of the Semana de Arte Moderna).

CHAPTER 2. The Feminization of Social Space in Patrícia Galvão's *Parque industrial*

Epigraph translation

The streetcar is stuffed. With department store girls. Receptionists. Stock boys. The whole population of the most exploited, of the least exploited. To their slum houses in the immense proletarian city, Braz.—Patrícia Galvão, *Industrial Park* (16)

Epigraph note: Although Tosta does not mention Galvão's novel in his examination of the *bonde* in the literature of Brazilian modernism, he does mention Oswald de

Andrade's "Poema à Pagu," in which he imagines taking the streetcar with his pregnant wife (45).

Author's note: This essay originally appeared in *Brasil/Brazil* 19.33 (2005–06), 23–46. It is used here with the permission of the editors. Unless otherwise noted, all translations are from the University of Nebraska 1993 edition of *Industrial Park*.

1. Her son, however, notes that Galvão repudiated this nickname in 1940, upon her resignation from the Communist Party (Ferraz, "Introdução" 3).

2. Galvão, however, is accorded an excellent entry in Melo's 1954 *Dicionário de autores paulistas* (250). This is particularly significant, since the *Dicionário* is an official publication of the city's IV Centennial.

3. See Wolfe concerning worker history in São Paulo; what is important particularly is his inclusion of women's experiences.

4. These two epigraphs have disappeared from the Mercado Aberto/ EDUFS Car edition (I have at hand the third printing, dated 1994); thus I will quote them from the 1981 facsimile edition; both epigraphs are retained in the Jackson and Jackson translation.

5. THE STATISTICS AND THE HISTORY OF THE HUMAN TRIBE THAT MAINTAINS THE INDUSTRIAL PARK OF SÃO PAULO AND THAT SPEAKS THE LANGUAGE OF THIS BOOK IS TO BE FOUND, UNDER THE DOMAIN OF CAPITALISM, IN THE JAILS AND TENEMENT, IN THE HOSPITALS AND MORGUES (my translation).

6. Another study might concern itself with the stylistic texture of Galvão's language in the novel, its use of certain women-centered metaphors, the emphasis on highly visual and telegraphic (perhaps futuristic) vocabulary and syntax, and the very effective colloquial register of many passages. Such a study would be substantially different from my examination here of language as social discourse, both feminist and contestational.

7. In an attempt to understand why *Parque industrial* was for so long ignored by Brazilian literary history, Hilary Owen focuses on how the novel depicts social discourses that become allegedly discarded because of how Galvão examines women's issues in a way that distances them from the patriarchal and family-oriented ideology of social movements in Brazil.

8. Galvão is unsympathetic to homosexuality in other writings as well, such as the journalistic note "Saibam ser maricons" (Learn How to Be Fags), where the context makes it evident that she is speaking out against one paradigm of bourgeois decadence routinely attacked by the left in general and the rhetoric of the Communist Party in particular (for an overview of research on this topic, see Wilkerson). Yet, it is important to note that Galvão is unquestionably attacking effeminate male homosexuals, not the "masculine" ones (Unruh points that out emphatically in her comments on the essay, *Performing Women* 207). Oswald de Andrade's homophobia, attributed to his links with the Communist Party, is mentioned in passing by Trevisan (278).

9. It is interesting to note that in Loos's characterization of the naturalistic features of Azevedo's novel, although she refers to how "most of the characters . . . are obsessed with sex" (47), no mention is made of lesbianism in the novel.

10. All page references to *Parque industrial* are, unless otherwise noted, to the 1994 Mercado Aberto/EDUFSCar edition.

11. For an excellent analysis of the relationship between modernization and gender inequality in the workplace, see Besse. Unfortunately, Besse does not take *Parque industrial* into account as one form of documentary proof of her analysis; Daniel examines the documentary dimensions of the novel.

12.—Loafers! That's why nothing gets done! You tramp!

Bruna awakens. The youth lowers his head in disgust. You have to keep your mouth shut!

That's the way it is, in all the proletarian sectors, every day, every week, every year! (9)

13.—Let's go to the latrine to talk. The girl asks:

—May I go outside?

—Again?

—I'm taking a laxative.

The walls above the tile mosaic record the laborer's complaints. Each corner is a tabloid of insults against the bosses, managers, foremen, and comrades who sold out. There are ugly names, cartoons, social teachings, fingerprints.

In the dirty latrines the girls spend a joyful minute stolen from the slave labor (10).

14. How could anyone dare record the language of the streets? How could anyone dare, after all, exalt in that way the lot of women?

15.—What's the meaning of this word 'fascism'? (10).

16. Madame runs again to accompany her customer, who jumps into an automobile with a mustachioed young man [. . . .] One of them mutters, in a twitching of needle-pricked fingers that crumple the fabric.

—And they say we're not slaves! (15–16).

17. a few lazy tramps (15).

18. Contemporary with Galvão's novel is the poem by the Argentine, Evaristo Carriego on "La costurerita que dio aquel mal paso" (The Little Seamstresses Who Took a Wrong Turn): "Daba compasión / verla aguantar esa maldad insufrible / de las compañeras, itan sin corazón!" (It made you sad / to see her taking the insufferable evil / of such heartless fellow workers!) (132–33).

19. See the early twentieth-century brothel photographs published by Ava Vargas; see also Lobanov-Rostovsky.

20. The following day, a flashy guy takes her to a brothel in Braz.

—Dressed like that no one will want you.

He opens her blouse, tears her brassiere and pushes her toward the windows by the door.

In twenty-five identical houses, in twenty-five identical doors, there are twenty-five identical pathetic women.

She remembers that with the other seamstresses she mocked the women of Ipiranga Street. She feels repugnance, but she cowers. Between tears, she does as the others.

—Hey! Sweetheart! Come here! I'll give you my button . . .

Little by little her erotic vocabulary enlarges (46).

21. The entry of a luxury automobile excites the collective houses. Eleonora steps out, elegant, constrained.

—Matilde! I got your address. How awful, you living here . . .

—What do you want? Momma lost her job. She's getting old.

—She's pretty as ever, you idiot! If she wanted to live with me! (62).

22. Matilde arrives, pale in her extremely modest outfit. Her Russian beret hides her tender eyes [. . . .]

Ming serves aperitifs.

Her childish little smile disappears little by little with the kisses. Ming left. Matilde was undressed and loved (63).

23. The issue of lesbianism in *Parque industrial* deserves a separate treatment, one that would take into account the history of the author's relations with other women (the facts of which are only known sketchily and are more insinuated than demonstrated, as in Bengell's film) and her writings as a whole. Such a study could also take into account the asymmetry between male and female homosexuality: although the latter might also be viewed as exemplifying bourgeois decadence (as in the case of the seduction of the shop worker by a wealthy woman in *Parque industrial*), lesbianism needs also to be understood as a manifestation of a woman's solidarity with other women, as it is in Adrienne Rich's famous postulation of the "lesbian continuum" and Monique Wittig's assertions to the effect that lesbianism refers to an opting out of the patriarchal, heterosexist paradigm (13). Galvão's creation in the fictional imaginary of a virtually all-female social space figures as a form of lesbian separatism, one that was impossible in her social reality (that is, the Brazil of the 1930s). It is important to note that Bengell herself is an out lesbian. She is mentioned by Bottassi and Fernades, although Galvão is not. Galvão is also absent from Mott's extensive account of lesbian writing in Brazil. Bengell, it might be noted, engaged in the first lesbian love scene in Brazilian film with Odete Lara in Walter Hugo Khouri's *Noite vazia* (Empty Night, 1954). Previously, she had performed the first fully female nude scene in Ruy Guerra's *Os cafajestes* (The Jerks, 1962).

24.—You didn't have this apartment or these delicious drinks . . . (63).

25. The tiny voice of the revolutionary rises in the flushed faces of the rally.

—Comrades! We can't remain silent in the midst of this struggle! We must be at the side of our men in the streets, as we are when we work in the factory. We have to fight together against the bourgeoisie that drain our health and turn us into human rags! They take from our breast the last drop of milk that belongs to our little ones to live on champagne and parasitism! (80).

26. The police advance, fire. A small woman lies on the ground, crying out with her leg shattered. Her blond Lithuanian hair flows smoothly over her sweaty forehead. Resembling Rosinha (100–101).

27. Braz of Brazil! Braz of the whole world (88).

28. It is important to note the role played by women in urban social movements in São Paulo. Corcoran-Nantes takes special note of women's space and women's voice in these movements. Paoli provides an overview of the history of the Brás and Mooca industrial districts.

CHAPTER 3. Appendix: Patrícia Galvão

Epigraph translation

Because I will not be able to count the bursts of laughter that I'm already practicing.

Author's note: This essay appeared originally in *Letras femeninas* 33.3 (2007), 73–86. It is used here with the permission of the editors. All translations from this text are my own.

1. Galvão, of course, would have been too young to actually intervene in the founding activities of the Semana, although she seems to have been involved in its ongoing project well before the end of the 1920s. See the chronology of her life provided by Ferraz in his introduction to the edition of her *Safra macabra*. Earl Fitz explicitly recognizes Galvão's relationship to the so-called modernist revolt (183–85), and connects that important event to the emergence of women writers in Brazil in the mid-twentieth century.

2. The American feminist scholar Vicky Unruh has written of Galvão's relationship to modernism, along with that of another overlooked and often-maligned female writer, the Argentine Norah Lange.

3. For example, there is no entry for her in the electronic database, DEDALUS, which encompasses the libraries of the Universidade de São Paulo, considered the premier academic institution in the country. Nor is she mentioned in the three-volume *História da literatura brasileira*, which, although published in Portugal, involved extensive collaboration by Brazilian scholars, and she is given only two passing references in the volume dedicated to Brazil in Roberto González Echevarría and Enrique Pupo Walker's *The Cambridge History of Latin American Literature*.

4. Bengell, in her film, insinuates a subsequent erotic relationship between Galvão and Tarsila, although there appears not to be much in the way of independent verification of such a biographical detail. Bengell also insinuates a relationship between Galvão and the American-Brazilian singer Elsie Houston, who comes to Galvão's rescue when she is released from prison in France, where she was being held on account of her antifascist militancy there; Bengell plays the part of Houston in *Eternamente Pagu*.

5. In reality, the Library of Congress's 1945 first edition appears not to bear Ferraz's name, as it is not part of the cataloguing record. The OCLC first search record for the first edition does, however, include Ferraz's name, although the 1959 edition, along with Ferraz's single-authored novel *Doramundo*, does give due credit to both authors. OCLC reports that only seven copies of the first edition are located in cooperating institutions worldwide, and only twenty-four report owning copies of the 1959 reedition.

6. I went around lonely at the time.

7. The fact is that at that time I didn't understand the setting. I remember that I considered myself very good and everyone thought I was bad. The other children's mothers did not want me playing with their daughters, and one day I was even thrown out of Álvaro George's house, the one who owned the bookstore, because he didn't want me to have any contact with his children. Only my sisters were allowed to go. I was never able to perceive my perversity. They had made me that way and placed me within strange walls. I went around lonely at the time.

8. The first distantly conscious fact of my life was the handing over of my body.

9. I was never sexually precocious.

10. I don't know, Geraldo, if you can understand what I felt that night [when Oswald sought out my body for the first time, after Rudá was born]. Oswald went overboard. And I felt repugnance for him. Repugnance and hatred for the deception that wounded me. I felt the sexual act to be based on an eternal repugnance. I would never again be able to tolerate Oswald and I felt like I would never again be able to tolerate masculine contact [.... And I thought] about that man lying beside me, aiding the sexual act with an offer of machos.

11. Pace Andrea Dworkin's legendary assertion, in her book *Intercourse*, that all (hetero)sexual intercourse is basically a variation on the rape of women by men.

12. I felt his arms close around me, but I also felt everything was useless. There was something obscene about contact with him. I still yielded a lot on this contact, but I did not hide my repugnance. Oswald continued to collect sexual organs. His mouth made me think continually about the female organ that I was obliged to kiss (114).

13. A truly lesbian trope here would be, precisely, for a woman to report a repudiation of the man's bearded mouth in favor of osculation with the female genitals, along with perhaps the allusion to the former as a ludicrous simulation of the latter.

14. There is another way of construing this passage: Galvão may be seeing imposed on Andrade's face the genitals of other women with whom he has been and whose bodies she is forced to kiss through kissing him. This would be consistent with her complaints not only regarding Andrade's infidelities, but also his indiscriminate sexual conduct. I am grateful to my colleague Isis Costa McElroy for this line of thought.

15. It was with a tone of infinite distaste that R. attacked what he designated as degrading sentimentalism. And with the full intent to hurt me he uttered these words: "And what if your son were to die today?"

I barely felt myself burning and I managed to reply:

"The children of the workers are dying of hunger every day. What is important is our task right now."

Why did I speak in this fashion? I felt my feelings were betrayed. I was also beginning to form attitudes. I hated myself for my stupidity and my dishonesty with myself.

16. I think that's asking too much of revolutionary women. I'm no prostitute.

17. A family treasure that a son must pass on in the future to his son and so on.

18. An appropriation, most assuredly, which I in turn appropriate by repeating it in the text of this essay.

19. One cannot help but think of parallels to be drawn as regards the entwined fates of Octavio Paz and Elena Garro in Mexican letters. However, there is no evidence that Andrade set out to destroy Galvão's reputation as Paz is reputed to have done in the case of Garro, nor did Garro, despite all that, ever experience the oblivion that Galvão did, no matter how benign Andrade may have been with regard to her literary fate.

CHAPTER 4. Downtown in São Paulo
with Hildegard Rosenthal's Camera

Epigraph translation

Because of various circumstances, the trove of Hildegard Rosenthal's photographs becomes a very useful instrument for researchers concerned about how the city of São Paulo was utilized and experienced by its protagonists, the everyday citizens.

Author's note: This essay originally appeared in the *Luso-Brazilian Review* 42.1 (2005), 118–35. It is used with the permission of the University of Wisconsin Press. It also appeared in *Revista tecnologia e sociedade* 1 (2005), 41–58.

1. Morse's history of São Paulo remains the definitive source on this spectacular growth; see also Font, who concentrates particularly on the economy of São Paulo. The third São Paulo that Toledo (*São Paulo*) examines is the one photographed by Rosenthal and Lévi-Strauss (the first and second, respectively, are the colonial city and the early, pre-1922, republican one).

2. See Warren Dean on the industrialization of the city.

3. Yet, the blithe pro-business spirit of São Paulo has not gone unchallenged, and Pochmann examines how the labor structure of the city actually creates un- and under-employment. This is a misery and poverty that is highlighted, for example, in recent Paulistano fiction and film, but hardly in Rosenthal's photography, which remains firmly entrenched in the boosterism of the period. Abreu et al., however, note that the period of 1937–42, precisely that of Rosenthal's photography, was one of economic stagnation (223). This makes her veritable boosterism all the more impressive. Kossoy records Rosenthal's "rápida viagem pela propaganda [comercial]"—the impressive list of slogans, brand names, and commercial icons that appear in her photos (27; a rapid trip through advertising).

4. The casual public dress of the citizens of Rio de Janeiro has often been contrasted with the formal dress of those of São Paulo, but the relaxation of dress codes in contemporary life and the blurring of distinctions between the two cities brought about by internal migration has led to less differentiation than was evident in the 1930s. This is also true with regard to the greater presence of people of color in Rio at that time and the very clear whitening effect of the massive European migration experienced in São Paulo (pace the accompanying Japanese presence in the latter).

5. Foster, *Social Realism* examines Argentine socialist realism/proletarian writing; I have found no similar study for Brazilian literature.

6. As do texts of a social realist stamp by Spanish-language writers, like the Peruvians César Vallejo and Ciro Alegría, the Colombian José Eustasio Rivera, and the Guatemalan Miguel Ángel Asturias.

7. See Abreu et al. on industrialization and import substitution in Brazil.

8. In general, Rosenthal's images capture the modern masculinist city, and this is an important political reality in itself. However, one set of images involves the new Estádio Municipal (Municipal Stadium, also known as Pacaembu), which is very much influenced by 1930s fascist-style architecture, a fact confirmed by the geometric display

of human bodies (that is, the index of [the attempt to construct] a strictly regulated society) arranged in some sort of public ceremony being held within its confines.

9. Meskimmon examines self-portraits by women artists, including photographers: "Self-portraiture is a way of coming into representation for women, in which the artist is both subject and object. . . . She presents an embodied subject" (xv). The early twentieth century was certainly the period in which women routinely began to become social subjects and represent themselves in their art, as in the case of Galvão's autobiographical essay or the self-portrait of a painter like Tarsila do Amaral.

10. Rosenthal, however, seemed to adhere to the basic Henri Cartier-Bresson principle that photographs should not be manipulated technically. As Camargo and Mendes assert: "Rosenthal não vê o trabalho de laboratório, a intervenção, como fotografia" ([41] Rosenthal does not see laboratory work, the intervention in the image, as photography).

11. There is one photomontage included in *Cenas urbanas*, however. It is built on a photograph that provides a perspective of the bustling downtown area, with cars, pedestrians, trollies, and multistoried commercial buildings. To the right, looming up behind the five- or six-story buildings, but at an angle as though partially toppled by an earthquake, is a truly imposing late nineteenth-century building, about twenty stories in height, with multiple cornices to alleviate the uniformity of a single façade, altogether quite rococo in appearance. To the right, striding as tall as the latter building, with his spread feet planted over the comings and goings of the street far below his gaze, is a newspaper boy, hawking with both arms copies of the *Jornal da manhã*, one of the major forums of Paulistano commerce and finance. The perspective of this towering figure is foreshortened by the depiction of gathered clouds in the background, such that there is no perspective into the distance and one must focus on the dominance of the central motif of the newspaper, a crucial element in the dynamic of the liberal capitalism of the city.

12. There is a another photograph, a couple of images later in the collection, that shows five women, all dressed in the same peasant fashion, captured face-on by the camera; four are very much interested in the photographer's interest in them. Behind these women—figures in the daily workforce of female peasants—stands the market, with a line of modern vehicles and, most eloquently, the file of telephone and light poles that are essential to the functioning of the modern city.

13. That is, anonymous subjects in a photograph such as this are under-individuated in a prima facie manner; the hiding of the face, typically considered to be the most revealing feature of the human body, only increases and reaffirms that under-individuation.

14. Another image in the collection demonstrates that open-air markets still existed in São Paulo at the time of Rosenthal's work; the image in question follows the two that I have just analyzed, and it shows the role of male children in the work of the marketplace. In this case, a well-dressed man in shirtsleeves, hat, and tie (other indicators in the photograph reveal that it is summertime, such as the parasols carried by both vendors and customers) contemplates the photographer going about her documentary work.

15. Kossoy provides an intriguing registry of all of the commercial images and slogans captured by Rosenthal's camera in her gaze on what was by then already becoming the financial center of Latin America. In the section of his essay titled "A São Paulo de Hildegard Rosenthal," he speaks of how "seu olhar se volta para os elementos-símbolo da metrópole" (26; her gaze turns to the symbolic elements of the metropolis).

16. Varig, the Brazilian national airlines, had an ad about thirty years ago that contrasted the "two Brazils": one, the Brazil of São Paulo, is represented by a very European-looking man decked out in formal business attire and consuming a *cafezinho*, the French café demitasse; while in the second we see purportedly a laid-back denizen of Rio—with an open denim shirt and a wide mulatto smile—drinking from a large cup, perhaps a hearty glass of beer. Such a racially and socially charged conception of the two Brazils is not likely to be found in contemporary advertising.

17. A famous Argentine tango by Homero Manzi and Aníbal Troilo, "Cafetín de Buenos Aires" (Neighborhood Buenos Aires Café), has a narrator nostalgically recount how he became a man by hanging around this typical male establishment, first peering in the window from the street and then directly participating in its male-dominated world on the inside.

18. See the photograph in the collection of the magnificent art deco façade of the Banco de São Paulo, an image that is rotated—in comparison with the majority of the others—90° in order to capture the soaring sweep of that façade. The foreground is populated by men, presumably going and coming from its inner depths.

19. In the camarão photo, there are thirty-three individuals standing on the street around the trolley. Only eight can with certainty be identified as women.

20. De Franceschi describes the São Paulo of Rosenthal's images as "ainda gentil," which leads one to consider the way in which a standard of gentility, while it may be associated with women as its guardians, characterizes very much the universe of masculinist privilege. Thus, the taxi driver shows himself to be deferential toward his female passenger, but he very much exercises a control over her access to the streets and the route followed through them.

CHAPTER 5. *Saudades do Brasil*

Epigraph translation

I therefore arrived in São Paulo prepared to find something much more than a new picture of life: one of those experiences in real time and space generally closed to the social sciences as a consequence of the slowness with which phenomena change and the material and moral impossibility of acting upon them.

Author's note: This essay originally appeared in *Chasqui*, special issue no. 3 (2006), 98–125. It is used here with the permission of the editors.

1. The term does not, as I understand it, refer primarily to *gaulesa* as a synonym for *francesa*, but rather to the presumed USP's sense of being a privileged social space, a

territory that remains unconquered by the barbarians, in the way in which it is used in the Asterix comic books ("Asterix 3D&T"; Costa, passim). However, one can speculate that this mentality is the direct consequence of the USP's privileged French origins.

2. He speaks, in the "Prefácio" to *Saudades de São Paulo*, of the conflicts he had with another member of the French university mission, who prejudiced his position vis-à-vis the controlling newspaper, *O estado de São Paulo*, such that when he chose to resign and spend a year on anthropological research "nenhum esforço foi feito para me reter" (10; no effort was made to retain me); see also Cardoso 182–83.

3. Vargas is never listed in the index of *Tristes tropiques*. Lesser recalls Lévi-Strauss's reference to how the Vargas regime denied him a visa in 1941 when he sought to travel to New York via Brazil (122; see Lévi-Strauss, *Tristes tropiques* 23: this passage contains a veiled reference to Lévi-Strauss's problems as a Jew). It might be appropriate to mention here the extensive involvement of Jews in the history of photography; see George Gilbert. *Tristes tropiques* literally means "sad tropics," although the English translation retains the French title.

4. *Saudades do Brasil* means "Nostalgia for Brazil."

5. *Saudades do Brasil* closes with a clever photograph by David Allison of three Cashinaua boys from Amazonian Peru scrutinizing a paperback copy of the English translation of *Tristes tropiques*.

6. Novaes analyzes Lévi-Strauss's dismissive attitudes toward photography, which may explain why this material took so long to find its way into print and why it remains virtually unknown in studies on Lévi-Strauss. Although she argues that Lévi-Strauss's negative attitude toward photography was misguided, she underscores how, from an ethnographic point of view, photographs were like scholars' notebooks, a form of documentation but never a valid analysis (68); moreover, photography, unlike real works of art, is characterized by appearing to be a "literal reproduction" (69), a position that contemporary theorists like Roland Barthes and Susan Sontag have emphatically refuted.

7. Here is what he had to say in *Tristes tropiques*: "I never thought that São Paulo was ugly: it was a 'wild' town, as are all American towns. . . . São Paulo, at that time, was untamed" (97).

8. Although such matters lie beyond the scope of the analysis of Lévi-Strauss's photographs, it is interesting to speculate on how, even from the start, the duplication of European architecture in Brazil necessitated and permitted structural modifications as a consequence of the singularly non-European locale, such as, perhaps, the absence of the need to install much in the way of central heating, as the São Paulo winter is notably mild by contrast with the severe Parisian one.

9. The "also" of this caption ties into the observation that introduces the photographs as a whole: "In 1935 the city of São Paulo, still a frontier town, was visibly turning into an industrial and financial metropolis. Changing from day to day, it offered a fascinating spectacle to the geographer, the sociologist, the anthropologist" (*Saudades do Brasil* 26).

10. Lévi-Strauss bemusedly recalls, in a footnote to his introduction to *Saudades do Brasil*, the matter of the pollution that has now become one of the signature features of

São Paulo: "Speaking to young colleagues and students at the University of São Paulo in 1985, I mentioned the very special quality of the air, a combination of high altitude and the tropical latitude, which I had recognized as I stepped out of the plane. The whole audience burst out laughing at this, as if I had said something incongruous. Nevertheless, this quality was still present, far from the city; but my audience, plunged daily into the São Paulo inferno, did not identify it as such. They were unable to conceive that an already urbanized existence could be carried on in a still-unpolluted atmosphere" (18).

11. São Paulo is still capable of filling the Teatro Municipal with a Brazilian audience willing to pay a goodly ticket price to hear Ibsen performed in English with an imported American actor like Joel Grey, as was the case on the occasion of one of my visits to the city in the mid-1990s.

12. In *Tristes tropiques*, Lévi-Strauss speaks of these buildings as a "frozen jumble," like large herds of motionless mammals around the waterhole of the valley of Anhangabaú park (99).

13. Quezado Deckker surveys the development of Brazilian architecture beginning in the 1930s. She notes the enormous impact of Le Corbusier's "'discovery' of Argentina and Brazil in 1929" and his influence on subsequent growth, especially in Rio de Janeiro and São Paulo (13).

14. Lest one get the impression that all of the buildings from the period are drab boxes, attention should be called to the thirty-story Martinelli building, which, when it was inaugurated in 1929, became Latin America's first skyscraper. Topped off with an Italian palazzo motif, it remains one of the city's most interesting landmarks and an abiding symbol of the better cultural aspirations of the period in which it was built. Various other office buildings in the central core attest to successful architectural ambitions.

15. Of passing note are the menial employee Macabea's initial experiences with São Paulo busses and subways; Macabea is a country bumpkin literally killed by the capitalist city in Suzana Amaral's 1985 film *A hora da estrela*, based on Clarice Lispector's 1977 novel of the same name (see Foster, *Gender and Society* 70–82).

16. It is worth noting that Langue's four-page review, typical of briefer notes, ignores completely the photography of São Paulo in *Saudades do Brasil*, as if it were only prefatory to the supposedly more important anthropological work.

17. I am disappointed that Lévi-Strauss is not included in *The Brazil Reader*, neither for his anthropological writing about Brazil nor for his perceptive comments on São Paulo.

CHAPTER 6. Films by Day and Films by Night in São Paulo

1. Although his comments are brief in nature, Kovacs is very clear in recognizing the scant representation of São Paulo in film, especially when compared to Rio de Janeiro.

2. Some sources write the acronym "S.A." out, which means Sociedade Anónima, the Brazilian equivalent of "Inc." However, in the context of the film, the subtitle becomes ironic, since it carries both the business sense and the nonmetaphorical meaning of

"anonymous society," which is one of the ways in which Person's film views modern São Paulo.

3. Unfortunately, the film is omitted from the discussion by Travero of the influence of Italian neorealism in Brazil.

4. Reichenbach's short commentary on the film refers to the "progesso perverso e desordenado que assolou a metrópole de 1957 a 1961" (perverse and disorderly progress that devastated the metropolis from 1957 to 1961).

5. The transition from European (especially German) economic dependence to American dependence as a consequence of Brazil's alliance with the United States is the basis of Chico Buarque de Holanda's 1978 play, *A opera do malandro* (The Gangster's Opera), made into a film of the same name by Ruy Guerra in 1986. See the analysis by Foster, *Society and Gender* 37–45.

6. The reference is to Sloan Wilson's 1955 novel, usually considered the paradigmatic representation of the American "company man."

7. There is a certain nostalgia for the Germanic in the film, but that must remain unexplored here. Yet both the Volkswagen and the Karmann-Ghia were being made in Brazil (the sticker on the back window of the latter announces the fact), and Carlos mocks his employer for driving a monstrous imported American car.

8. Amácio Mazzaropi is often identified in critical sources with the first name Amâncio; the latter is a common Brazilian name but, as Mazzaropi liked to stress, he was born in the paradigmatic São Paulo Italian neighborhood (Barra Funda) and his correct first name is, consequently, Italian.

9. For example, Trelles Plazaola does not include him in his registry of South American filmmakers, while none of his thirty-plus films make their way into *South American Cinema*. On the other hand, Nuno César Abreu provides a superb encyclopedia entry on Mazzaropi's career. Mazzaropi is also discussed by Dennison and Shaw, 149–55 and passim.

10. Mazzaropi takes his character from a collection of short stories about a rural São Paulo provincial of that name, *Urupês*, originally published in 1914.

11. As Dennison and Shaw point out, the highbrow Cinema Novo movement is tied to Rio de Janeiro (141), where Mazzaropi is solidly a product of the state and the city of São Paulo.

12. Candace Slater discusses popular poetry relating to internal migration to Sao Paulo, but does not mention Mazzaropi's films.

13. After devoting so much energy to filmmaking, Mazzaropi made the transition in the 1970s to pop television, which by then had become a major forum of Brazilian popular culture.

14. There is a very clear consciousness in the film of the deleterious influence of American values and their corruption of the traditional Brazilian way of life that Punduroso represents. He at one time demands the suppression of linguistic tokens in English in favor of "speaking Portuguese." At the same time, there is a clear juxtaposition in the film between the father's backlands pronunciation of Portuguese (a characteristic that Mazzaropi exploited over and over again in his films, such that his Jeca Tatu was a

veritable case study of nonurban or pre-urban speech) and the linguistic hipness of his city-dwelling children.

15. Dennison and Shaw relate Mazzaropi's persona as an actor to the tradition of the circus clown in Brazilian culture (15).

16. Shown in English as both *The Invader* and *The Trespasser*.

17. Shown in English both as *Elite Squad* and *The Elite Squad*.

18. See Marta Peixoto's article on Rio's favelas in recent Brazilian filmmaking for excellent comments on Lacerda's film (175–76).

19. See Caldeira's effect metaphor of "a city of walls."

20. Whether this is true or not, the dynamic involved here is that the police will pursue aggression committed by social inferiors against social superiors, but will not pursue that carried out in the other direction, nor between social equals of whatever social class unless there is a higher social consideration, such as an upper-class victim who turns out to have more powerful allies than an upper-class perpetrator. This social dynamic is very much operant in a film like *Tropa de elite*, where multiple social players are involved (particularly a police unit that is socially superior to the regular police), affording a veritable *ars combinatoria* of the power relations involved.

21. The soundtrack of *O invasor* is an anthology of São Paulo rap music, some of it by Paulo Miklos, who plays the part of Anísio. In addition to Miklos's own music, tracks by Rica Amabis, Daniel Ganjaman, Sabotage, and Tejo are featured prominently.

22. Two major sources on Cinema Novo are Johnson and *Cinema Novo and Beyond*.

23. *Anjos* is the only feature-length film Barros made, although he is an important production figure in the Brazilian film industry. See the encyclopedia entry on his work by Arthur Autran, who notes that he was a key figure in the São Paulo incarnation of the Cinema Novo.

24. Nelson Brissac Peixoto (165–66) identifies the inspiration for this scene in Vincente Minelli's *The Band Wagon* (1953), where the Astaire-Charisse dance scene takes place in Central Park. Peixoto also speaks of other Hollywood reprises in the film and a certain noir dimension as well.

25. Despite the prizes it won and the critical acclaim it received, *Anjos* is not mentioned in Johnson and Stam's *Brazilian Cinema*, perhaps because it breaks too radically from the sort of social-commitment filmmaking that prevails in their study.

26. The film is referenced ten times in Moreno's study of the "homosexual" character in Brazilian filmmaking, although it is never analyzed in any satisfactory way.

27. She tied with Betty Faria for the 1987 Gramado award for best actress. Faria's film, *Anjos de arrabalde* (Angels from the Outskirts), directed by Carlos Reichenbach, also involved São Paulo, but in a dirty-realist fashion.

28. Note that the actress's name is an oblique reference to the significant Jewish community in São Paulo. This is one more indication of Barros's desire to accurately capture the social demographics of the city.

29. See Néstor Perlongher's famous study on the taxi-boys (os michês) of São Paulo and the gay urban culture they represent.

30. Aside from the delight of seeing the camera pull back to reveal the added lights

necessary to film the dance sequence (which could not possibly have been adequately illuminated by the usual nighttime sources of light), one particularly hilarious example is when, in her boudoir, the escort reaches for the breast of the actress and she puts up her hand to block the gaze of the camera as though on the actual set she is objecting to the way in which the director is allowing for an unfavorable representation of her body. This gesture is particularly effective because it abruptly interrupts the mood of the scene of erotic foreplay to remind us that we are witnessing a film and its staged action. The fact that Pêra strategically overacts her role throughout can also be seen as reminding us that it is a film, not life, that we are viewing.

31. In terms of a Cinema Novo film on the night—set, as usual, in Rio—one thinks of Walter Hugo Khouri's *Noite vazia* (1964), which includes the first lesbian scene in a Brazilian film, although hardly with the sense of queer jouissance found in Barros's *Anjos*; indeed, sex in *Noite vazia* is a metonym for the wasted and empty lives of the two couples who are the main characters of the film (see the discussion of the film by Araujo).

32. This was the global title given to the dozens of episodes of television series in the 1990s based on Rodrigues's famous chronicles about life in Rio (see Rodrigues).

33. There is also a sequel directed by Kemeny and Lustig, *São Paulo em 24 horas* (São Paulo in Twenty-Four Hours; 1934), lasting only six minutes. Silva Neto cites the following synopsis: "2a Symphonia da Metropole [*sic*] Paulista" (534; 2nd Symphony of the São Paulo Metropolis).

CHAPTER 7. Madalena Schwartz

Author's note: This essay appeared originally as a chapter in *Latin American Jewish Cultural Production*, edited by David William Foster (Nashville: Vanderbilt University Press, 2009). It is used here with the permission of Vanderbilt University Press.

1. Fellow singer and musician Caetano Veloso comments on Clementina's participation in the Tropicália movement (99–100).

2. Paralleling the image of Brazilian Archbishop Dom Hélder Câmara, which appears in *Personae* (54).

3. Despite the degree to which the authoritarian governments that followed the 1964 military coup went to extremes in the project of "purging" Carnival in the name of social hygiene and international tourism, a segment of which, nevertheless and undeniably, had recourse to these *carnes tollendas* precisely in search of such "disreputable" qualities.

4. James Green provides a characterization of the importance of the group (257–58). Green alludes specifically to a "gender bending and androgyny to shake up standard representations of the masculine and feminine [and their] provocative portrayals of gender roles and identities" (257). Green cites, in his footnote on page 62, various sources of information on Dzi Croquettes (340). "Dzi" is a Portuguese version of English "The"; there is no agreement on the origin of "Croquettes." Since completing this chapter, a major documentary on this group has appeared, titled *Dzi Croquettes* and directed by Tatiana Issa and Raphael Álvarez (2009).

5. One might say that the basic posture of the average Brazilian with respect to homosexuality is to accept the right of the Other to be homosexual/gay/queer as long as it does not impinge on their world—including their family—and as long as homosexuals keep their place in the sense of "such goings-on having nothing to do with me or mine."

6. The transvestite artist represented by Harvey Feierstein at the beginning of the main part of the film he directed (based on his stage play by the same name), *Torch Song Trilogy* (1988; the play won Tony awards in 1982), monologues with the spectator of the film through his makeup mirror as he prepares for his show. At one moment, he stops short to stare at the camera from his mirror and defiantly challenges the audience not to complain: "It's still under construction." Feierstein's gravelly voice only serves to increase the comic effect that, in turn, is enhanced grotesquely because the author is so unfeminine (at least in conventional terms): Feierstein has what one might call the build of a truck driver.

7. It is necessary to bear in mind that the theater generally requires an element of makeup of the actor, masculine as well as female, even if it is customarily part of the conditions of stage performance. Such makeup, however, functions in a way that is quite semiotically different from how it functions for Dzi Croquettes.

8. One is fully aware of the feminist demand to hold on to some versions of the sexual binary as part of the re-vindication of the rights of women after at least five thousand years of patriarchal subjugation. But such a demand and the questioning of the construction of the sexual binary are not mutually exclusive theoretical—and, here, artistic—undertakings.

9. See, for example, the publicity photographs that appear on the webpage of Mix Brasil: http://mixbrasil.uol.com.br/cultura/especiais/dizcroquettes/dzi.asp

10. I leave for another study the analysis of the work Schwartz did among the poor and common people of Brazil in, for example, the vast rural reaches of that country. See the image of a young Afro-Brazilian from the Brazilian Northeast that illustrates the cover of the dossier *Retratos* (Portraits).

CHAPTER 8. Days and Nights at the Copan

Epigraph translation

"The Copan is busier than a whore's ass" [. . . .] "It's that dumb ass Niemeyer. Like everything he did, it's good for taking pictures, but lousy to live in."—Regina Rheda, *First World Third Class and Other Tales of the Global Mix* (27)

Author's note: This essay appeared originally in *Tradições portuguesas/Portuguese Traditions: In Honor of Claude L. Hulet* (San José, California: Portuguese Heritage Publications of California, 2007), 121–29. It is used here with the permission of the editors. All translations are from the 2005 University of Texas Press edition, *First World*.

1. To be sure, there are those for whom the Copan is yet one more Niemeyer masterpiece. It is featured in Khan's anthology of great modernist architecture (198). For a technical description, see Séron-Pierre.

2. In this regard, it is significant to note that the Copan has its own postal code: 01066–900.

3. The Copan appears in the chronological listing, under the year 1950, of Niemeyer's work provided by Botey (238), and it is discussed, along with images, in the overview of Niemeyer's work (64–66). See the official site of the building: *http://www.copansp.com .br/*. There are many images of the Copan on the Internet; one of the most dramatic is by Madalena Schwartz, whose work is studied elsewhere in this book. See the image at: http://www.usp.br/jorusp/arquivo/2004/jusp671/pag10.htm

4. In a visit to São Paulo in mid-2008, I was able to appreciate how attempts are being made to renovate the building. A fascinating document is Friedl's series of interviews, aptly titled *Trabalhando no Copan/Working at Copan*, with major building employees.

5. Another interesting use of a Brazilian building for sociocultural commentary is in the documentary *Edifício Master* (2002) by Eduardo Coutinho, one of Brazil's major documentary filmmakers. Built around thirty-seven interviews of families living in apartments in the modest-but-imposing twelve-story Edifício Master in Copacabana in Rio de Janeiro, the film attempts to provide a slice of life of Brazil's urban lower middle class.

6. For more biographical information and a complete bibliography of Rheda's publications, including translations, see the bilingual website: http://home.att.net/~rheda/ (in Portuguese: http://home.att.net/~rheda/RRHPPortg.html).7. Where the nonurban is present, as in the third part of *Pau-de-arara classe turista* (1996), it is so grimly primitive that the ugly brawl of the megalopolis comes off as seductively inviting.

8. The Copan continues to be counted as one of São Paulo's signature buildings in guidebooks like the Insight series; see Taylor, *Insight Guide: Brazil* (160). See also the excellent Web site: www.http://sampacentro.terra.com.br/.

9. There is a strong likelihood, on the basis of the way in which he is identified in the story, that the "bad neighbor" is a sly reference to the dirty-realist playwright Plínio Marcos (1935–99), one of the most famous inhabitants of the Copan.

10. "The bathrooms in this section, for example, have no windows. If you fart you'll asphyxiate" (11).

11. "The following days Mrs. Albuquerque didn't do any cleaning. She sat quietly at home, her nose alert to every movement of air, eager to catch the stench rising from the rotting flesh in her neighbor's apartment" (15).

12. Dunn, in his "Introduction," refers to the Copan as "a sort of national allegory" (xiv), as "evoking the ruins of Brazilian democratic modernity" (xiv), and as "a microcosm of urban Brazil" (xiv).

13. Perrone points out that the subtitle of the book has become the only title of the English translation because of Rheda's subsequent desire, as part of her evolution to veganism, to exclude anything that might imply a pejorative connotation for animals ("Preface" viii); he also underscores the lack of any religious connotation. My point is that the inhabitants of the Ark, the dwellers of the City of Man, are alone in a world without any beneficent delegate of the Lord, a role hardly fulfilled by the agents of the Condomínio Edifício Copan.

14. Quick as a flash, Leonor pushed her colleague into the abyss. Margarete reacted,

grabbing Leonor by the blouse. Screams were heard on the terrace but, before any tanned body had time to get up from the mat, the two were already flying out over the metropolis, headed for the inexorable pavement.

It isn't known whether Margarete fainted during the fall or if, conscious, she found room for resentment in her vertiginous terminal flux of thoughts. But it is known that the therapist suffered greatly over the tragedy. As for Leonor, she forgave them both before smashing into the ground. (69)

15. Another clever utilization of such omniscience is to be found in the story "A menina dos gatos" ("The Cat Girl"). Her legion of cats actually functions as a feline signaling system as part of her involvement with a drug ring. Although she disrupts the life of her neighbors with her comings and goings, one day when she disappears, they carry on happily without her. Meanwhile, the narrator deals with the loose ends of what actually happens to the cat girl outside the universe of the Copan: "Quanto ao paradeiro da menina dos gatos, a polícia nunca descubriu nada. Mas, eu, que escrevi este conto, sei que ela morreu atropelada numa avenida escura de São Paulo, numa emboscada, e que o assassino fugiu" (56; "As for the cat girl's fate, the police never discovered anything. But I, who wrote this story, know that she was ambushed and run over in a dark alley of São Paulo, and that the perpetrator got away" [31]).

16. At that moment the doorbell rang. Hildebrando, her husband, the trunk around which Vera had twined her life, the mast she had hoisted her dreams on, the cross she had bound herself to, her only path to the future, had returned. He had brought several gift-wrapped packages. Full of newfound goodwill, he opened them himself. There were porn magazines, videos, photographs, and playing cards, which he scattered on the bed with jovial energy. Vera threw herself into his arms.

Across the avenue, at the hotel window, a valet watched them. The wife began to draw the curtains, but her husband stopped her. With an impetuous gesture, he threw them open to the curiosity of the valet, who bore witness to Ms. Vera's and Mr. Hildebrando's possible, necessary, and inescapable love. (80)

17. The fact that, outside the narrative universe of the story, the Hilton Hotel is no longer operating is inconsequential for the story's integrity of meaning, however much such important changes in the urban landscape may inevitably have an impact on human affairs. A story that would incorporate the closing of the hotel would necessarily involve an examination of the consequences of Vera and Hildebrando's sexual theatrics.

CHAPTER 9. Trekking the Urban

Epigraph translations

As far as I am concerned, life in the city is not as disagreeable as people make it out to be.

Astronauts head for the moon / Urbenauts head for the streets.

Author's note: This essay originally appeared in *Studies in Latin American Popular Culture* 24 (2005), 1–16. It is used here with the permission of the University of Texas Press.

1. According to the Web site "City Population" (http://www.citypopulation.de/world.html), although Fenianos claims that São Paulo is the third-largest city (*Expedições* 12), undercounting may mean that Mexico City is in fact the largest in the world, although it vies for this distinction with Tokyo. Also, subsequent quotes are from *Expedições* unless otherwise noted.

2. It is usually assumed that the outrageous dimension of Newville de Almeida's *A dama do lotação* (1978) is that an upper-middle-class woman (played by Sônia Braga) would spend her day riding city buses in search of cheap sexual thrills, but perhaps it lies rather with the very idea of a woman of her station riding the bus in the first place.

3. Lúcia Sá, in the only other academic essay on Fenianos's expedition, uses Walter Benjamin's trope of the flâneur to describe the Urbenauta's intersection with the neighborhoods of São Paulo. I am not completely comfortable with this understanding of his travels within the city, since one mostly associates with the flâneur a detached or, at best, bemused gaze, while I would prefer to underscore Fenianos's deep human involvement with urban space and its inhabitants. See Sheilds's discussion of Benjamin's notion of the flâneur.

4. A radical adventure

5. The Urbenaut has two waste containers, one for organic material and another for recyclable waste, that can be used by the populace, thereby contributing in a simple, more educated way to urban cleanliness.

6. The details of this expedition, including the ways in which Roosevelt went against the original plans of the Museum, are told fascinatingly by Candice Millard, a former editor of *National Geographic*.

7. My São Paulo is not Oswald de Andadre's or Mário de Andrade's. My São Paulo is that of Christopher Columbus and Charles Darwin.

8. Although the two utterances "I do X" and "I experience X" are similar syntactically as active constructions (a first-person pronoun and a transitive verb that agrees with that pronoun, followed in turn by a direct object), on a semantic level, the first-person pronoun of the first verb is the agent of the predicate, while in the case of the second verb, the first-person pronoun is a patient or non-agent of the predicate. This explains why it is only the first class of active propositions that allow for passivization in Spanish and Portuguese, while the second class routinely do not: when they are used passively, they sound strange, as if the speaker is forcing an agentive meaning on the predicate.

9. More specifically, it deviates from his formal training in Comunicação Social e Direito (per the black flap of *Expedições Urbenauta*). The back flap of *Almanaque Kurytyba* only identifies him as a "jornalista."

10. To tame and recognize that portion of the Cantareira Jungle that lies within the municipality of São Paulo.

To demarcate the north and south cardinal points of the city.

During the navigation of the rivers, to seek out other angles and points of view for the city, staking out the view of the city from the river and not of the river from the city, as usually takes place.

To alert the governing bodies and the population about the importance of the preservation of natural resources, principally water, which runs serious risks of becoming scarce even by the twenty-first century.

11. Reality began to appear greater than my imagination.

12. I cross the Marginal Tietê standing. Friday. I wish I could be home, fix something to eat, take a bath, and then go out. But the reality is that this is what I chose.

I have a maverick headache and my neck really hurts. At first I suffered from being cooped up in the vehicle, but now I'm happy today that I no longer have to climb stairs, open a drawer, open the closet door. All I have to do is reach back with my right hand and grab the medicine from the Urbenaut's pharmacy. I'm more organized in my new way of life.

I take the remedy and turn the sound on in the Urbeship to my lucky music, and in a ritual manner I imagine myself in the Northern Zone. First objective: find a place to sleep. I only have one contact up my sleeve: Manuel, an office-boy I met at Barra Funda the same day I slept in the street. It's either him or sleep in the street again.

13. Around six o'clock, having just left for Pirituba, I realized that I had no place to sleep. First I asked a woman who was indulgent with me in a very friendly fashion when I stopped the Urbenaut [or Urbeship], contemplating a lovely corner in the area, without realizing that others would need to be on their way about their business in Brazil's largest city. I had no luck. Then I saw some kids messing around [with a ball] on their way to the grocery store. I played a bit with them, and when I said enough, the star of the group made a clever observation: "Boy what a strange beggar you are! You have a big jeep and no place to sleep."

14. close with a golden key the expedition in the Northern Zone and sleep for two days in the house of a former girlfriend.

15. Since the movies of the expedition are being filmed in large part by the residents themselves, once we get acquainted I show them my equipment and proceed to show the crowd how to work the video and the photographic camera. Then I hand the camera to one of them who might want to grab it from me. I show him how it works and place in his hands the responsibility of showing me the world in which he lives. In place of mistrust, complete trust. It's a pact.

16. We talk until dawn. We both sleep with the doors open and the street gave one more marvelous and wise grandmother.

17. I gave everyone hugs and thanks, curious to know what will happen to us afterwards. I see everyone returning to their lives. And me getting ready to return to mine. The square empties. . . . Before climbing aboard the Urbeship and returning home, I see a man pointing his finger toward me and saying to someone else: "He's returning from a long trip. He's gone around the world and is just getting back now."

Basically, he was right. The challenge of Around the World today is knowing how to live with the solitude of the multitudes and to not feel alone while surrounded by six billion human beings and the planet that shelters them. The challenge of Around the World today is to know how to construct cities without destroying the planet and ourselves. The world does not need people who think only of the moon. The planet needs people who think of the street.

I looked around the Cathedral Plaza one more time and thought to myself: "São Paulo is surely a radical adventure! When we think we've reached its borders, the city reminds us that we are just setting out!"

18. Observe the ends of these three major Brazilian narratives:

Euclides da Cunha, *Os sertões*:
É que ainda não existe um [Henry] Maudsley [early psychiatrist] para as locuras e os crimes da nacionalidade. (409)

João Guimarães Rosa, *Grande sertão: veredas*:
O diabo não há! É o que eu digo, se for . . . Existe é homem humano. Travessia. (460)

Mário de Andrade, *Macunaíma; o herói sem nenhum caráter*:
Me acocorei em riba destas folhas, catei meus carrapatos, ponteei na violinha e um toque rasgado botei a boca no mundo cantando na fala impura as frases e os casos de Macunaíma, herói de nossa gente.
Tem mais não. (135)

Euclides da Cunha, *Os sertões* (*Rebellion in the Backlands*)
The fact is that there is still no Maudsley for the madness and the crimes of nationality. . .

João Guimarães Rosa, *Grande sertão: veredas* (*The Devil to Pay in the Backlands*)
The devil doesn't exist! And I would say even if he did . . . Man the human being exists. Journey.

Mário de Andrade, *Macunaíma; o herói sem nenhum caráter* (Macunaíma; The Hero with No Character)
I curled up on the bank among these leaves, took stock of my chiggers, strummed on my guitar and sang forth to the world in impure speech the sayings and deeds of Macunaíma, the hero of our people.
There is no one else.

19. There are openings for Urbenauts.

20. Urbenaut Manifesto: 120 reasons for you to travel in the city in which you live or to defy the Jungles of Stone.

CHAPTER 10. Drawing São Paulo

Author's note: This essay originally appeared in *Ciberletras* 19 (July 2008), *http://www. lehman.edu/ciberletras/v19/foster.html*. It is used here with the permission of the editors.

1. According to Smylie (505), Eisner is to be credited with inventing the term "graphic novel" to characterize his widely acclaimed *A Contract with God* (1978) (see also Eisner's various discussions of this narrative form).

2. The aforementioned *Wikipedia* entry states that "Graphic novels are typically

bound in longer and more durable formats than familiar comic magazines, using the same materials and methods as printed books, and are generally sold in bookstores and specialty comic book shops rather than at newsstands." This statement concerns the sales venue of the graphic novel, which is part of what makes it particularly urban, since bookstores and specialty comic book shops are typically found only in urban settings.

3. Such as those pioneered by Classics Illustrated as early as the 1940s; much equivalent production is available in Spanish and Portuguese. A notable example signed by Moon and Bá is their elegant version of Machado de Assis's famous short story, *O alienista* (*The Psychiatrist*; 1881). The Moon-Bá version appears in a series titled Grandes Clássicos em Graphic Novel (Graphic Novels of the Great Classics); note the use of the English term rather than the reasonable Portuguese cognate "romance gráfico," although the latter term is used for an entry on the graphic novel in the (quite inferior) Portuguese Wikipedia.

4. It would appear from their interview with Shook that the text was written originally in English, rather than translated from Portuguese (45).

5. I note, however, that a modest amount of work by Brazil's Ziraldo (Ziraldo Alves Pinto) and Mexico's Rius (Eduardo de Ríos) has been translated into English. For an overview of Latin American graphic art, see Foster, *From Mafalda to Los supermachos*.

6. Also of considerable importance in the Moon-Bá oeuvre are their illustrations for Shane L. Amaya's four-volume *Roland: Days of Wrath* (1999), based loosely on the French epic *La Chanson de Roland* (mid-twelfth century) and winner of the 1999 Xeric Foundation Grant. Moon-Bá have also collaborated with Amaya in the episodes of the anthology *Gunned Down* (2005), which contains Brazilian versions of stories of the Old American West.

7. My colleague Isis Costa McElroy has pointed out to me that the intersecting discourses of the characters in these strips, with the abundant use of ellipses signifying reticence in full articulation and expectation for the other to complete the thought, are typical of online chat. It would be entirely reasonable for Moon-Bá to have an interest in such a typically contemporary urban phenomenon.

8. There is a problem with the English translation here: " . . . until you bumped into that girl on your way to the bathroom. . . . . . / . . . and dropped her drink" (56, 61). The unspaced ellipses are in the text, and the forward slash indicates the transition from one speech balloon to another. One assumes that the underlying Portuguese is equivalent either to "and made her drop her drink" or "knocked her drink out of her hand."

9. Since most men in Brazil are uncircumcised, the rituals of hygiene are different from those of a society in which most men are circumcised.

10. One must note at this point that the sexual politics represented in this and other Moon-Bá strips reflect a considerable degree of sexism that one must assume characterizes the social milieu being portrayed.

11. Although in the strip "qu'est-ce que c'est" (what is it), which takes place in Paris and deals with violence on the subway, the combined narrative voice of the two protagonists states "We live in a much more violent city, in Brazil . . . / . . . but no matter how violent it may get, it's home. It's where we belong" (74). This utterance does provide

a singular, anchoring identity for the urban space of the strips: it is identity-specific because it is one's own. But such a solipsistic determination does not replace any sort of specific characterization of a uniquely remarkable space.

12. According to Shook's interview, Moon-Bá are now preparing a second volume of *De:Tales* (45).

Conclusion

1. I have studied the eastern area of the city in a photographic essay that has not yet been published.

2. One can see how the Edifício Copan can be examined in reference to the neighboring ground zero of the city, the Praça da República, or how it could be viewed in terms of other architectural monuments: the Edifício Martinelli (which appears in Lévi-Strauss's photography), the Jornal do Brasil building, the Banco do Brasil building, the Edifício Itália, the Teatro Municipal, the Estação da Luz (now the seat of the magnificent Museu da Língua Portuguesa), and others in a city of skyscrapers, many of which are monumental.

Works Cited

Abreu, Marcelo de Paiva, Afonso S. Bevilaqua, and Demosthenes M. Pinho. "Sustitución de importaciones y crecimiento en el Brasil (1890–1970)." *Idustrialización y estado en la América Latina: la leyenda negra de la posguerra.* México: Fondo de Cultura Económica, 2003. 210–39.

Abreu, Nuno César. "Mazzaropi, Amácio." *Enciclopedia do cinema brasileiro.* Org. Fernão Ramos and Luiz Felipe Mirando. São Paulo: Editora SENAC São Paulo, 2000. 366–67.

Amaya, Shane L., et al. *Roland: Days of Wrath.* Santa Barbara: Terra Major, 1999.

Andrade, Mário de. *Hallucinated City. Paulicea desvairada.* Trans. Jack E. Tomlins (bilingual ed.). Nashville: Vanderbilt University Press, 1968.

———. *Macunaíma, o herói sem nenhum caráter.* 1928. 21a ed. Texto revisto por Telê Porto Ancona Lopez. Belo Horizonte: Editora Itatiai, 1985.

———. *Poesias completas.* Ed. crítica de Diléa Zanotto Manfio. Belo Horizonte: Villa Rica, 1993.

Anjos da noite. Dir. Wilson Barros. Brazil, 1987. Duration: 110 min.

Araujo, Inácio. "*Noite vazia;* Empty Night." *Cinema brasileiro: The Films from Brazil.* Ed. Amir Labaki. São Paulo: Publifolha, 1998. 48–50.

"Asterix 3D&T." <http://www.geocites.com/asterix_gaules/3det.htm> Accessed April 20, 2004.

Autran, Arthur. "Wilson Barros." *Enciclopédia de cinema brasileiro.* Org. Fernão Ramos and Luiz Felipe Miranda. São Paulo: Editora SENAC São Paulo, 2000. 49–50.

Barros, Wilson. *Anjos da noite* [script]. Porto Alegre, R.S.: Tchê!, 1987.

Barthes, Roland. *Camera Lucida: Reflections on Photography.* Trans. Richard Howard. New York: Hill and Wang, 1981.

Bastos, Eliana. *Entre o escândalo e o sucesso: a Semana de 22 e o Armory Show.* Campinas, S.P.: Editora da Univeresidade Estadual de Campinas, UNICAMP, 1991.

Benjamin, Walter. *The Arcades Project.* Trans. Howard Eiland and Kevin McLaughlin. Cambridge, Mass.: Belknap Press, 1999.

Bernardet, Jean-Claude. "Trajectory of an Oscillation." *Brazilian Cinema.* Ed. Randal Johnson and Robert Stam. Expanded ed. New York: Columbia University Press,

1995. 281–89. The original Portuguese version may be found in Bernardet's *Brazil em tempo de cinema*. 3a ed. Rio de Janeiro: Paz e Terra, 1978. 110–17.

Besse, Susan K. *Restructuring Patriarchy: The Modernization of Gender Inequality in Brazil, 1914–40*. Chapel Hill: University of North Carolina Press, 1994.

Bloch, Jayne H. "Patrícia Galvão: The Struggle against Conformity." *Latin American Literary Review* 14.27 (January–June 1986): 188–201.

Borges, Jorge Luis. "Borges y yo." *Obras completas*. Buenos Aires: Emecé, 1974. 808.

Botey, Josep Ma. *Oscar Niemeyer*. Barcelona: Editorial Gustavo Gil, 1996.

Bottassi, Miriam, and Marisa Fernandes. "Brazil." *Lesbian Histories and Cultures*. Ed. Bonnie Zimmerman. New York: Garland, 2000. 129–30.

Brasil: de la antropofagía a Brasilia, 1920–1950. Valencia: IVAM Centre Julio González, 2000.

The Brazil Reader: History, Culture, Politics. Durham: Duke University Press, 1999.

Bueno, Eva. *O artista do povo: Mazzaropi e Jeca Tatu no cinema do Brasil*. Maringá, Paraná: Eduem, Editora da Universidade Estadual de Maringá, 1999.

Caixa modernista. Org. Jorge Schwartz. São Paulo: EDUSP; Imprensa Oficial, Governo do Estado de São Paulo; Belo Horizonte: Editora UFMG, 2003.

Caldeira, Teresa P. R. *City of Walls: Crime, Segregation, and Citizenship in São Paulo*. Berkeley: University of California Press, 2000.

Camargo, Mônica Junqueira de, and Ricardo Mendes. *Fotografia: cultura e fotografia paulistana no século xx*. São Paulo: Secretaria Municipal de Cultura, 1992.

Campos, Augusto de. *Pagu: vida-obra*. São Paulo: Editora Brasiliense, 1982.

Cancelli, Elizabeth. *O mundo da violência: a polícia da era Vargas*. Brasília: Editora Universitária de Brasaília, 1993.

Cardoso, Irene de Arruda Ribeiro. *A universidade da comunhão paulista*. São Paulo: Cortez, 1982.

Carneiro, Maria Luisa Tucci. *O anti-semitismo na era Vargas: fantasmas de uma geração (1930–45)*. São Paulo: Editora Brasiliense, 1988.

Carriego, Evaristo. *Poesías*. Prólogo y notas de Juan Carlos Ghiano. Buenos Aires: Los Libros del Mirasol, 1964.

Castro, Sílvio. *História da literartura brasileira*. Lisboa: Publicações Alfa, 1999.

———. "A Semana de Arte Moderna de 1922 e a proposta modernista." *História da literatura brasileira*. Ed. Sílvio Castro. Vol. 3. Lisboa: Publicações Alfa, 1999. 38–66.

Catani, Afrânio Mendes. "Person, Luís Sérgio." *Enciclopédia do cinema brasileiro*. Org. Fernão Ramos and Luiz Felipe Miranda. São Paulo: Editora Senac, 1997. 425–27.

Cendrars, Blaise. *Au Coeur du monde: poésies completes: 1924–1929*. Paris: Gallimard, 1968.

Cinema Novo and Beyond. New York: Museum of Modern Art, 1998.

Cirne, Moacy. *História e crítica dos quadrinhos brasileiros*. Rio de Janeiro: FUNARTE, 1990.

Cócaro, Nicolás, and Emilio E. Cócaro. *Florida, la calle del país*. Buenos Aires: Fundación Banco de Boston, 1984.

Corcoran-Nantes, Yvonne. "Women and Popular Urban Social Movements in Sao Paulo, Brazil." *Bulletin of Latin American Research* 9.2 (1990): 249–64.

Costa, Caio Túlio. *Cala-se: a saga de Vennuncchi Leme, a USP como aldéia gaulesa, o show proibido de Gilberto Gil*. São Paulo: A Girafa, 2003.

Cultura paulista: antologia 2005. Coord. Célio Debes, Hernâni Donato, and Ives Gandra da Silva Martins. São Paulo: Academia Paulista de Letras; Imprensa Oficial do Estado de São Paulo, 2006.

Cunha, Euclides da. *Os sertões: campanha de Canudos*. 1902. 32a ed. Rio de Janeiro: Livraria Francisco Alves Editora, 1984.

Daniel, Mary L. "Life in the Textile Factory: Two 1933 Perspectives." *Luso-Brazilian Review* 31.2 (Winter 1994): 97–113.

Dassin, Joan. *Política e poesía em Mário de Andrade*. São Paulo: Livraria Duas Cidades, 1978.

De Franceschi, Antonio Fernando. "Uma São Paulo ainda gentil." Rosenthal 5–7:

Dean, Warren. *The Industrialization of São Paulo 1880–1945*. Austin: University of Texas Press, 1969.

Dennison, Stephanie, and Lisa Shaw. *Popular Cinema in Brazil, 1930–2001*. Manchester, Eng.: Manchester University Press, 2004.

Diaféria, Lourenço, et al. *Um século de Luz*. São Paulo: Editora Scipione, 2001.

DiAntonio, Robert. "Conscious Primitivism in the Poetics of Mário de Andrade." *Mester* 14.1 (Spring 1985): 12–19. This is an expanded version of "Study of Mythopoetic Primitivism in a Brief Poem by Mário de Andrade." *Ilha do desterro/Exile's Island* 3.7 (July 1982): 67–73.

Dicionário mulheres do Brasil de 1500 até a atualidade: biográfico e ilustrado. Ed. Schuma Schumaher and Érica Vital Brazil. Rio de Janeiro: Jorge Zahar Editor, 2000.

Dunn, Christopher. "Introduction: On the Ground in the Global Mix." Rheda xiii–xviii.

Dworkin, Andrea. *Intercourse*. New York: Free Press, 1987.

Dzi Croquettes. Dir. Tatiana Issa and Raphael Álvarez. Brazil, 2009. Duration: 110 min.

Eisner, Will. *Comics and Sequential Art*. Tamarac, Fla.: Poorhouse Press, 1985. Rev. ed. 1990.

———. *Graphic Storytelling*. Tamarac, Fla.: Poorhouse Press, 1996.

Eternamente Pagu. Dir. Norma Bengell. Script: Márcia de Almeida, Geraldo Carneiro, and Norma Bengell. Sistema Globo de Comunicação, 1987.

Faria, Vilmar Evangelista. "São Paulo." *The Metropolis Era*. Ed. Mattei Dogan and John D. Kasarda. Vol. 2, *Mega-Cities*. Newbury Park, Calif.: Sage Publications, 1988. 294–309.

Fenianos, Eduardo Emílio. *Almanaque Kurytyba*. Curitiba: Univer Cidade, 1999.

———. *Expedições Urbenauta: São Paulo, uma aventura radical*. São Paulo: Univer Cidade, 2002.

———. *O urbenauta: manual de sobrevivência na selva urbana*. Curitiba: Univer Cidade, 1998.

Fernandes Junior, Rubens. "Modernidad y fotografía en Brasil." *Brasil: de la antropofagia a Brasília, 1920–1950*. Valencia: IVAM Institut Valencià d'Art Modern, 2000. 207–61.

Ferraz, Geraldo Galvão. "Cronologia de Patrícia Galvão." *Safra macabra: contos policiais*. By King Shelter (pseud. of Patrícia Galvão). Rio de Janeiro: José Olympio Editora, 1998. 10–15.

———. "Introdução: a *pulp fiction* de Patrícia Galvão." *Safra macabra: contos policiais.* By King Shelter. Rio de Janeiro: José Olympio Editora, 1998. 1–9.

———. "Prefácio." *Industrial Park: A Proletarian Novel.* By Patrícia Galvão. Trans. Elizabeth and K. David Jackson. Lincoln: University of Nebraska Press, 1993. 12–16.

Fitz, Earl. *Brazilian Narrative Traditions in a Comparative Context.* New York: Modern Language Association of America, 2005.

Font, Mauricio A. *Coffee, Contention, and Change in the Making of Modern Brazil.* Cambridge, Mass.: Basil Blackwell, 1990.

Foster, David William. "Annemarie Heinrich: Photography, Women's Bodies, and Semiotic Excess." *Journal of Latin American Popular Culture* 25 (2006): 253–70.

———. *Buenos Aires: Perspectives on the City and Cultural Production.* Gainesville: University Press of Florida, 1998.

———. *Contemporary Argentine Cinema.* Columbia: University of Missouri Press, 1992.

———. "Dreaming in Feminine: Grete Stern's Photomontages and the Parody of Psychoanalysis." *Ciberletras* 10 (2003): 10 pages. <http://www.lehman.cuny.edu/ciberletras/v10/foster.htm >.

———. *From Mafalda to Los supermachos: Latin American Graphic Humor.* Boulder, Col.: Lynne Rienner, 1981.

———. *Gay and Lesbian Themes in Latin American Writing.* Austin: University of Texas Press, 1991.

———. *Gender and Society in Contemporary Brazilian Cinema.* Austin: University of Texas Press, 1999.

———. "Masculinidades argentinas: *Hombres* de Silvio Fabrykant." *Arizona Journal of Hispanic Cultural Studies* 9 (2005): 87–97.

———. *Mexico City in Contemporary Mexican Cinema.* Austin: University of Texas Press, 2002.

———. *Queer Issues in Contemporary Latin American Cinema.* Austin: University of Texas Press, 2003.

———. "Some Formal Types in the Poetry of Mário de Andrade." *Luso-Brazilian Review* 2 (1965): 75–95.

———. *Social Realism in the Argentine Narrative.* Chapel Hill: University of North Carolina Studies in Romance Languages and Literatures, 1986.

Friedl, Peter. *Trabalhando no Copan/Working at Copan.* Trans. Portuguese-English, Elizabeth Jackson. Berlin: Sternberg Press, 2007.

Furlani, Lúcia Maria Teixeira. *Pagu: Patrícia Galvão: livre na imaginação, no espaço e no tempo.* 3a ed. Santos: Editora da UNICEB, 1991.

Gabara, Esther. "Modernist Ethics: Really Engaging Popular Culture in Mexico and Brazil." *The Ethics of Latin American Literary Criticism.* New York: Palgrave Macmillan, 2007. 63–102.

Galvão, Patrícia. *Industrial Park: A Proletarian Novel.* Trans. Elizabeth and K. David Jackson. Lincoln: University of Nebraska Press, 1993.

———. *Paixão Pagu: a autobiografia precoce de Patrícia Galvão.* Org. Geraldo Galvão Ferraz. Rio de Janeiro: Agir, 2005.

———. *Parque industrial*. 3a ed. Porto Alegre: Mercado Aberto; São Paulo: EDUFS-Car, 1994.

———. *Parque industrial*. São Paulo: Editorial Alternativa, 1981. Facsimile edition of original 1933 edition, signed Mara Lobo.

———. "Saibam ser maricons." *Homem do povo* 1.6 (7 de abril de 1931): 2. Rpt. in Campos, *Pagu: vida-obra* 85.

Gatti, André P. "Uma metrópole em busca da sua autodeterminação cinematográfica." <http://www.mnemocine.com.br/cinema/historiatextos/andre_gati_spsin.htm>. Accessed May 31, 2008.

Gilbert, George. "Jews in Photography; A Significant Contribution to Civilization." Hebrew History Federation, Fact Paper 7. <http://www.hebrewhistory.org/factpapers/photo7.html>. Accessed April 4, 2004.

Gomes, José Maria B. *Mário de Andrade e a revolução da linguagem: a gramatiquinha da fala brasileira*. João Pessoa: Editora Universitaria/UFPb, 1979.

González Echevarría, Roberto, and Enrique Pupo-Walker, eds. *The Cambridge History of Latin American Literature*. Vol. 3: *Brazilian Literature, Bibliographies*. Cambridge: Cambridge University Press, 1995.

"Graphic Novel." *Wikipedia*. <http://en.wikipedia.org/wiki/Graphic_novel>. Accessed July 25, 2008.

Green, James. *Beyond Carnival: Male Homosexuality in Twentieth-Century Brazil*. Chicago: University of Chicago Press, 1999.

Greimas, A. J., and J. Courtés. *Semiotics and Language: An Analytical Dictionary*. Trans. Larry Crist, et al. Bloomington: Indiana University Press, 1982.

Higonnet, Patrice. *Paris: Capital of the World*. Trans. Arthur Goldhammer. Cambridge, Mass.: Belknap Press of Harvard University Press, 2002.

História da cidade de São Paulo. Org. Paula Porta. São Paulo: 2004.

O invasor. Dir. Beto Brant. Brazil, 2002. Duration: 97 min.

Iturbide, Graciela. *Juchitán de las mujeres*. Fotografía: Graciela Iturbide. Texto: Elena Poniatowska. Edición: Pablo Ortiz Monasterio. México, D.F.: Ediciones Toledo, 1989.

Jackson, David K. "Afterword." *Industrial Park: A Proletarian Novel*, by Patrícia Galvão. Trans. Elizabeth and K. David Jackson. Lincoln: University of Nebraska Press, 1993. 115–53.

Jagose, Annamarie. *Queer Theory: An Introduction*. New York: New York University Press, 1996.

Johnson, Randal. *Cinema Novo x 5: Masters of Contemporary Brazilian Film*. Austin: University of Texas Press, 1984.

Johnson, Randal, and Robert Stam. *Brazilian Cinema*. 2nd ed. New York: Columbia University Press, 1995.

Khan, Hasan-Uddin. *International Style: Modernist Architecture from 1925–1965*. Köln: Taschen, 1998.

Kossovitch, Elisa Angotti. *Mário de Andrade, plural*. Campinas: Editora da Universidade Estadual de Campinas, UNICAMP, 1990.

Kossoy, Boris. "Apontamentos para uma biografia." Rosenthal, 15–30.

Kovacs, Steven. "Visions of the Metropolis: São Paulo and the Cinema." *Review: Latin American Literature and Arts* 28 (1981): 56–59.

Langue, Frédérique. *Saudades do Brasil.* Rev. ed. *Caravelle* 65 (1995): 283–86.

Leach, Edmundo. *Claude Lévi-Strauss.* Rev. ed. New York: Viking, 1974.

Lesser, Jeffrey. *A Discontented Diaspora: Japanese Brazilians and the Meanings of Ethnic Militancy, 1960–1980.* Durham, N.C.: Duke University Press, 2007.

———. *Welcoming the Undesirables: Brazil and the Jewish Question.* Berkeley: University of California Press, 1995.

Lévi-Strauss, Claude. *Anthropologie structurale.* Paris: Plon, 1958.

———. *Le Cru et le cuit.* Paris: Plon, 1964.

———. "Prologue." *Saudades do Brasil,* 9–23. Also, *New York Review of Books* 42.20 (December 21, 1995): 19–21.

———. *Saudades de São Paulo.* Org. Ricardo Mendes. Trans. Paulo Neves. São Paulo: Companhia das Letras, Instituto Moreira Salles, 1996.

———. *Saudades do Brasil; A Photographic Memoir.* Trans. from French by Sylvia Modelsi. Seattle: University of Washington Press, 1995.

———. *Les Structures élémentaires de la parenté.* Paris: Presses Universitaires de France, 1949.

———. *Tristes tropiques.* Trans. from French by John and Doreen Weightman. New York: Penguin, 1992. Also published as *World on the Wane.* Trans. John Russell. New York: Criterion Books, 1961.

Lima, Luiz Costa. *Lira e antilira (Mário, Drummond, Cabral).* Rio de Janeiro: Civilização Brasileira, 1968.

Literatura em quadrinhos no Brasil: acervo da Biblioteca Nacional. Moacy Sirne, et al. Rio de Janeiro: Nova Fronteira, Fundação Biblioteca Nacional, 2002.

Lobanov-Rostovsky, Sergei. "Prostitution." *Encyclopedia of Feminist Literary Theory.* Ed. Elizabeth Kowaleski-Wallace. New York: Garland, 1997. 319–20.

Loos, Dorothy Scott. *The Naturalistic Novel of Brazil.* New York: Hispanic Institute in the United States, 1963.

Lopes, Rodrigo Garcia. "Cityscape." *Nômada.* São Paulo: Lamparina Editora, 2004. 130.

Lowe, Elizabeth. *The City in Brazilian Literature.* East Brunswick, N.J.: Fairleigh Dickinson University Press, 1982.

Machado de Assis, Joaquim Maria. *O alienista.* Adaptação de Fábio Moon e Gabriel Bá. Rio de Janeiro: Agir, 2007.

Mapping Desire; Geographies of Sexualities. Ed. David Bell and Gill Valentine. London: Routledge, 1995.

Maricato, Ermínia. *Metrópole na periferia do capitalismo: ilegalidade, desigualdade e violência.* São Paulo: Editora Hucitec, 1996.

Martins, Wilson. *The Modernist Idea; A Critical Survey of Brazilian Writing in the Twentieth Century.* Trans. Jack E. Tomlins. New York: New York University Press, 1970.

Massey, Doreen B. *Space, Place and Gender.* Cambridge, Eng.: Polity Press, 1994.

Matos, Grégorio de. *Crônica do viver baiano seiscentista.* Ed. James Amado. Bahia: Janaina, 1969.

Melo, Luis Correia de. *Dicionário de autores paulistas*. São Paulo: Comissão do IV Centenario da Cidade de São Paulo, 1954.

Meskimmon, Marsha. *The Art of Reflection: Women Artists' Self-portraiture in the Twentieth-Century*. London: Scarlet Press, 1996.

Millard, Candice. *The River of Doubt: Theodore Roosevelt's Darkest Journey*. New York: Anchor Books, 2006.

Moon, Fábio, and Gabriel Bá. *10 pãezinhos: mesa para dois*. São Paulo: Devir, 2006.

———. *De:Tales; Stories from Urban Brazil*. Milwaukie, Or.: Dark House Books, 2006.

———. *O girasol e a lua: uma história*. São Paulo: Via Lettera Editora e Livraria, 2000.

———. *Meu coração, não sei por que*. São Paulo: Via Lettera Editora e Livraria, 2001.

———. *Úrsula*. San Francisco: Air/PlanetLar, 2004.

Moreno, Antônio. *A personagem homossexual no cinema brasileiro*. Rio de Janeiro: Ministério da Cultura, FUNARTE; EdUFF, Editora da Universidade Federal Fluminense, 2001.

Morse, Richard M. *From Community to Metropolis: A Biography of São Paulo, Brazil*. New and enlarged ed. New York: Octagon Books, 1974.

Mott, Luiz. "As lésbicas na literatura brasileira." *Lesbianismo no Brasil*. Porto Alegre: Mercado Aberto, 1987. 63–138.

Nist, John. *The Modernist Movement in Brazil: A Literary Study*. Austin: University of Texas Press, 1967.

Novaes, Sylvia Caiuby. "Lévi-Strauss: razão e sensibilidade." *Revista de antropologia* 42 (1999): 67–76.

Nunes, Benedito. "Mário de Andrade: as enfibraturas do modernismo." *Revista iberoamericana* 50.126 (enero-marzo 1984): 63–75.

Owen, Patricia. "Discardable Discourses in Patrícia Galvão's *Parque industrial*." *Brazilian Feminisms*. Ed. Solange Ribeiro de Oliveira and Judith Still. Nottingham, Eng.: University of Nottingham Monographs in the Humanities, 1999. 68–84.

Paoli, Maria Cecília. "Working-Class São Paulo and its Representations, 1900–1940." *Latin American Perspectives* 14.2 (1987): 204–25.

Peixoto, Marta. "Rio's Favelas in Recent Fiction and Film: Commonplaces of Urban Segregation." *PMLA: Publications of the Modern Language Association of America* 122.1 (2007): 170–78.

Peixoto, Nelson Brissac. "*Anjos da noite*: Night Angels." *Cinema brasileiro: The Films from Brazil*. Ed. Amir Labaki. São Paulo: Publifolha, 1998. 163–67.

———. "Latin American Megacities: The New Urban Formlessness." *City/Art: The Urban Scene in Latin America*. Ed. Rebecca E. Biron. Durham: Duke University Press, 2009. 233–50.

Perlongher, Néstor Osvaldo. *O negócio do michê: prostituição viril em São Paulo*. São Paulo: Editora Brasiliense, 1987.

Perrone, Charles A. "Performing São Paulo: Vanguard Representations of a Brazilian Cosmopolis." *Latin American Music Review* 23.1 (2002): 60–78.

———. "Preface: A Regina Rheda Reader—Titles, Subtitles, Versions, Reversions." Rheda, vii–x.

——. "Presentation and Representation of Self and City in *Paulicéia desvairda*." *Chasqui; revista de literatura latinoamericana* 31.1 (May 2002): 18–27.

Pinto, Edith Pimentel. *A gramatiquinha de Mário de Andrade: texto e contexto*. São Paulo: Livraria Duas Cidades, 1990.

Pochman, Márcio. *Metrópole do trabalho*. São Paulo: Editora Brasiliense, 2001.

Proença, M. Cavalcanti. *Roteiro de Macunaíma*. Rio de Janeiro: Civilização Brasileira, 1969.

Quezado Deckker, Zilah. *Brazilian Built: The Architecture of the Modern Movement in Brazil*. London: Spon Press, 2001.

Quinlin, Susan Canty. *The Female Voice in Contemporary Brazilian Narrative*. New York: Peter Lang, 1991.

"Pagu." *Dicionário mulheres do Brasil de 1500 até a atualidade biográfico e ilustrado*. Org. Schuma Schumaher and Érica Vital Brazil. Rio de Janeiro: Jorge Zahar Editor, 2000. 463–64.

O puritano da Rua Augusta. Dir. Amácio Mazzaropi. Brazil, 1965. Duration: 102 min.

Rago, Margareth. *Os prazeres da noite: prostituição e códigos da sexualidade feminina em São Paulo (1890–1930)*. Rio de Janeiro: Paz e Terra, 1991.

Rebollo, Lisbeth, and Armando Silva. "Sketch of São Paulo." *Urban Imaginaries from Latin America*. Ed. Armando Silvo. Trans. Vincent Martin. Ostfildern-Ruit, Germany: Hatje Cantz, 2003. 134–44.

Reed, Justin A. "Obverse Colonization: São Paulo, Global Urbanization and the Poetics of the Latin American City." *Journal of Latin American Cultural Studies* 15.3 (2006): 281–300.

Reichenbach, Carlos. "*São Paulo, S.A.*; São Paulo, S.A." *Cinema brasileiro: The Films from Brazil*. Ed. Amir Labaki. São Paulo: Publifolha, 1998. 51–53.

Reis, Roberto. "Aluísio Azevedo." *Latin American Writers on Gay and Lesbian Themes: A Bio-Critical Sourcebook*. Ed. David William Foster. Westport, Conn.: Greenwood Press, 1994. 49.

Rheda, Regina. *Arca sem Noé: histórias do Edifício Copan*. 1994. 2a rev. ed. Rio de Janeiro: Book Link, 2002. Trans. into English as *Stories from the Copan Building* and included as Part 1 of Rheda's *First World Third Class and Other Tales of the Global Mix*. Trans. Adria Frizzi, R. E. Young, David Coles, and Charles A. Perrone. Austin: University of Texas Press, 2005. 1–86.

Rich, Adrienne. "Compulsory Heterosexuality and Lesbian Experience." *Blood, Bread and Poetry: Selected Prose, 1979–85*. New York: W. W. Norton, 1986. 23–75.

Riffaterre, Michael. *Semiotics of Poetry*. Bloomington: Indiana University Press, 1978.

Rivera, José Eustacio. *La vorágine*. 1924. Prólogo y cronología Juan Loveluck. Caracas: Biblioteca Ayacucho, 1985.

Rodrigues, Nelson. *A vida como ela é—: o homem fiel e outros contos*. Sel. Ruy Castro. São Paulo: Companhia das Letras, 1992.

Rodríguez Monegal, Emir. *Mário de Andrade/Borges: um diálogo dos anos 20*. São Paulo: Editora Perspectiva, 1978.

Roig, Adrien. "Le Langage poétique de *Paulicéia desvairada* de Mário de Andrade." *Quadrant* 12 (1995): 81–114.

Roosevelt, Theodore. *Through the Brazilian Wilderness*. 1914. New York: Charles Scribner's, 1920.

Rosa, João Guimarães. *Grande sertão: veredas*. 1956. 13a ed. Rio de Janeiro: José Olympio Editora, 1979.

———. "A terceira margem do rio." *Primeiras estórias*. 1962. Rio de Janeiro: Nova Fronteira, 2001.

Rosenberg, Fernando J. *The Avant-Garde and Geopolitics in Latin America*. Pittsburgh, Penn.: University of Pittsburgh Press, 2006.

Rosenthal, Hildegard. *Cenas urbanas*. São Paulo: Instituto Moreira Salles, 1998.

Rosso, Mauro. *São Paulo, 450 anos: a cidade literária*. Rio de Janeiro: Editora Expressão e Cultura, 2004.

Sá, Lúcia. *Life in the Megalopolis: Mexico City and São Paulo*. London: Routledge, 2007.

Sacchetta, Vladimir. "Pequeno retrato de uma pioneira." Rosenthal 33–35.

Said, Edward W. *Orientalism*. 1978. New York: Vintage, 1979.

São Paulo, S.A. Dir. Luis Sérgio Person. Brazil, 1965. Duration: 107 min.

São Paulo, sinfonia da metrópole. Dir. Adalberto Kemeny and Rudolf Rex Lustig. Brazil, 1929. Duration: 90 min.

Schelling, Vivian. "Mário de Andrade: A Primitiva Intellectual." *Bulletin of Hispanic Studies* 65.1 (January 1988): 73–86.

Schwartz, Jorge. *Caixa modernista*. São Paulo: EDUSP; Belo Horizonte: Editora UFMG, 2003.

Schwartz, Madalena. *Personae: fotos e faces do Brasil/Photos and Faces of Brazil*. São Paulo: Companhia das Letras, 1997.

———. *Retratos*. São Paulo: Instituto Moreira Salas, c. 1998.

Segawa, Hugo. *Prelúdio da Metrópole: arquitetura e urbanismo em São Paulo na passagem do século XIX ao XX*. 2a ed. São Paulo: Ateliê Editorial, 2004.

Selby, Nick, et al. *Brazil*. 1989. 4th ed. Hawthorn, Victoria: Lonely Planet, 1998.

Séron-Pierre, Catherine. "Oscar Niemeyer: complexe residentiel Copan, São Paulo, 1951–1957." *Moniteur architecture* 123 (March 2002): 76–79.

Sevcenko, Nicolau. *Orfeo extático na metrópoli: São Paulo, sociedade e cultura nos fermentes anos 20*. São Paulo: Compañía das Letras, 1992.

———. "São Paulo, The Quintessential, Uninhibited Megalopolis as Seen by Blaise Cendrars in the 1920s." *Megalopolis: The Giant City in History*. Ed. Theo Barker and Anthony Sutcliffe. New York: St. Martin's Press, 1993. 175–93.

Shields, Rob. "Fancy Footwork: Walter Benjamin's Notes on *Flânerie*." *The Flâneur*. Ed. Keith Tester. London: Routledge, 1994. 61–79.

Shook, David. "An Interview with Fábio Moon & Gabriel Bá." *World Literature Today*, special issue, "Graphic Novel" (March-April 2007): 42–45.

Silva, Nadilson Manoel da. *Fantasias e cotidiano nas histórias em quadrinhos*. São Paulo: Annablume; Fortaleza: Governo do Estado do Ceará, Secretaria da Cultura e Desporto, 2002.

Silva Neto, Antônio da. *Diccionario de filmes brasileiros: curta e média metragem*. 1a ed. São Paulo: Assahi Gráfica e Editora, 2006.

Slater, Candace. ""Setting Out for São Paulo": Internal Migration as a Theme in Brazilian Popular Literataure." *New Scholar* 8.1–2 (1982): 245–56.

Smylie, John. "Graphic Novel." *Encyclopedia of the Novel.* Ed. Paul Schellinger. Chicago: Fitzroy Dearborn, 1998. Vol. 1, 505–9.

Sontag, Susan. *On Photography.* New York: Farrar, Strauss and Giroux, 1990.

——. *Regarding the Pain of Others.* New York: Farrar, Straus and Giroux, 2003.

South American Cinema: A Critical Filmography 1915–1994. Ed. Timothy Barnard and Peter Rist. New York: Garland, 1996.

Stern, Grete. *Sueños: fotomontajes de Grete Stern. Serie completa.* Ed. de la obra impresa en la revista Idilio (1948–51). Buenos Aires: Fundación CEPPA, 2003.

Suárez, José I., and Jack E. Tomlins. *Mário de Andrade: The Creative Works.* Lewisburg, Penn.: Bucknell University Press; London: Associated University Presses, 2000.

"Tarsila do Amaral." *Dicionário mulheres do Brasil de 1500 até a atualidade biográfico e ilustrado.* Org. Schuma Schumaher and Érica Vital Brazil. Rio de Janeiro: Jorge Zahar Editor, 2000. 503–4.

Taschner, Suzana P., and Lucia M. M. Bógus. "São Paulo, uma metrópole desigual." *Revista EURE* 27.80 (2001): 87–120.

Taylor, Edwin, ed. *Insight Guides: Brazil.* Rev. and updated. Boston: Houghton Mifflin, 1994.

Toledo, Benedito. *São Paulo: três cidades em um século.* São Paulo: Livraria Duas Cidades, 1981.

Toledo, Benedito Lima de. "Um olhar encantado pelos tipos humanos." Rosenthal 8–13.

Tosta, Antonio Luciano de A. "Exchanging Glances: The Streetcar, Modernity, and the Metropolis in Brazilian Literature." *Chasqui: revista de literatura latinoamericana* 32.2 (2001): 35–52.

Tosta, Clorindo. "Placeres del ser urbano." *La ciudad subterránea.* By Fabiana Barreda. Buenos Aires: Metrovías, 1998. Np.

Travero, Antonio. "Migrations of Cinema: Italian Neorealism and Brazilian Cinema." *Italian Neorealism and Global Cinema.* Ed. Laura E. Ruberto and Kristi M. Wilson. Detroit: Wayne State University Press, 2007. 165–86.

Trelles Plazaola, Luis. *South American Cinema: Dictionary of Film Makers.* Río Piedras, P.R.: Editorial de la Universidad de Puerto Rico, 1989.

Trevisan, João Silvério. *Devassos no paraíso: a homossexualidade no Brasil, da colônia à atualidade.* 5a ed. revised and extended. Rio de Janeiro: Editora Record, 2002.

Trigo, Luciano. *O viajante imóvil: Machado de Assis e Rio de Janeiro do seu tempo.* Rio de Janeiro: Editora Record, 2001.

Uhl, Michael. *Frommer's Comprehensive Travel Guide: Brazil.* 3rd ed. New York: Prentice Hall Travel, 1993.

Underwood, David. *Oscar Niemeyer and the Architecture of Brazil.* New York: Rizzoli International Publications, 1994.

Unruh, Vicky. "Las águilas musas de la modernidad: Patrícia Galvão y Norah Lange." *Revista iberoamericana* 182–83 (1998): 271–86. An expanded version of the discussion of Galvão appears as "A Refusal to Perform: Patrícia Galvão's Spy on the Wall," in Unruh's *Performing Women,* 195–221.

———. *Performing Women and Modern Literary Culture in Latin America.* Austin: University of Texas Press, 2006.

Updike, John. *Brazil.* New York: Fawcett Crest, 1994.

Vargas, Ava. *La casa de citas en el barrio galante.* Prólogo de Carlos Monsiváis. México, D.F.: Grijalbo; Consejo Nacional para la Cultura y las Artes, 1991.

Veloso, Caetano. *Tropical Truth: A Story of Music and Revolution in Brazil.* Trans. Isabel de Sena. Ed. Barbara Einzig. New York: Alfred A. Knopf, 2002.

Wilkerson, William. "Communism and Homosexuality." *Reader's Guide to Lesbian and Gay Studies.* Ed. Timothy F. Murphay. Chicago: Fitzroy Dearborn Publishers, 2000. 154–55.

Williams, Daryle. *Culture Wars in Brazil: The First Vargas Regime, 1930–1945.* Durham N.C.: Duke University Press, 2001.

Wittig, Monique. "One Is Not Born a Woman." *The Straight Mind and Other Essays.* Boston: Beacon Press, 1992. 9–20.

Wolfe, Joel. *Working Women, Working Men: São Paulo and the Rise of Brazil's Industrial Working Class, 1900–1955.* Durham, N.C.: Duke University Press, 1993.

Index

Breathed, Berkeley, 136
Bueno, Eva Paulino, 86

Cafajestes, Os (dir. Ruy Guerra), 162n23
Caldeira, Teresa P. R., 171n19
Câmara, Dom Hélder, 172n2
Camargo, Mônica Junqueira de, 166n10
Campos, Augusto de, 35, 46
Candomblé, 103
Carriego, Evaristo, 161n18
Cartier-Bresson, Henri, 166n10
Castro, Fidel, 59
Castro, Sílvio, 28
Cela, Camilo José, 136
Certeau, Michel de, 157n12
Chanson de Roland, La, 179
Charisse, Sid, 95, 171
Chiclete com banana, 136
Cidade de Deus (dir. Fernando de Meire-
lles and Kátia Lund), 90
Cinema Novo, 83, 86, 94, 96, 170n11,
171nn22–23, 172n31
Cixous, Hélène: "The Laugh of the Me-
dusa," 52, 53, 113
Clementina de Jesus, 9, 100–101, *100*, 103
Coelho, Luciano, 124
Columbus, Christopher, 127
Corcoran-Nantes, Yvonne, 162n28
Coutinho, Eduardo, 174n5
Crumb, Robert, 136
Cunha, Euclides da: *Os sertões*, 127
Curitiba, 10, 123–24

Dama do lotação, A (dir. Newville de
Almeida), 176n2
Daniel, Mary L., 161n11
Darwin, Charles, 127
Dean, Warren, 165n2
Deckker, Quezado, 169n13
De Franceschi, Antonio Fernando,
167n20
Dennison, Stephanie, 170nn9,11, 171n15
Denser, Márcia, 34
DiAntonio, Roberto, 19

Dicionario de mulheres do Brasil, 46
Double Day, The (dir. Helena Solberg-
Ladd), 36
Duarte de Perón, Eva (Evita), 98
Dunn, Christopher, 174n12
Dworkin, Andrea, 164n11
Dzi Croquettes, 9, 106–10
Dzi Croquettes (dir. Tatiana Issa and
Raphael Álvarez), 172n4

Edifício Copan, 9–10, 112–21, 152, 180n2
Edifício Itália, 113, 180n2
Edifício Martinelli, 8, 9, 80, 113, 156n4,
180n2
Edifício Master (dir. Eduardo Coutinho),
174n5
Editora Abril, 102
Editora Três, 102
Eisner, Will, 136, 178n1
Estação da Luz, 24, 180n2
Estádio de Pacaembu, 8, 99, 165n8
Estado Novo, 2, 60
Eternamente Pagu (dir. Norma Bengell),
28, 42, 45, 48, 50

Fabrykant, Silvio, 102; *Hombres argenti-
nos*, 102
Facio, Sara, 102
Faria, Betty, 171n27
Feierstein, Harvey, 173n6
Feminist space and language, 27–44
Fenianos, Emilio Eduardo, 10, 152, 157n12;
*Expedições Urbenauta: uma aventura
radical*, 10, 122–34; *O Urbenauta:
manual de sobrevivência na selva
urbana*, 10, 124
Ferraz, Geraldo, 46–54; *Doramundo*,
163n5; *A famosa revista*, 48, 163n5
Ferraz, Geraldo Galvão, 37, 46, 47, 52,
160n1
Ferreira-Pinto, Cristina, 28
Film and São Paulo, 8–9, 82–97
Fitz, Earl, 163n1
Font, Mauricio A., 165n1

David William Foster is Regents' Professor of
Spanish and Women and Gender Studies at Arizona
State University. His research focuses on urban culture
in Latin America, with specific emphasis on gender,
queer issues, and Jewish diaspora culture. In July 2010 he
led a National Endowment for the Humanities Seminar
for College and University Professors on urban culture
in Brazil, held in São Paulo. He is editor of *Chasqui:
revista de estudios latinoamericanos.*